Duels in the Sky

Duels in the Sky

WORLD WAR II NAVAL AIRCRAFT IN COMBAT

by Captain Eric M. Brown, RN

Naval Institute Press
Annapolis, Maryland

Library of Congress Cataloging-in-Publication Data

Brown, Eric Melrose.
  Duels in the sky.

  Includes index.
  1. Air warfare. 2. Airplanes, Military. 3. Naval
aviation. 4. World War, 1939–1945—Aerial operations.
5. World War, 1939–1945—Naval operations. I. Title.
UG700.B76   1988   940.54′4   88-15258
ISBN 0-87021-063-7

Designed by Moira Megargee

Printed in the United States of America

Contents

Captain Eric M. Brown, R.N., 1969

Preface

THE WEALTH OF documentation we have on World War II, almost certainly the last major conflict of its kind, has given not only historians but also those who dabble in theory a wide field over which to range. Perhaps armchair theorists are attracted to aerial combat more than any other facet of the war because aviation technology made such huge strides in the period from 1939 to 1945 and therefore invited numerous questions. How often I have listened to argument rage about whether the Spitfire was a greater fighter than the Zero, or the Junkers 87 a better dive-bomber than the Dauntless.

Few pilots have had the privilege of flying a wide assortment of World War II aircraft. It has been my fortune to have sampled many, an experience I hope can be applied to this controversial area with the object of clearing up some of the uncertainty.

I have drawn on recorded history to set the scene for technical descriptions and subjective impressions of Allied naval aircraft and their opponents. Most of the information on individual planes is based on my experience of flying them. Following the descriptions are scenarios in which aircraft are pitted against one another in single combat. Each scenario has been kept pure, presented without the complication of extraneous considerations, so that in effect I am flying both opposing aircraft and fighting for my life against myself. The historical narrative should put my flight evaluations and combat verdicts into perspective.

Finally, I assess the features of the best aircraft of World War II to determine which of each type is the most outstanding. Granted, this material is theoretical; I hope I have successfully diluted theory with the test pilot's analytical approach and given a touch of realism to flights of fancy in order to answer at least some of the questions about this most exciting phase in the history of aerial combat.

I would like to thank the following individuals for their help with photo research: Peter M. Bowers; Joe Mizrahi, editor, Sentry Books; Alastair Simpson, Airlife Publishing; staff at the National Air and Space Museum; and Linda Cullen and photo library staff, U.S. Naval Institute.

Duels in the Sky

1

Prewar State of the Art

IN THE 1930S EUROPE was a cauldron of simmering discontent stirred by the hands that signed the unreasonable Treaty of Versailles. Huge reparations demanded of Germany caused uncontrollable inflation, which in turn generated social unrest and deep resentment. The Weimar Republic, born of the shame of defeat, tried unsuccessfully to steer the nation. In short, the Treaty of Versailles bankrupted a nation and drained it of pride.

The German air force was officially dissolved in May 1920, the terms of the Treaty of Versailles allowing no military air force of any kind. However, a professional long-service army not exceeding 100,000 men was permitted for such tasks as border policing, and in this body cells of aviation experts were concealed by the Germans. There was also the new Civil Aviation Department, formed with Allied permission in 1922 and headed by an experienced wartime officer to ensure that civil aviation developed in response to military needs.

The Rapallo negotiations led to liaison between the German and Russian armies, and thus Germany was able to partially circumvent restrictions on its military strength. Russia would supply facilities for the development and testing of weapons.

A German military flying school was established at Lipetsk, and from this source some 120 fully qualified German fighter pilots emerged between 1925 and 1933. But even before 1924 aviation was being encouraged in Germany, by the institution of a network of gliding clubs, a system of airfields and civil aircraft factories, pilot training, and instruction in passive air defense.

On 26 February 1935, when Adolf Hitler had risen to his position of supreme power, the Luftwaffe became public. In the same year Germany obtained air parity with Great Britain, and its massive pro-

1

Senior Luftwaffe Officers at Rechlin Aircraft Test Establishment, 1939 (Bundesarchiv)

duction machine was getting into its stride. Concurrently, Italy's fascist dictator Benito Mussolini, long suspicious of the upstart Hitler, decided to become his ally. Mussolini bought as part of the dowry to this unholy marriage a significant air force, producing a new Axis strength that stirred Britain out of its political apathy, especially when Italy invaded Abyssinia. The Abyssinian invasion was an act of revenge for the defeat suffered by Italy in 1915 at Adowa, and it now became starkly evident that Germany might seek to exact a similar retribution for the ignominy at Compiègne, where the German surrender was signed in 1918.

In 1936 I visited Berlin during the Olympic Games and made my first acquaintance with the new Luftwaffe in the person of Colonel Ernst Udet, enthusiastic proponent of dive-bombing and then head of the technical department in the German Air Ministry. In the early 1930s he had witnessed a demonstration by U.S. Navy Curtiss Helldivers at Cleveland, Ohio, and was so impressed that he influenced the placing of a contract for the design of such aircraft on 27 September 1933. The Junkers (Ju) 87 was the result; the prototype made its first flight in late spring 1935 with a proud Udet as witness.

Things were moving in the aircraft production business in Germany at this time. In January 1936, at Berlin's Tempelhof Airport, there was the first public showing of the Heinkel (He) 111, Ju 86, and Focke-Wulf (Fw) 200. The following year the Messerschmitt (Me) 109, the Dornier (Do) 17, and He 112 appeared. All these aircraft, with the exception of the He 112, were to play significant roles in World War II.

The first flexing of Nazi muscles came with the occupation of the Rhineland on 7 March 1936, when Germany's fighter arm made its public debut. It was commanded by Major Ritter von Greim, whom Hitler would later appoint head of the Luftwaffe in the Berlin bunker, shortly before he committed suicide.

Meanwhile Europe was rocked by another political and human catastrophe with the outbreak of the Spanish Civil War, a direct clash between fascism and communism. Both Hitler and Mussolini reacted to this event by sending military aid, mainly in the form of air support. Germany's Condor Legion was equipped with the new Luftwaffe aircraft, and Spain was to be their proving ground. The legion came away with 340 victories, a resounding success that could be attributed to three factors: weak opposition, sound German design, and determined Luftwaffe pilots.

Nineteen thirty-eight brought the stark reality of an Axis threat to the rest of Europe, particularly a threat from the air. Nations scrambled to catch up in the race for air power, but Germany had had a substantial head start. On its first leg Great Britain replaced biplane fighters such as the Gloster Gladiator with the modern, eight-gun Hawker Hurricane monoplane, and by September of that year it had five squadrons. Germany at that time had 920 fighters, a large proportion of them Me 109s, so in air strength there was a great disparity between the two countries.

In mid-1939 I traveled to Germany and was immediately struck by the bustling activity and feeling of supreme confidence that pervaded the country. Everywhere the panoply of Nazi ceremony could be seen, and it was exciting if you did not breathe too deep and catch the smell of underlying evil. I traveled around freely and visited the glider training sites of the National Sozialistisches Flieger Korps, where the Hitler Youth had facilities. Here was the nursery from which the mighty Luftwaffe was to get its supply of pilots. There was no attempt to conceal these activities from foreigners; indeed, they were shown off as models of discipline and dedication to the regime.

The invasion of Poland on 1 September 1939 heralded the outbreak of World War II and found Germany with a strength of 1,090 fighters and 1,553 bombers. Its manpower had been significantly increased by ten million Austrians and Sudetens annexed to the Reich in 1938. At the outbreak of war Great Britain, though it had set up the Ministry of Aircraft Production in a desperate attempt to catch up with Germany, still had only half the strength of the Luftwaffe.

In the United States aircraft production was beginning to speed up largely because of European interest in boosting modest stocks with American models. Although at this stage there seemed little chance of the United States becoming directly involved in the European conflagration, it was inevitably going to have to take measures of self-defense; this also served to keep pressure on aircraft production.

Naval Aviation

The Axis dictators regarded their air forces as the cutting edge of their power and as their own noble creations; unlike Germany's and Italy's other proud, long-established services, their air forces would give unswerving loyalty to the regime. Total control of all military aviation, whether land- or sea-based, was vested in the air force. Thus it was that in Germany an air general was placed in the Naval High Command as the commander in chief of naval aviation, and the Luftwaffe met all naval and coastal air requirements. This was to include carrier aviation, for Hitler had decided in 1934 to build an aircraft carrier; the 23,200-ton *Graf Zeppelin* was launched at Kiel on 8 December 1938.

Mussolini unified all the Italian air arms in a single air force in 1923; he did not contemplate an aircraft carrier, the Italian peninsula itself acting as a sort of giant carrier in the middle of the Mediterranean. In Great Britain a similar unification of air arms had taken place in 1918, but in 1924 a branch of the Royal Air Force was formed known as the Fleet Air Arm, seventy percent of whose pilots were to be naval officers. This anomalous setup persisted until 1937, when the Fleet Air Arm, largely owing to the influence of Winston Churchill, came under the control of the Admiralty.

France had shown an early interest in carrier aviation, as in all aspects of air power, and had converted a battleship hull into a carrier in 1927. The *Béarn* remained its sole vessel of this type until the outbreak of war.

Thus on 1 September 1939 Great Britain was the leading carrier power in the world, with seven carriers in service and six under construction. This compared with six plus two in Japan and five plus two in the United States. However, the picture was not as rosy in fact as it looked on paper; British carriers were equipped with obsolescent aircraft built in small numbers. The Fleet Air Arm's total inventory was 30 Skua fighter/dive-bombers, 18 Sea Gladiator biplane fighters, and about 180 Swordfish torpedo/spotter/reconnaissance biplanes. In addition, there were a few four-gun, turreted versions of the Skua, but these never joined carriers. Total embarked strength was actually 18 Skuas, 12 Gladiators, and 147 Swordfish.

The comparative lineup of British and German aircraft types in 1939 was as follows:

	British	German
Fighters:	Supermarine Spitfire I (RAF) Hawker Hurricane I (RAF) Gloster Gladiator (RAF/ FAA)	Messerschmitt 109E (Germany) Messerschmitt 110C (Germany)
Dive-Bombers:	Blackburn Skua (FAA)	Junkers 87B (Germany)
Torpedo-Bombers:	Fairey Swordfish (FAA)	Heinkel 111H (Germany)

I have flown all these and they make interesting comparison, but I will confine myself at this stage to the Allied naval types and their German counterparts and opponents.

GLOSTER SEA GLADIATOR

The Gladiator was built as a private venture to meet an Air Staff requirement bridging the gap between conventional, open-cockpit, two-gun fighters and more sophisticated multigun monoplanes. Developed from the highly successful Gauntlet from the same stable, it made its first flight on 12 September 1934. First-production aircraft were not available until January 1937. In September of that year they were inspected by Major General Ernst Udet and General Erhard Milch during an invitation tour of RAF units in Britain.

In 1937 the Admiralty approached the Air Ministry wanting to know which aircraft already in the RAF's service or under development would be most suitable for conversion and use by the Royal Navy. The Gladiator was nominated, and in March 1938 Gloster received an Admiralty order for thirty-eight Gladiators, followed in June by another order for sixty out of the main-production batch of Gladiator IIs.

The Gladiator differed from its RAF counterpart only in the installation of catapult points, an arrester hook, and a collapsible dinghy in a fairing beneath the fuselage and between the landing-gear legs.

This single-seater was a good-looking airplane, with remarkably clean lines for a biplane, and the streamlined effect was enhanced by a neatly enclosed cockpit canopy. Wing span was 32 ft 3 in. All-up weight was 5,020 lbs.

The engine, a nine-cylinder, 840-hp, air-cooled Bristol Mercury

Gloster Sea Gladiator (Flight International)

VIII AS, was neatly cowled and drove a Fairey three-blade, fixed-pitch metal propeller. It was started by hand cranking.

Takeoff was short and the climb to 10,000 ft took 4.75 min. At that altitude maximum speed was 250 mph and maneuverability was outstanding, with beautiful harmony of control. The view ahead was restricted, especially in the climb, and the view below was poor because of the lower mainplane. Service ceiling was 32,300 ft.

With stalling speed only 55 mph, a speed of 62 mph was comfortable for carrier landing, although the view ahead at that speed was poor. The arrester hook was placed almost halfway along the fuselage, a location that, together with rather bouncy landing gear, created problems unless a three-point attitude was achieved at touchdown.

Armament consisted of two fixed, synchronized Browning .303 machine guns mounted in troughs in the fuselage sides and two machine guns, mounted under the lower mainplanes, that fired outside the propeller disc.

Only 83 imperial gals (99.67 U.S. gals) of fuel were carried, giving a range of 425 statute miles (370 nm) and an endurance of 2.25 hrs.

Assessment: The Gladiator, in service with fourteen air forces in the world, was undoubtedly one of the greatest biplane fighters ever built, but, appearing almost simultaneously with the first of the new breed of heavily armed monoplane fighters and bombers, it was pitched into a combat era where it was outgunned and outperformed, though never outmaneuvered.

BLACKBURN SKUA

The Skua, designed to an Air Ministry specification issued in 1934, was to be the Fleet Air Arm's first shipboard monoplane. The gestation period for this two-seat fighter/dive-bomber was elephantine; the first flight did not take place until 9 February 1937. The reason was its advanced design. This consisted of a flush-riveted Alclad fuselage incorporating watertight buoyancy compartments beneath the pilot's floor and aft of the gunner's cockpit; a three-piece, two-spar wing with sealed watertight bays between the main spars of the outer panels and a heavy-duty center section bolted under the fuselage, so that its upper surface formed the bottom of the forward watertight compartment; and a cantilevered metal tail assembly with movable, fabric-covered surfaces.

Catering to its dive-bombing role, the Skua's wing carried a flap of modified Zap type, which, housed in a recess between aileron and root, acted as both normal flap and dive-brake. An unusual feature of the tail assembly was the placement of the entire elevator surface aft of the rudder trailing edge to prevent blanking and aid spin recovery. This and slightly upturned wingtips were hallmarks of the Skua.

Because of the manual wing-folding arrangement, the landing gear struts were attached to the extremities of the center section, giving a relatively narrow wheeltrack of 9 ft 7 in, a feature that caused a number of ground accidents.

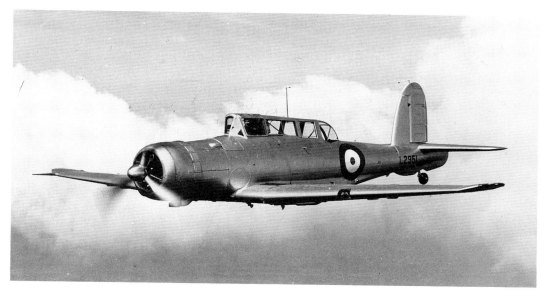

Blackburn Skua (Flight International)

The Skua was powered by a 905-hp sleeve-valve Bristol Perseus XII, a nine-cylinder, air-cooled radial engine driving a three-blade, two-pitch De Havilland propeller. The wing-span was 46 ft 2 in, the folded width, 16 ft 2 in. Loaded weight was 8,228 lbs with a total fuel capacity of 163 imperial gals (195 U.S. gals).

Armament consisted of four .303 machine guns in the outer wing panels, and one .303 manually operated Lewis gun in the rear cockpit. One 500-lb bomb was carried on retractable ejector arms in a recess below the fuselage, these arms swinging the bomb clear of the propeller arc in a diving attack.

Being seated in the cockpit was like being in a greenhouse, an effect produced by the deep, aft-sliding hood and the near-vertical, flat-paneled windscreen. The windscreen was meant to improve visibility in wet weather.

Takeoff was ponderous, and it was essential to get the tail up early to aid acceleration. For carrier operations TAKE-OFF (25-degree) flaps were used, but with the requirement for open engine cowl gills and a two-pitch propeller, a free-run takeoff was quite unimpressive.

The initial rate of climb was poor for a fighter at 1,580 ft/min and decreased to 930 ft/min at 6,000 ft. The service ceiling was a mere 19,000 ft, and maximum speed at 6,700 ft was a stately 195 knots (225 mph).

The all-up stall occurred at 72 knots without warning, causing a sharp wing drop and incipient spin. Since spin recovery was poor, a spin parachute was fitted in a compartment aft of the rudder and between the elevators. Together, the poor maneuver margin and the likelihood of drastic results from high-speed stalling hardly inspired confidence in the Skua as a fighter.

It was in the dive-bomber role that the Skua came into its own. Approaches to the target were normally made at 8,000 ft at right angles, with the target kept in sight until it disappeared under the leading edge of the wingtip. The aircraft then pulled up, until the target reappeared at the trailing edge, and winged over into a steep 70-degree dive, extending its Zap flaps fully and keeping the target at the top of the engine cowling. Release height was 3,000 ft, where pullout was commenced and, simultaneously, flaps were retracted. Pullout was completed at around 1,500 ft to avoid bomb blast and light flak. The elevator force required to pull out was heavy.

The Skua behaved well when trimmed in the dive; it was steady longitudinally, and yet its ailerons remained moderately light and effective. The rudder force had to be trimmed out, otherwise a heavy foot load resulted, but there was a tendency for the two-position propeller to overspeed before terminal velocity was reached.

As a carrier aircraft the Skua had a poor record. Its approach speed of 80 knots was high for that era, it was nose-heavy on closing the throttle, and its oleopneumatic shock-absorber landing gear was of the high rebound type. This was a good recipe for a trip into the crash barrier.

At the outbreak of war three squadrons of Skuas were aboard HMS *Ark Royal,* and on 25 September 1939 a flight of these aircraft shot down a Dornier 18 flying boat off Heligoland—the Fleet Air Arm's first "kill" of World War II.

Assessment: The Skua, obsolescent as a fighter, had little hope of success except against slow aircraft, and it was vulnerable because of its poor performance. However, as a dive-bomber it performed effectively, provided it was not intercepted before reaching the target area. Having dropped its bomb load, it reverted in effect to a fighter and so had a reasonable chance of escape.

Fairey Swordfish

This torpedo/spotter/reconnaissance biplane began as a private venture in 1933 and evolved into the Swordfish prototype, which made its first flight on 17 April 1934. It entered service in February 1936 and was obsolete in both concept and design by the time World War II broke out, when the Fleet Air Arm had thirteen Swordfish squadrons embarked in five carriers. Thus this anachronism became the mainstay of British naval aviation, and although the enemy must have quietly smiled at the old "Stringbag," it was to enjoy several incredible successes in action.

The Swordfish was ungainly in appearance, with its massive girderlike struts angled out from the fuselage to support the lower center wing section, a braced tailplane, substantial main landing gear, a large tailwheel, and an engine that looked as if it had been added to the fuselage as an afterthought. The two cockpits were open; the rear two-seat cockpit was a cavernous unprotected hole in the fuselage, giving the impression that the aircraft had been badly shot up.

The effect of this mountain of appendages was a meager 25-knot speed range to cover climbing, cruising, and landing. Even then, anything could be hung on the Swordfish—torpedo, mines, bombs, rockets, or whatever—with negligible effect on an already negligible performance.

The Swordfish was a two-bay, unequal-span, staggered biplane with ailerons on all four wings. The aircraft structure, including flying controls, was covered in fabric. The wing span was 45 ft 6 in, which narrowed to a width of 17 ft 3 in when folded. Folding was done manually.

This fairly large aircraft was powered by an air-cooled, super-

Fairey Swordfish (Flight International)

charged radial engine, a 690-hp, nine-cylinder Bristol Pegasus III M.3. The engine drove a three-bladed, fixed-pitch Fairey-Reed metal propeller. The aircraft had an empty weight of 4,700 lbs and could carry virtually double this with an overload weight of 9,250 lbs. The engine was started by cranking an external inertia flywheel, then engaging the clutch from the cockpit until the hideously noisy machine sprang into life.

Takeoff was made without flaps. The run was short, and the aircraft exhibited little tendency to swing. The deck run at maximum loaded weight in a 20-knot wind was 540 ft. The climb at 70 knots was barely worthy of the name, requiring 10 min to reach 5,000 ft.

In cruising flight at 85 knots, the Swordfish was stable about all axes and easy to fly on instruments. Harmony of control was somewhat spoiled by an overly sensitive rudder, although this effect was canceled because the rudder aided the slightly heavy ailerons in endowing the aircraft with agility totally out of keeping with its ungainly

appearance. Its rate of turn was phenomenal. In essence, the Swordfish was virtually without vice when it came to flying.

The stall consisted of a gentle sink at 52 knots, and recovery was
immediate. Carrier landings were made at 60 knots without flaps,
which would have encouraged float. Indeed the flaps, simply an 8-
degree symmetrical drooping of the ailerons, were only used for cat-
apulting. That the view was not ideal for landing mattered little, for
this airplane virtually landed itself.

The armament of the Swordfish consisted of one fixed, forward-
firing .303 Vickers machine gun in the starboard fuselage decking and
one .303 Lewis machine gun with 600 rounds on a Fairey high-speed
flexible mounting in the rear cockpit. An 18-in torpedo or a 1,500-lb
bomb load could be carried.

In 1939 the Swordfish saw active service only on fleet protection
and convoy escort duties; this was the calm before its stormy wartime
career. With a range of 474 nm at full load, it was useful in such
duties.

Assessment: The Swordfish was an obsolete design that could
only survive in an environment of air superiority. It possessed good
handling qualities but, except for being a good weight lifter, it performed poorly.

MESSERSCHMITT 109E

The Me 109, when it was designed by Willy Messerschmitt of the
Bayerische Flugzeugwerke A. G., was officially designated the Bf 109,
and as such it had by 1939 acquired an awesome reputation as a high-
performance aircraft and a killer in combat. A specially modified
version held the world speed record for land planes, 481.4 mph, and
showed itself to be the outstanding fighter in the Spanish Civil War
while in service with the Condor Legion.

The Me 109E was a cantilevered, low-wing, single-seat monoplane built of metal with flush-riveted duralumin skin. The fuselage
was an oval monocoque structure; the single-spar wing was fitted
with automatic leading edge slats, and the inboard portions of the
trailing edge carried slotted flaps. The tailplane was braced and could
be adjusted by handwheel in the cockpit. It had a fixed tailwheel and
a narrow track landing gear with a splayed look.

The aircraft had an 1,150-hp, twelve-cylinder, inverted-V, liquid-
cooled engine, a Daimler-Benz 601A. It drove a three-blade, electrically operated, controllable-pitch, full-feathering airscrew. The main
fuel tank behind the pilot's seat held 88 imperial gals (105.68 U.S.
gals). The aircraft was started by a hand-cranked inertia flywheel
engaged from the cockpit.

Messerschmitt 109E (U.S. Naval Institute)

The Me 109E always looked sleekly sinister to me, and it felt sinister once I was seated in that small, narrow cockpit which made movement of the head difficult—hardly ideal for a combat fighter. The auxiliary services were mostly electrical; apart from the undercarriage and radiator, which were hydraulically operated, and the flaps, which were directly connected to a manually operated handwheel and, consequently, tediously slow in lowering.

Takeoff was commendably short, engine response to throttle movement commendably good. The strong swing to port could easily be held on rudder, but it was advisable to raise the tail as quickly as possible owing to the poor forward view. This could be done fairly coarsely, without fear of the airscrew hitting the ground, as the high thrust line of the inverted-V engine gave ample clearance. However, the airplane had to be flown off; because the wing slats opened unevenly, any attempt to pull it off the ground early resulted in aileron snatching.

The main wheels retracted quickly, but airscrew pitch changed slowly. The flaps were raised manually by means of the outer of two concentrically mounted wheels to the pilot's left, the inner wheel adjusting tailplane incidence. Thus as the flaps came up the wheels could be moved together to counteract the change in trim.

The Me 109E climbed steeply at an initial rate of 3,100 ft/min. Stability proved excellent in the longitudinal and lateral planes but was almost neutral directionally. Control harmony was poor for a fighter, the rudder being light, the ailerons moderately light, and the elevators extremely heavy. There was no rudder trimmer, which meant it was necessary to apply moderate right rudder during the climb and considerable left rudder during a dive.

Cruising speed at 62.5 percent rated power was 298 mph, a condition in which it was pleasant to fly. Maximum speed was 354 mph at 12,300 ft. Service ceiling was 36,000 ft.

The clean stall at 105 mph was preceded by elevator buffet and the uneven opening of slats about 20 mph above the stall, accompanied by unpleasant aileron snatching. The stall itself was fairly gentle, with the nose dropping about 10 degrees. In the landing configuration the stall occurred at 99 mph and with identical symptoms, apart from heavier elevator buffeting.

The landing approach at 118 mph was steep, but elevator feel was positive and gave delightfully accurate control. Attitude had to be substantially changed on flaring before touchdown. Care had to be taken to prevent speed from decaying too much in the flare, otherwise a wing could drop as a result of the uneven snatching of slats. On the ground run there was a tendency to swing because of the narrow track landing gear.

Armament provided for one 20-mm engine-mounted cannon firing through the center of the airscrew spinner, although this was not normally fitted in the early 109Es. Two 7.7-mm MG 17 machine guns were mounted on the engine crankcase and synchronized to fire through the airscrew. Two 20-mm Oerlikon cannon were mounted on the wings and fired outside the airscrew disc. A 550-lb bomb could be carried on a rack under the fuselage.

During 1939–40 ten Me 109Es were converted by the Fieseler factory at Kassel to 109Ts for operation from the aircraft carrier *Graf Zeppelin*. They had increased span, manually folding outer wings, wing spoilers, an arrester hook, and catapult spools. They never actually became carrier-borne. Even with extra wing area to reduce landing speed, and with spoilers to give more lift control on the approach and to kill float on touchdown, the aircraft would have been difficult to land on deck because of its poor view and tendency to drop a wing.

Assessment: The Me 109E was a formidable fighter of proven ability, but one with certain handling shortcomings that could be exploited in combat if known to the opposition. Above all it was a survivor; in its developed forms the Me 109E fought right through World War II, and it was built in larger numbers than any other airplane except the Russian Ilyushin Il-2. The Me 109 was also the exclusive mount of the highest-scoring fighter pilot in the world, Major Erich Hartmann, who had 352 victories.

MESSERSCHMITT 110C

The Me 110C design was developed from a 1934 Luftwaffe specification for a long-range strategic fighter. The aircraft was a cantilevered, low-wing monoplane built of metal, with flush-riveted, stressed, duralumin skin. The fuselage was an oval monocoque structure with an elongated and extensively glazed canopy enclosing the crew of two. The tailplane was mounted above the rear of the fuse-lage with endplate fins and rudders. The wing carried leading-edge automatic slats and trailing-edge slotted flaps.

The Me 110C was powered by two 1,100-hp, twelve-cylinder, inverted-V, liquid-cooled engines, Daimler-Benz DB601As, with di-rect fuel injection in place of conventional carburetors. The engines drove VDM three-bladed, controllable-pitch, fully feathering air-screws. The airplane was started by electrically energized inertia starters.

Its takeoff run was long and directional control poor until the tail could be raised. The angle of climb was steep at an initial rate of 2,500 ft/min. Cruising speed at 10,000 ft was 280 mph with the controls fairly light, well harmonized, and effective up to 250 mph, but thereafter they began to grow heavy, particularly the elevator. Stability was good fore and aft and directionally, but neutral laterally.

When the flaps were first moved during landing, attitude changed nose-up abruptly, an effect reversed with further flap movement and resulting in no change of trim. The ailerons began to droop as the flaps moved, their control suddenly lightening but without apparent loss of effectiveness. The approach attitude at 100 mph was rather steep, but the view ahead was excellent. As with the Me 109, care had to be taken not to hold off too high when the automatic slats were activated, for speed decayed and this could cause a wing to drop.

The Me 110C had a useful turn of speed with a maximum of 349 mph at 23,000 ft, which was slightly slower than that of the Me 109E. It had a service ceiling of 32,000 ft and a cruising range of 680 miles. It carried two 20-mm Oerlikon cannon under the nose and four 7.9-mm machine guns in the upper portion of the nose. One move-able 7.9-mm machine gun on an Arado mounting was located in the rear gunner's cockpit. The Me 110C could carry a 4,800-lb bomb load.

This aircraft first saw action against the British RAF on 18 December 1939, when twenty-two Wellington bombers on an armed reconnaissance of the Heligoland Bight were intercepted by a mixed force of 110s and 109s and fourteen bombers were lost.

Assessment: The Me 110C was a useful night-fighter, but as a day-fighter it lacked the agility to mix with single-seat interceptors. Its forward-firing armament proved lethal against bombers, but it was poorly defended from the rear. Its basic flying characteristics were strikingly similar to those of the Me 109.

JUNKERS 87B

When Germany placed its first contract for a *Sturzkampflugzeug* or dive-bomber on 27 September 1933, the Ju 87 was born. Five of the

Messerschmitt 110C (U.S. Naval Institute)

first-production Ju 87B-1s were dispatched to Spain in October 1938 and enjoyed considerable success in the environment of air superiority provided by the Condor Legion. The same subtype fired the opening shots in World War II and became the backbone of the Nazi blitzkrieg in Europe, thus earning for itself a reputation as a ferocious weapon. It had the appearance of a predatory bird in the dive and this, along with its devastating bombing accuracy and banshee-like scream when fitted with a siren, created a powerful psychological effect on the unfortunate populace below.

The Stuka, as it came to be known, employed the Junkers double-wing principle for its inverted gull wing and its sturdy tailplane. Massive fixed landing gear with streamlined fairings, square fin and rudder, chin radiator, and greenhouse crew compartment canopy all gave an angular look to the airplane. Dive brakes were fitted underneath the wings and turned through 90 degrees to present a flat plate area to the airflow.

The single unit powering the Ju 87B was a 1,200-hp, twelve-cylinder, inverted-V, liquid-cooled engine, a Junkers Jumo 211Da driving a three-bladed VDM controllable-pitch airscrew. It was started by an inertia system, which was standard in most Luftwaffe aircraft.

For takeoff, the tailwheel had to be locked and the takeoff flap setting used. There was little swing and the unstick distance was short. After the flaps had been retracted, the climb was made at 133 mph, a laborious affair at the full-load weight of 9,370 lbs. The view even in this nose-up attitude was excellent because of the highly positioned pilot's seat and good visibility through the large greenhouse canopy.

Cruising at a speed of 160 mph at 10,000 ft, the aircraft exhibited positive stability about all three axes. All the controls were reasonably light and effective. In summary, the Ju 87B was a pleasant airplane to handle; this combined with its automatic pullout mechanism were the secrets of its operational success.

The preparations for diving were to set the landing flaps, trim-

Junkers 87B (U.S. Naval Institute)

mers, and airscrew pitch in the cruise position; switch on the contact altimeter and set it to the release altitude; put the supercharger on automatic; close the cooler flaps, throttle right back; and open the dive brakes. This last action activated the pullout mechanism and made the aircraft nose over into a dive.

Dive angle was established by aligning with the horizon the required one of a series of lines of inclination marked on the front starboard side screen of the cockpit. The Ju 87B could be stood on its nose, for acceleration was slow; it took some 4,500 ft for the aircraft to reach 335 mph, and thereafter it crept gradually to the absolute permitted limit of 373 mph (600 kilometers).

As speed built up, the nose of the Ju 87B was used as its aiming mark. The elevators were moderately light in the initial stages of the dive, but they grew considerably heavier with increased speed. Any alteration in azimuth to keep the aiming mark on target could be made accurately with the ailerons. These also grew heavy with speed, but they always remained effective. Use of the elevator or rudder trimmers in a dive or pullout was strictly forbidden. During a dive the signal light on the contact altimeter would come on; it warned the pilot to depress the knob on the control column and thereby initiate the automatic pullout at 6 "g," a 1,475-ft height margin being required to complete the maneuver.

Once the aircraft had its nose safely pointed above the horizon from the pullout, the dive brakes were retracted, the airscrew pitch was set to takeoff/climb, and the throttle and radiator flaps were opened.

Landing was easy, the Ju 87B approaching at 93 mph with an excellent view and progressively reducing speed to 75 mph at holdoff. Powerful brakes and tail-heaviness ensured a short landing run after a three-pointer touchdown.

Armament for the two-man crew, sitting back to back, consisted of two fixed, forward-firing 7.9-mm MG 17 machine guns, one on either side of the fuselage and firing outside the airscrew disc, and one similar-caliber gun on a flexible mounting in the rear cockpit. There were two standard bomb loads, either one 1,100-lb bomb under the fuselage, or one 550-lb bomb under the fuselage and four 110-lb bombs under the wings, two on each side outboard of the dive brakes. The fuselage bomb was carried on swing links so that, before release, it could be swung down to clear the airscrew.

When hostilities began in Europe, the aircraft carrier *Graf Zeppelin* was 85 percent complete and was supposed to carry a squadron of Stukas. This special version, designated the Ju 87C, was fitted with catapult spools, an arrester hook immediately ahead of the tailwheel, main landing gear legs (for emergency landing on water these could be jettisoned), flotation equipment, and manually folded outer wing panels. A small batch of these aircraft had been built and a later version with electrical wing folding was under construction when work on the carrier was suspended in October 1939.

In my opinion the Ju 87B would have been a good deck-landing aircraft, but judging from its airfield landing performance, one can conclude that its rather weak main landing gear and tailwheel would have required strengthening.

Assessment: The Ju 87B was a most effective dive-bomber, but its poor performance and weak defensive armament meant that unless it was operated in an environment where air superiority reigned, it was extremely vulnerable. It was a powerful psychological weapon because of its spectacular record of success against weak opposition, and it became a symbol of the Nazi jackboot. The Ju 87B also gave Germany its greatest war hero, Hans-Ulrich Rudel, who flew 2,530 Stuka sorties in the plane and survived the war.

HEINKEL 111H

The He 111 was designed early in 1934 as a high-speed transport but, ultimately, as a bomber for the still-secret Luftwaffe. The prototype made its first flight on 24 February 1935 and gave a performance comparable to that of contemporary fighters. Eventually, in early 1937, the Luftwaffe sent thirty He 111B-1s to the Condor Legion in Spain, where they proved eminently successful.

In the first months of World War II the He 111H was used in antishipping strikes against British naval and merchant units. In this role it was manned mainly by former naval pilots and navigators who found themselves pressed into the Luftwaffe by Field Marshal Goering's edict, "Everything that flies belongs to me."

The He 111H was a thing of aerodynamic beauty; it had a sleek, cigar-shaped fuselage and elliptical wings and tail unit. But all is not gold that glitters, as I found out on flying it for the first time. The long glazed nose of the bomber made me feel as though I was looking down a glass tunnel. Indeed, in inclement weather the view ahead was so bad that the pilot's seat had to be elevated, allowing the head to emerge through a sliding panel in the upper decking, where it was partially protected from the slipstream by a small retractable windscreen.

This monoplane's low wings had ailerons on the outer sections and hydraulically operated slotted flaps on the inner sections. The ailerons drooped when the flaps were lowered. Flettner trimming tabs were fitted to the elevators.

Normally the He 111H carried a crew of four. The pilot sat on the port side of the unsymmetrical glazed nose, the navigator/bomb aimer/nose gunner on the right. The flying controls were conventional enough. An arm at the top of the control column could be swung over to enable the crew member on the right to control the elevators and ailerons. There were no dual engine or rudder controls, but the elevator and rudder trimmer controls, on the pilot's right, could be reached by the navigator, as could the coolant radiator-control handles. The throttles, supercharger control levers, and airscrew-pitch control levers were all on the pilot's left.

The radio/operator/gunner and second gunner in the rear were separated from the forward crew members by the bomb bay, although there was a narrow catwalk between the two rows of vertically stacked bombs.

The He 111H-4 was powered by two 1,100-hp, twelve-cylinder, inverted-V, liquid-cooled engines, Junkers Jumo 211Ds. These drove three-bladed VDM full-feathering controllable-pitch airscrews. Total fuel capacity was 762 imperial gals (915 U.S. gals). The engines were started with the standard electrically energized or hand-energized inertia system.

The takeoff run was short, with the airplane exhibiting little tendency to swing, and rate of climb was good at about 800 ft/min fully loaded. The aircraft handled beautifully, being stable around all axes and offering good harmony of control. The maximum permissible acceleration at 24,251 lbs was 2.7 "g" with maximum bank in turns of 65 degrees. Cruising speed was 225 mph using 61 percent power at 17,000 ft. Maximum speed was 260 mph at 17,000 ft. Maximum permissible speed in a dive was 298 mph.

Armament consisted of two 7.9-mm MG 17 machine guns in the nose, one fixed and one flexible; a 7.9-mm machine gun in the upper shielded mounting over the wings; and in the ventral position, a 7.9-mm machine gun and a 20-mm cannon, one firing forward and the other aft. Internal stowage accommodated eight 550-lb bombs.

Assessment: The He 111 was undoubtedly the outstanding medium bomber of the 1930s, both with regard to performance and versatility, but it was vulnerable to fighter attack because of its lack of adequate defensive armament. It was well liked by pilots and navigators, though the internal layout made it unpopular with the rear crew members; lack of mutual support detracted from morale and combat efficiency.

1939 Operations

In the first four months of World War II the British and German air forces had only casual, accidental contact and only carried out limited probe operations against each other. Both sides were cautious at first, forbidding the dropping of bombs on enemy territory, attacks on merchant ships, and overflights of neutral countries. The only legitimate targets were enemy warships on the open sea or in channel approaches to harbors; there were some stirring skirmishes in the Heligoland Bight and Firth of Forth, but little else.

The Fleet Air Arm's activities at this stage were virtually confined to antisubmarine patrols from carriers, occasional intruder chases, and reconnaissance flights such as those in the famous *Graf Spee* encounter in the South Atlantic.

The sum total of this "phoney war" was an absence of fighter-versus-fighter combat, though there were a number of occasions on which multiple fighters met bombers.

SINGLE COMBAT

Often the outcome of aerial combat in war is influenced by factors other than performance, handling qualities, and the firepower of the aircraft involved. There is the skill of the crew, the tactical situation (air superiority, escort cover, ground defenses), weather, balance of forces, intelligence information, and so forth. The removal of these external factors enables us to make at least a theoretical comparison of aircraft in single combat. The outcome of an encounter can be cross-checked for accuracy by reference to operational results, where, of course, the other factors come into play. In the considerable number of cases in which combatants never fought, verdicts must remain theoretical.

Sea Gladiator Versus Messerschmitt 109E

This was obsolescence versus modernity, with the biplane's only hope of survival resting in its remarkable maneuverability. Any foolhardy attempt by the Me 109E pilot to engage the Gladiator in a dogfight and he would have to pull high "g" turns, opening the slats and causing aileron snatching, which would ruin his aim if he could bring his guns to bear at all. If the Me 109E tightened the turn beyond this point it would lose longitudinal control in a high-speed stall and, for a rare few seconds, be helpless in the face of the Gladiator.

However, German pilots were well trained and not caught this easily. Their best tactic was to maneuver at speed around, over, and under the Gladiator, keeping out of his view as much as possible, then pouncing when he reversed bank or eased his turn. Just one short burst of the Me 109E's powerful armament was lethal against the fabric-covered biplane.

Verdict: The superiority of the Me 109E was virtually total in this encounter.

Sea Gladiator Versus Messerschmitt 110C

The Me 110C was less maneuverable than the 109E and with similar handling characteristics was less likely to weave a confusing web around the Gladiator. However, it had the advantage of a pair of eyes in the back of its head—a rear gunner with a good field of fire on either beam—so an encounter would become a cat and mouse game, with the German gunner directing his pilot when necessary, knowing that his own aircraft had immunity from attack by the Gladiator because of its 100-mph speed advantage.

A single machine gun may not seem a very powerful rear armament, but against a fabric-covered airplane it was highly effective. I can vouch for that, having witnessed a Me 110C rear gunner blast a Hawker Hart biplane, not unlike the Gladiator, out of the English skies in the summer of 1940.

Verdict: This contest, if anything, was probably even more one-sided than a contest involving the single-seat Me 109E. If tracer ammunition was used by the German aircraft, there was a high risk of the Gladiator becoming a "flamer."

Sea Gladiator Versus Junkers 87B

With a significant advantage in speed and climb and infinitely better maneuverability, the Gladiator could deal effectively with the Ju 87B, provided it attacked from dead astern to restrict the German rear gunner's field of fire. If a renewed attack were necessary, the Gladiator would have to break away down and beyond the enemy gun's angle of depression before climbing back up for the attack.

A head-on attack was not a sound tactic for the Gladiator because of the Ju 87B's useful forward-firing armament and because the Gladiator lacked the speed margin necessary to catch up with the German aircraft if the first pass was not successful.

The Ju 87B's only defense against fighter attack was to try and bring its rear gun to bear. Although reasonably nimble for such a large aircraft, it was no match for one of the most maneuverable fighters ever built.

Verdict: The Ju 87B was one of the few aircraft in the German inventory that the Gladiator, despite its status as possibly the world's best biplane fighter, could handle. The Gladiator's margin of superiority was not so great that it could afford to lose respect for the Stuka.

Sea Gladiator Versus Heinkel 111H

The He 111H belonged to the new breed of high-performance bombers that could give most contemporary fighters a run for their money. Indeed, if it operated at its rated altitude of 20,000 ft, it could outrun the Gladiator. However, because it aimed its weapons visually, it usually operated at much lower altitudes, and this narrowed the speed gap to virtually zero. I chased two He 111Hs in a Gladiator over England in the autumn of 1940 at about 5,000 ft, and once I had dived off my slight height advantage, I could make little gain on them; fortunately, they fell to ground defenses before they could reach their target at Bristol, otherwise I might not have been able to close in with some twenty miles yet to run to the intended bomb-release point.

To close a bomber with defensive rear armament at a low relative speed is of course courting trouble, but if the Gladiator found itself in a favorable position to pick up reasonable closing speed for an astern attack it would have a fair chance of success. In this case, it would be vulnerable in the break unless it employed its full rate of turn.

Verdict: Near parity in performance would make the He 111H a hard nut for the Gladiator to crack. Unless the latter were favorably positioned for attack, it would probably be as much at risk as the bomber.

Skua Versus Messerschmitt 109E

Encounters between these two aircraft were not uncommon in 1940. If one took place at around 10,000 ft, while the Skua was en route to a target, the advantage lay heavily with the German fighter because it enjoyed higher speed, better maneuverability, and superior firepower against a sluggish performer with a bomb load. In such an encounter the Me 109E invariably attacked from the rear in a flat pass made possible by its high overtaking speed; its objective would be to make the Skua's rear gun ineffective by keeping within the narrow arc where the gunner could not fire without risk of hitting his own tail unit.

Even when diving the Skua was in grave danger from the Me

109E, which with its direct-injection fuel system could bunt steeply to follow without any loss of speed and without yaw effect from engine cutting. The only problem facing the German pilot was the heavy foot load necessary to counteract engine torque—he had no rudder trimmer to help him remove yaw while aiming his guns.

Once the Skua had released its bomb in a dive, its best chance of survival against the Me 109E was to descend to sea level, forcing the enemy fighter to come in on a shallow dive from astern or from the quarter; at this point the Skua could bring its rear gun to bear. My tactic, if the attack came from astern, was to open the dive brakes when the rear gunner estimated the German was just coming into firing range. This maneuver rapidly slowed the Skua, and the Me 109E would suddenly become more interested in avoiding collision than in opening fire.

In Norway, where most of the Skua operations took place, it was also a good tactic to hug the steep walls of the fiords when leaving the target zone, thus preventing a quarter attack and making a stern attack difficult, if not impossible. But fiords don't extend endlessly; one would eventually reach the open sea and there face increased risk of attack.

Verdict: The Skua was extremely vulnerable to the Me 109E, especially when carrying its bomb. There was no question of mixing with the German in a fighter-versus-fighter dogfight, so little was achieved by jettisoning the load. The Skua's survival hung heavily on the rear gunner, and even then was slim until sea level could be reached, where it would be considerably more difficult for the enemy to achieve a kill.

Skua Versus Messerschmitt 110C

While carrying a bomb load, the Skua would be in even more trouble against the Me 110C because of its heavier armament, which included a flexible rear gun. The Me 110C also had direct-fuel-injection engines and could bunt steeply, without losing momentum, to follow the Skua in a dive-bombing attack.

Once divested of its bomb, the Skua would not have the same survival prospects in a low-level flight profile because of the Me 110C's rear-gun flexibility. It would probably pay the Skua pilot to go into the fighter role, for then he had a slight edge in turning maneuverability and had useful front and equivalent rear armament. In such a dogfight the Skua pilot would be well advised to keep height at around 1,000 ft, negating the Me 110C's superior performance in speed, rate and angle of climb, and acceleration in the dive.

Verdict: The Skua with bomb aboard was even more vulnerable to the Me 110C than to the Me 109E, but it could probably create a stalemate in a fighter-versus-fighter encounter. The problem with this latter possibility was that, in the Skua's operational role as a dive-bomber in Norway, it was usually at maximum range from its Scottish base in the Orkneys and so could only afford some five minutes at maximum combat power.

Skua Versus Junkers 87B

Such a confrontation would of course only occur with the Skua in the fighter role. It would involve two large, obsolescent airplanes of the same vintage, each carrying a rear gunner. Of the three variables of performance, maneuverability, and armament, the only significant difference between the two combatants was the superior number of forward-firing guns carried by the Skua.

With that small advantage the odds hardly weighed heavily in favor of the Skua, so it boiled down to the skills of pilot and rear gunner. In this respect, it must be remembered that Skua pilots were trained primarily in fighter tactics, Ju 87B pilots in dive-bombing and defensive tactics.

Verdict: Taking everything into consideration, the Skua should have a slight edge over the Ju 87B because it would be the aggressor in such combat, while the German would have been on the defensive.

Skua Versus Heinkel 111H

The He 111H at this stage of the war was only used as a medium-level bomber; not yet adapted for torpedo dropping, it had a slight speed advantage over the Skua, which meant the latter required a height advantage to close the enemy. Even then, the relative speed difference would be small and the Skua would be under fire for a significant time during both attack and breakaway. A head-on attack would be the most effective, but it would be strictly a one-pass effort on account of the Skua's inferior performance.

Verdict: The Skua would be hard pressed to destroy the He 111H and, indeed, to avoid being destroyed itself. This would be a finely balanced encounter that could go either way.

Swordfish Versus Messerschmitt 109E

With the tremendous disparity in performance and armament between these two aircraft, this might look like a no contest situation. But the difference in speed, while it could pose a few problems for the fighter, would not affect the inevitable outcome.

When committed to the straight-and-level torpedo-aiming run, the Swordfish was a sitting duck for the Me 109E. On 12 February 1942, in the heroic attack conducted by six Swordfish against the German battle cruisers *Scharnhorst* and *Gneisenau* and the heavy cruiser *Prinz Eugen*, the German fighters used flaps and lowered their landing gear to get sufficient firing time to annihilate all six Swordfish.

Verdict: The Swordfish was no match for the Me 109E. Such an encounter could only have one result—destruction of the biplane.

Swordfish Versus Messerschmitt 110C

The twin fighter was an even more formidable threat to the Swordfish because of the flexibility of its armament, a powerful antidote to the biplane's maneuverability. Tight turns might slightly delay, but would not ultimately prevent, the coup de grâce.

Verdict: This would be a totally one-sided encounter, the result favoring the Me 110C.

The United States

When World War II broke out the United States remained neutral, pending government assessment of the situation. It initiated a neutrality patrol out to 300 miles off the East Coast and running south along the boundary of the Caribbean. Any foreign warships entering this zone were to be reported immediately. Naturally, the brunt of this task fell on the U.S. Navy.

In 1939 that navy was almost exclusively equipped with biplane dive-bombers, scouts, and fighters. It was fortunate to have over two hundred efficient PBY Catalina monoplane flying boats, which made excellent patrol aircraft. When hostilities commenced, the United States reacted by shifting its massive aircraft-production machine into top gear. Soon an impressive array of new designs were coming off the drawing board.

The Soviet Union

The signing of the Soviet-German Non-Aggression Pact on 23 August 1939 left Hitler in a position to concentrate his war effort on a single front, but it also gave Stalin a chance to close the frontiers of his vast empire. The Russians, who had always feared the Germans and their intentions, considered the passage from East Prussia to the Baltic States particularly vulnerable. The first step was taken in September 1939 when Russia and Esthonia, Latvia, and Lithuania signed the Pacts of Mutual Assistance; under their provisions, the Russians were able to garrison the tiny Baltic states. The second step proved much harder to take. On 30 November 1939 the Russians attacked Finland's thousand-mile frontier at eight points, the thrust of the action falling on the Karelian Isthmus. At the same time the Red Air Force bombed the capital of Helsingfors, giving the West its first evidence since the Spanish Civil War of Soviet air potential.

The Red Air Force comprised two independent forces, one in

the west and one in the Far East, as well as regional aircraft industries to support them. However, its equipment was significantly inferior to that being flown by the Germans and the Allies, and Soviet pilots, while not lacking courage, proved to be poorly trained in tactical flying. The Red Air Force suffered not only from inferior aircraft but also from inadequate numbers—Russian territory was enormous and the organization of its communist labor force, inefficient.

With regard to aircraft and engine design, Russia was not lacking invention, but generally it copied proven technology from the West.

I-16 RATA

The Rata is one of the few Russian aircraft I have flown. Designed by Nikolai N. Polikarpov, it was the world's first cantilevered monoplane with retractable landing gear and an enclosed cockpit. Its stubby, wooden, barrel-like monocoque fuselage merged with a low cantilevered wing by means of immense roots, fully half the overall length of the fuselage. The wings were fabric covered. The Rata made its first flight in December 1933, powered by a 450-hp license-built Gnome-Rhone Jupiter engine driving a two-bladed, two-pitch AV1 metal airscrew.

The version I flew had graduated to a 750-hp M-25V engine. Its appearance reminded me vividly of the Granville Gee Bee, an American racing plane of the 1930s, and the later Brewster Buffalo. On walking around it, I realized that none of the control surfaces were balanced and that the tailplane could be adjusted on the ground. The original sliding canopy had been replaced by a small, fixed windscreen. The telescopic gun sight that had pierced the original windscreen had been replaced by a rudimentary reflector sight. Apparently the early canopy had obscured the vision of Russian pilots fighting in Spain.

Once I was in the cockpit it became doubly clear why the canopy had been dispensed with—the view ahead was terrible. The cockpit was narrow and uncomfortable despite the tubby fuselage. The instruments were basic—there was no fuel gauge or radio—and chaotically arranged. Light armor had been installed in the back of the pilot's seat.

The engine, based on the American Wright Cyclone, used a Hucks-type starter connected to the propeller boss, but unlike the Cyclone it had a rather unsteady note when running, which belied the sturdiness and reliability it displayed in service. The Russians have always believed that military engines are short-lived, and with their cheap labor it is more cost effective to replace than to repair.

Takeoff on grass was rough and took longer than expected, possibly owing to the drag of the tail skid. On a hot day unstick did not

Polikarpov I-16 Rata (Pilot Press)

occur until 125 mph had been reached. During takeoff directional
control was poor. Once the Rata was airborne, landing gear had to be
wound up manually with eighteen or twenty turns of a handcrank
located under the throttle; the result was a wobbly climb. With the
gear up, all buffet smoothed out and the aircraft climbed nicely at
3,000 ft/min.

   Cruising at 225 mph, the Rata had marginal longitudinal but
neutral lateral and directional stability. The controls were all sensitive, and its featherlight ailerons gave a high rate of roll. The Rata
was agile and had outstanding zoom-climb capability. Top speed was
283 mph at 10,000 ft, but acceleration was surprisingly poor in the
dive, when the nose showed a tendency to rise and a rigidly mounted
engine caused the airplane to shake and rattle through the whole
flight envelope. This made the Rata a poor gun platform.

   The Rata was not easy to land, because once the landing gear
was down—and one never knew if it was—the aircraft became sluggish and buffeted. When the long-span, split-type ailerons drooped 15
degrees to serve as flaps, the nose jerked up and one had to react
smartly; there was a marked tendency to drop a wing if power was
not kept on and speed was allowed to fall below 110 mph.

   It was difficult to achieve a three-point touchdown, for with rigid
shock absorbers fitted to the landing gear the airplane bounced dangerously nose up. The brakes, the worst I have ever encountered in
an aircraft, were virtually useless.

   The original armament of two 7.62-mm wing Shpitalny-
Komaritsky machine guns, each with 900 rounds, was increased by

the addition of two similar guns, each with 650 rounds, mounted on the forward fuselage decking and synchronized to fire through the airscrew disc. These were highly accurate weapons with a rate of fire amounting to 1,800 rounds per minute. They had a tendency to jam but could be cleared by using the gun-charging handles in the cockpit.

With 93.4 imperial gals (112 U.S.) of fuel in a tank located ahead of the pilot, the range was 500 miles and the duration 1.9 hours.

Assessment: The Rata, incorporating some innovative design features at its debut in the early 1930s, remained a useful fighter because its engine and armament were updated. Its performance, allied with its agility, allowed it to live with the Fiat CR 32 and the Me 109B in the Spanish Civil War, although it was fully taxed against the German fighter. Its biggest shortcomings were the engine vibration, which made it a poor gun platform, and its fragility against gunfire of even the lightest-caliber weapons.

Japan

When Japan's Kwantung Army seized Manchuria in the winter of 1931, Japan used aircraft carriers with great success. It suffered setbacks in 1937 when its biplane fighters encountered Russian Ratas, flown by Chinese pilots that had been trained by former U.S. Army Air Corps officers. It was not until the low-wing A5M Claude monoplane fighter appeared that Japan got back on its feet.

Although it had fixed landing gear and was 10 mph slower in level-flight top speed, the Claude was more maneuverable and climbed faster than the Rata. The air superiority that the Claude restored to the Japanese was still a fact in 1939, when they had six aircraft carriers in service.

The Norwegian Theater

2
1940

Year of Isolation

THE "PHONEY WAR" of late 1939 and early 1940 ended on 8 April 1940 when Germany invaded Norway. During the assault on Oslo nine Norwegian Gloster Gladiators surprised eight escorting Me 110s by attacking out of the sun; they lost four of their small force, the Germans, two. This was the beginning of the end for Norway.

The German assault included landings in Bergen Fiord, during which the 6,000-ton light cruiser *Königsberg* was hit by Norwegian shore batteries. The damaged vessel was moored at a mole and the British Admiralty decided to try and destroy her. Two Skua squadrons based in the Orkneys were ordered to undertake the operation, involving a round trip of 660 miles, which was almost the limit of the aircraft's effective range. Sixteen Skuas made the sortie on the morning of 10 April, each carrying a 500-lb bomb. They achieved surprise and executed a brilliant dive-bombing attack, with three direct hits and no bomb more than 50 yards off target. The magazines of the German cruiser exploded, and she rolled over and broke in half. Thus she died, first warship to become a victim of air attack in World War II. Only one Skua was sacrificed.

HMS *Ark Royal* arrived off the Norwegian coast on 24 April from the Mediterranean. She used her Skuas spasmodically in support of the Allied Expeditionary Force, which made counterlandings in central Norway between 14 and 19 April. By the end of the campaign the Skuas had accounted for nine He 111s, two Ju 88s, and produced the Royal Navy's first ace, Lieutenant W. P. Lucy, who was killed by return fire from an He 111H. In this period of operations six Skuas were shot down and ten were lost when they ran out of fuel. As for the Swordfish, which proved ineffective in torpedo attacks because of shallow fiord waters, they suffered a number of losses.

The Sea Gladiators accounted for an He 111H, a Ju 87, and an He 115.

HMS *Glorious*, which arrived with the *Ark Royal*, carried eighteen RAF Gladiators that were flown ashore and operated from a frozen lake. In two days seventeen were lost, after having destroyed, according to their claim, fourteen German aircraft.

In late May HMS *Furious* returned to Norway with another eighteen RAF Gladiators, while HMS *Glorious* brought eighteen Hawker Hurricane fighters. They came too late. The Hurricanes landed in Norway on 28 May, the same day the Dunkirk evacuation started. The aircraft, together with the *Ark Royal* and the *Glorious*, were at least able to cover the evacuation of the Allied Expeditionary Force from Norway. Most of the RAF planes were recovered by the *Glorious* in a remarkable embarkation made possible by a 40-knot wind over the deck and using partially deflated tires to improve the braking action of the Hurricanes, which had no arrester hooks.

When this unusual event ended, on 8 June, the carriers set off for Britain on different routes. The course taken by the *Glorious* brought her into the path of the German battle cruisers *Scharnhorst* and *Gneisenau*. Their 11-inch guns, using radar fire direction at a range of 28,000 yards, blasted the British carrier into oblivion before she could fly off any of her aircraft. In this action the *Scharnhorst* received a torpedo hit from one of the two attendant British destroyers, both of which were sunk. With serious engine-room damage she took refuge at Trondheim, where she was spotted by RAF reconnaissance. The *Ark Royal* was ordered to attack. Fifteen Skuas, dispatched at midnight on 12–13 June, met intense antiaircraft fire and fighter opposition. Eight were lost and the attack ended in failure.

The month of June 1940 was probably the most dramatic of World War II. Norway fell to German might, and in France the British army was being pushed back relentlessly into the English Channel. The Luftwaffe had been ordered to administer the coup de grâce, and Britain, in hopes of fending it off, threw in every available fighter it had. The surviving Skuas in Norway were dispatched to the south of England to fly patrols over the Dunkirk beaches during the evacuation of the British Expeditionary Force. They were involved in skirmishes with both German bombers and fighters, but in the chaotic inferno of Bomb Alley, as the English Channel came to be known, it was difficult to verify any claims of kills. Suffice it to say that the Skuas gave as good as they got, surviving with the support of cover given by RAF Spitfires and Hurricanes.

Swordfish were also used during the evacuation to attack barges, gun positions, and concentrations of enemy troops. They were vulnerable by day, and when one squadron of twelve was set on by a swarm of Me 109s, seven were lost. After that they were mostly confined to minelaying at night.

On 10 June Italy declared war on Britain and France. A week later the French laid down their arms. Britain now stood alone and at bay against the Axis powers, its fate dependent on victory in the air. The Battle of Britain, fought in the high summer of 1940, culminated in victory on 15 September. But this was only a breathing space. A number of naval pilots seconded to RAF fighter squadrons for the battle acquitted themselves with distinction.

Taking on the Italian Fleet

With Italy's entry into the war and the possibility of French forces in North Africa falling to or siding with the Axis, the Royal Navy's interest switched from the Norwegian Sea to the Mediterranean. By mid-July, after a British naval force had disabled those elements of the French fleet not sworn to the Free French cause, the Royal Navy turned its attention to the Italian fleet, defense of the strategic island fortress of Malta, and keeping open the Suez Canal. Taking stock of this situation from an aerial standpoint, we can line up British and Axis aircraft types as follows:

	British	Axis
Fighters:	Hawker Hurricane (RAF) Fairey Fulmar (FAA) Gloster Gladiator (RAF/ FAA)	Fiat C.R. 42 (Italy)
Dive-Bombers:	Blackburn Skua (FAA)	
Torpedo-Bombers:	Fairey Swordfish (FAA)	Savoia-Marchetti 79 (Italy)

I have flown all these, including the Hurricane, but will leave it out of the reckoning at this stage because it was confined to operations in defense of Malta.

In the Mediterranean theater of war a strange new factor came into play with Italian fighters, namely, the tendency of their pilots to perform aerobatics in combat. This indulgence did not serve any apparent tactical purpose; rather, it seemed to be a foolhardy display of prowess. Perhaps it was because they were flying highly maneuverable but inadequately armed airplanes and hoped to flaunt their one asset. Whatever the reason, it certainly made for a different kind of dogfight.

FAIREY FULMAR

The British Admiralty issued specification 0.8/38 calling for a two-seat naval fighter at a time when the Fairey company had been flight-testing its sleek P.4/34 day bomber. In fact, the bomber's second prototype was modified to become, in effect, the prototype Fulmar. The first-production Fulmar flew on 4 January 1940, and eight months later the first squadron was in service.

Although big by shipborne fighter standards, the Fulmar was a neat-looking airplane. It was of flush-riveted, stressed-skin construction with fabric-covered control surfaces and sturdy, wide-track landing gear. It had a particularly good cockpit layout, and despite a longish nose, the view from the pilot's seat was commendable.

It was powered by the medium-supercharged, twelve-cylinder Rolls Royce Merlin VIII of 1,080 hp, which drove a three-bladed, constant-speed, full-feathering propeller. The engine was started by a Coffman percussion cartridge.

The takeoff run was short, but climb was rather mediocre, starting at 1,105 ft/min and only accelerating to 1,200 ft/min at 7,000 ft. The aircraft had a service ceiling of 22,400 ft.

While cruising the Fulmar was stable about all axes, and the controls were relatively light and responsive for such a large fighter. Directional trim was sensitive. The plane was extremely steady in a dive and enjoyed reasonable acceleration. It was not easy to produce a high speed stall, as the all-up stalling speed was only 66 knots. However, if a "g" stall was produced and allowed to develop into a spin, a good amount of height was required to recover. Top speed was 222 knots (255 mph) at 2,400 ft—not very exciting.

As a deck-landing aircraft, the Fulmar fell into the "easy" category. It was necessary to hold a lot of power so that the slipstream could give positive rudder and elevator action, but it was a forgiving airplane. Since all-down stalling speed was 55 knots, the approach speed was a gentle 63 knots, and this, combined with the reasonably good view and responsive controls, made it a popular aircraft on the deck.

Of course, the Fulmar's trump card was its eight-gun armament, which gave it tremendous hitting power. There were four .303 Browning machine guns in either wing, each with 500 rounds of ammunition. This two-seat fighter was different in having no rear cockpit gun, a fact that kindled the fires of survival in observers, some of whom used Verey pistols to distract the enemy, others, sheets of toilet paper.

One of the principal demands of the 0.8/38 specification was endurance, and the Fulmar more than met it: at a speed of 130 knots,

Fairey Fulmar (Pilot Press)

the airplane could stay up 4.75 hours at 10,000 ft. This was achieved with a fuselage tank holding 155 imperial gals (186 U.S. gals) and a flush-fitting ventral tank holding 60 gals (72 U.S. gals).

Assessment: The Fulmar's performance was well below that of contemporary single-seat monoplane fighters, but it had a killer punch if it could bring its forward-firing armament to bear on the enemy. It was reasonably maneuverable for its size and had an endurance that made it useful for combat air patrol in carrier service.

FIAT CR 42

The Freccia, or Arrow, as it was named, was developed from the CR 32, which had distinguished itself in the Spanish Civil War, displaying excellent maneuverability and astonishing acceleration for a biplane in a dive. When Italy entered the war, the Corpo Aero Italiano had 290 CR 42s ready for operation.

The CR 42 was a single-seat fighter biplane with unequal-span, rigidly braced, fabric-covered wings. It had ailerons on the top wings only. The fuselage was covered with metal panels forward and fabric aft. The horn-balanced rudder and elevators were covered partly with metal, partly with fabric. There was a Flettner tab in the rudder. Streamline fairings enclosed the fixed landing gear.

I had a rare chance to fly this aircraft, serial no. MM5701, which had been damaged by British fighters and forced down the day Mussolini decided to make a show of Italian strength in the English skies. A force of bombers protected by fifty CR 42s and forty-eight Fiat G 50s attempted to attack Allied convoys in the mouth of the river Thames on 11 November 1940. The Italians lost eight bombers and five fighters on this first and last foray against Britain, whose uncertain weather created navigation difficulties for the Italian pilots.

On first seeing the CR 42, I was struck by its close resemblance

Fiat CR 42 (Pilot Press)

to the Gladiator, though it was sleeker and, even with an open cockpit, more streamlined. It was powered by a fourteen-cylinder, radial air-cooled, geared and supercharged Fiat A.74R.1C.38 engine of 840 hp, driving a three-bladed, constant-speed Fiat airscrew.

The takeoff run was short, and the aircraft's fairly strong tendency to swing could easily be controlled by the effective rudder. The CR 42 climbed at a steep angle at an initial rate of 2,500 ft/min. All the controls were light and effective, particularly the elevator. Stability was marginal, the hallmark of a good fighter. The airplane was an aerobatic gem, and it also flew remarkably fast for a biplane with a top speed of 270 mph at 12,400 ft.

Stalling speed, at 65 mph, brought little buffet and a straight nose drop. The aircraft could recover from an induced spin quickly and straightforwardly. It exhibited no unpleasant characteristics in landing at 80 mph, although view ahead from the cockpit aft of the trailing edge of the wings was poor.

The CR 42 was not adequately armed for a fighter. It carried, in the fuselage, two 7.7-mm machine guns that fired through the airscrew. In later models the caliber of gun was increased to 12.7 mm.

Cruising range was 460 miles, endurance two hours. The service ceiling was 31,000 ft.

Assessment: The CR 42 was a superb biplane that gave an outstanding performance for its type, but as a fighter it was undergunned. Though highly maneuverable, like all aircraft with a lot of fabric covering, it was very vulnerable to enemy fire.

SAVOIA-MARCHETTI 79

Savoia-Marchetti's trademark was the three-engine layout, and the SM 79, one of its most famous products, typified this. It was a low-wing cantilevered monoplane bomber, widely used in the Mediterranean as a torpedo-bomber against Allied shipping. The trailing edge of the wing, from tip to engine mounting, was hinged, the inner section acting as camber-changing flaps and the outer section as ailerons or flaps. The wing's leading edges had Handley Page slots. The aircraft had a single rudder and a braced tailplane.

The three power units were nine-cylinder, radial air-cooled Alfa-Romeo 126 R.C. 34s, geared and supercharged to give 750 hp at 11,000 ft. They drove three-bladed, two-position, variable-pitch Savoia-Marchetti airscrews. The aircraft was started with a compressed mixture through an engine-driven gas distributor.

The SM 79 appeared rather hump-backed. Fabric covered the sides and bottom of the fuselage as well as the tail unit. The engine installations were neat, though there was a lack of viewing positions in the after main body of the aircraft.

The cockpit, large and roomy, gave the sort of view I would have associated with an airliner rather than a military bomber. The pilot's seat had heavy back armor plating. Behind the two front seats were another two, for the wireless operator and engineer. The bomb compartment located in the center of the fuselage; behind it was the bomb aimer's position, outfitted with duplicate rudder control, flight instruments, bomb sights and releases, and an automatic camera. All compartments were connected.

During a straightforward takeoff the aircraft exhibited little

Savoia-Marchetti 79 (Smithsonian Institution)

swing. Unstick distance was short. The initial rate of climb was 1,000 ft/min, and the aircraft proved stable.

While the SM 79 was cruising, its controls were heavy and slow in effect, but stability was positive, making it a good weapons platform. It was easy to handle if either outer engine failed. Maximum speed was 260 mph at 11,500 ft.

The stall was gentle, the nose drop straight at 62 mph in the landing condition. Landing speed was 75 mph, and the aircraft gave a feeling of great solidity on the approach.

Armament consisted of four 7.7-mm machine guns, one in the hump on a fixed mount firing forward, two on movable mounts aft of the wings, and one above and one below the fuselage. A fourth gun was installed on a sliding mount inside the rear portion of the fuselage for defense on both sides. Bomb load was 2,200 lbs; two torpedoes could be carried, in lieu of bombs, under the fuselage.

The SM 79 had a service ceiling of only 23,000 ft but a useful range of 1,000 miles. There were armor-protected main fuel tanks in the wings and two auxiliary tanks behind the engines, giving an endurance of four and a half hours.

Assessment: As a torpedo-bomber the widely used SM 79 was slow, sluggish to maneuver, and not heavily armed for defense. The largely plywood and fabric covering of wings and fuselage increased its vulnerability.

Fulmar Versus CR 42

This situation was anomalous in that the biplane's performance was superior to that of the monoplane. Of course, the biplane was much more maneuverable. Indeed, it had all the handling assets except speed in a dive, and so the obvious tactic for the Fulmar was to get a height advantage over the biplane and, with overtaking speed thus gained, to bring its heavy armament to bear. The Fulmar could even pursue the CR 42 round a loop to capitalize on the possibility of overtaking it sufficiently in the downward part of the maneuver for firing. I know of actual cases of this happening.

The CR 42 was so underarmed that its chances of succeeding against a robust aircraft like the Fulmar were poor. It was, in effect, always on the defensive, even though the British fighter had no rear-firing gun.

Verdict: The spritely CR 42 was not easy prey for the somewhat pedestrian Fulmar, but one short burst of the latter's eight-gun armament was enough to cause catastrophic damage to the fabric biplane. Except as a defensive tactic, the CR 42's superior maneuverability was of little avail because of its inadequate armament.

Fulmar Versus Savoia-Marchetti 79

The Fulmar had speed parity with the Italian bomber and could afford to attack from any angle, but a beam attack turning to quarter and sliding astern would yield the best results, as no more than two guns could be brought to bear in defense. Again, the powerful armament of the Fulmar was likely to be decisive against the lightweight structure of the SM 79.

In its torpedo-dropping role the SM 79 was badly set up for defense: it had to restrict its speed for a successful drop, and the fighter would inevitably have a height advantage.

Verdict: The SM 79 would be a sitting duck if caught on a torpedo-bombing sortie by the Fulmar. Its meager armament, relatively slow speed, and light construction all worked against its chances of survival. Still, it was quite well armored in critical areas and had three engines, and so a lot of lead might be needed to down it.

Sea Gladiator Versus CR 42

This would have been a fascinating duel between the two best biplane fighters in the world. The CR 42 had a slight speed advantage, the Gladiator a slight armament advantage. In the matter of maneuverability the aircraft were about equal, and each was lightweight in construction.

Verdict: This combat would be decided on the skills of the opposing pilots. The outcome could go either way.

Sea Gladiator Versus Savoia-Marchetti 79

There was little speed difference between the British biplane and the Italian monoplane, a fact weighted in the Gladiator's favor when the SM 79 was on a torpedo-dropping sortie. In such circumstances, the Gladiator's best mode of attack would be a diving quarter, turning astern so it would become a two-gun versus four-gun battle. The four-gun Gladiator would be able to absorb less punishment than the bomber.

Verdict: This combat could go either way, with the relative skills of the fighter pilot and the bomber's defensive gunners largely determining the outcome. The odds would probably favor the Gladiator, because it would have the aggressor's initiative.

Skua Versus CR 42

In performance and handling, the Skua had the disadvantage in this encounter, but it was a better armed airplane and more robust. With no hope of besting the biplane in a dogfight, it would inevitably find itself in a defensive position.

The CR 42 would gain the greatest advantage from a quarter attack, sliding astern to keep fire from the rear gunner to a minimum, while the Skua's best counter would be to initiate a turn into the attacker, giving the rear gunner maximum firing time.

Verdict: The CR 42's remarkable agility should get it into an advantageous attacking position against the clumsy Skua, but it would probably take a number of firing passes before the biplane, with its light armament, would achieve a kill.

Skua Versus Savoia-Marchetti 79

Provided the Skua could catch the Italian bomber on a torpedo-dropping run, it would have a chance of approaching within striking distance and carrying out a stern attack. With its four guns against the SM 79's two, firing in defense, the odds should be in the Skua's favor.

Verdict: The Skua should have slightly more than a fifty-fifty chance of success, if contact could be made with a height advantage. In any other situation, the Skua would be hard pressed to catch the Italian bomber.

Swordfish Versus CR 42

This contest would involve two biplanes with tight turning circles and a large disparity in speed and agility. Both were covered in fabric and therefore vulnerable, and both were lightly armed.

The Swordfish's only real defense would be to hug the surface of the sea and wrap into a tight turn as the CR 42 came within firing range. This tactic could make things difficult, indeed dangerous, for the CR 42, but it would only be postponing the moment of truth.

Verdict: The Swordfish would be outclassed by the CR 42 in every department, which would make the outcome virtually inevitable.

Malta and the Mediterranean

The Italian fleet was modern and equal or superior in numbers to the British fleet in the Mediterranean, but it had no aircraft carrier or naval air arm, and without an indigenous supply of fuel oil, it was dependent on Germany.

British naval forces in the area consisted of the Mediterranean Fleet at Alexandria, with the *Eagle* carrying seventeen Swordfish, and Force H at Gibraltar, with the *Ark Royal* carrying Swordfish and Skuas. Between them stood the strategic island of Malta, a static carrier in effect, only 58 miles off Sicily.

Malta's strategic value lay in its location on the Italian supply route to Libya; air, surface, and submarine attacks could be conducted from Malta against ships on that route. It was necessary to keep the island intact with air defense in particular, and thus the Royal Navy was given the task of ferrying RAF Hurricane fighters by aircraft carrier to within flying distance of Malta, a shuttle service that became a long-term commitment. The carriers were not only ferrying but also protecting the convoys of merchant ships carrying supplies to the beleaguered island. They were constantly shadowed by Italian flying boats and seaplanes and attacked by SM 79 bombers, which were shot down in large numbers by the protecting Fulmars and, to a much lesser degree, by the Skuas.

In late August Force H was reinforced by a new carrier, HMS *Illustrious*, bringing eighteen Swordfish and fifteen new Fulmars along with radar and an armored flight deck. She was in fact only with Force H for the passage to Malta. Afterwards she joined the Mediterranean Fleet.

On 28 October Italy invaded Greece, and about the same time its naval strength was increased by two new battleships, giving it superiority in the Mediterranean. The British decided to attack the Italian fleet at its Taranto base, where on 11 November all six of its battleships lay at anchor. Twenty Swordfish from the *Illustrious* made this historic night attack, which crippled three battleships and damaged a cruiser and destroyer. Only two aircraft were lost.

The next month saw a drastic change in the balance of Mediterranean air power with Hitler's decision to bolster the Italians in Libya, where they were suffering defeats at the hands of the British army. The German plan was to neutralize Malta and thereby protect German forces going to Libya. The Luftwaffe Fliegerkorps X, the anti-shipping air corps so successful in the Norwegian campaign, was sent to Sicily with 226 aircraft, including 50 He 111s, 80 Ju 87s, 70 Ju 88s, and 26 Me 110s.

Toward the end of 1940 American aircraft ordered by European nations, which had already succumbed to German invasion, were diverted to the United Kingdom. These included Brewster F2A Buffalo and Grumman F4F Wildcat fighters. The latter scored the first victory by an American-built aircraft during the war; on 25 December 1940 two Wildcats shot down a Ju 88 over the Scapa Flow naval base in the Orkneys.

Thus 1940 drew to a close with Great Britain fighting against odds but having registered two major aerial victories in the Battle of Britain and at Taranto. Both of these morale-building successes also had strategic value. The Battle of Britain compelled the Germans to reconsider their plans to invade England, while the victory at Taranto

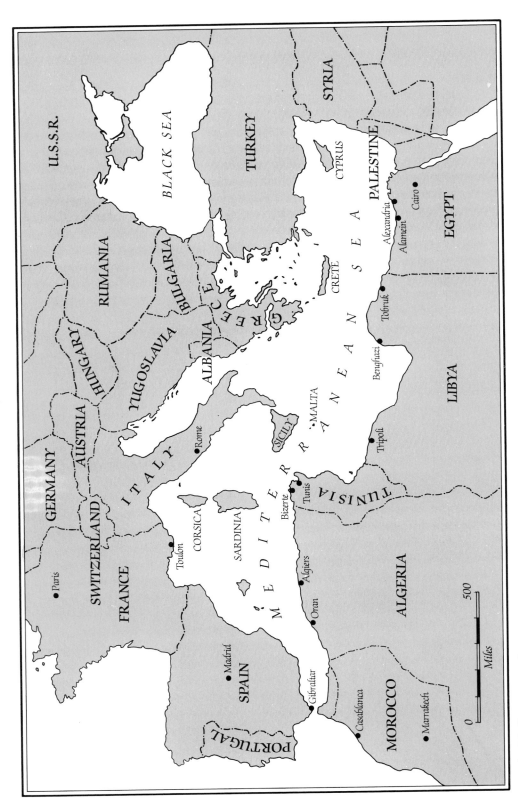

The Mediterranean Area

HMS Illustrious, *the First Carrier to Be Fitted with an Armored Flight Deck* (U.S. Naval Institute)

passed the balance of naval power in the Mediterranean from the Italians to the Royal Navy.

War had taken a heavy toll on Britain's gold reserves. In recognition of this and in response to Churchill's appeal, President Roosevelt had conceived a lend-lease plan and ordered its preparation for submission to Congress.

The United States of America

In September 1940 the United States concluded a transaction with Great Britain whereby fifty U.S. destroyers were exchanged for the lease of a series of bases in the West Indies and Bermuda.

Before the war the United States had been governed by the Neutrality Act, which forbade the shipment of arms to any belligerent nation. At the end of November 1939 the act was repealed and replaced by the new principle of "cash and carry," which preserved the appearance of neutrality by permitting the sale of weapons to Germany as well as the Allies. Three days after the passage of the new law the British Purchasing Commission began its work. One of its first buys was the Brewster Buffalo naval fighter.

Brewster F2A Buffalo

Early in 1940 the British Purchasing Commission placed contracts for 170 Buffalo; these were B-239Es, a version of the F2A-2 without arrester gear or catapult spools. I first flew a Buffalo in early 1941, and the appearance of the portly, stubby little fighter reminded me of the Granville Gee Bee racer of the 1930s.

The Buffalo was powered by a 1,100-hp, nine-cylinder radial

A Reconnaissance Photo of the Italian Fleet after the Taranto Attack
(Imperial War Museum)

engine, a Wright Cyclone R-1820-G105A, with a two-speed blower driving a Hamilton Standard Hydromatic propeller. It had a gross weight of 6,782 lbs, borne on wide-track, double-strutted landing gear and a retractable tailwheel. With a span of 35 ft, it did not require wing folding for carrier stowage.

Once in the roomy cockpit, I found the view ahead rather poor because of the aft location of the pilot and the high position of the nose. The cockpit instruments were metric, the aircraft being one of an original Belgian batch. The other unusual feature was the lack of automatic boost control; the throttle had to be opened carefully for takeoff. The tail was raised on takeoff to improve acceleration. Rudder control managed to keep the aircraft straight on its short run.

The climb, steep, was initially made at 2,000 ft/min, but it fell noticeably as altitude increased. Longitudinal stability was decidedly

Brewster F2A Buffalo (U.S. Navy)

bad and would make instrument flying difficult. A dangerously high level of carbon monoxide leaked into the cockpit from engine fumes.

In normal cruise at 160 mph the Buffalo was unstable longitudinally, neutrally stable laterally, and positively stable directionally. Maximum speed was 290 mph at 16,500 ft, and the service ceiling was only 25,000 ft—not very impressive. Its handling, however, was good: the ailerons were highly effective throughout the speed range, the elevators almost equally so, and the rudder performed well.

The all-up stall occurred at 76 mph, with a sudden but mild wing drop followed by the nose. The all-down stall occurred at 67 mph with similar but slightly more pronounced characteristics.

The landing approach at 80 mph gave a reasonable view but required almost full backward elevator trim. During touchdown at 75 mph, when the power was cut, the pilot had to give a good pullback on the stick to achieve a three-pointer.

Armament was four 0.5 machine guns, two located in the upper engine cowling and synchronized to fire through the airscrew, and one in each wing.

Assessment: The Buffalo was a true anomaly for an airplane, with delightful maneuverability but poor fighter performance. Above

10,000 ft it labored badly. The oil and cylinder-head temperatures were high in temperate climates and would obviously pose problems in tropical conditions.

Finland

The invasion of Finland by the Soviet Union on 30 November 1939 precipitated the Winter War. In December 1939 the U.S. Navy's contract with Brewster changed from F2A-1 Buffalo to F2A-2s, and so forty-three F2A-1s were released for immediate delivery to Finland's air force, the Ilmavoimat. These together with the original prototype were transported to Sweden, where they were assembled and flown to Finland. Only six had arrived by 13 March 1940 when the Soviet terms for surrender were accepted by the Finnish government and the Winter War ended.

The B-239s, as the export Buffalo were known, had to receive new engines, as no export license was available for the R-1820-34 engine, which was then the latest military production model of the Wright Cyclone. The Finnish B-239s were supplied with the R-1820-G5, an export model Cyclone rated at 950 hp for takeoff with a Hamilton Standard propeller. This aircraft had a gross weight of only 5,820 lbs, which gave it a reasonably lively performance below 10,000 ft.

The Soviet Union

By the end of September 1940 it was certain that Hitler had abandoned any immediate plan of invading Britain, and like Napoleon he turned his thoughts east toward Russia. On 18 December 1940 his historic directive for the invasion of Russia was issued. Meanwhile, the Soviets had not relaxed their aircraft production. As a result of their air force's poor showing in Finland, they had been stimulated into a drive to improve design, mainly by copying or adapting the best foreign techniques to their own requirements. A ponderous Soviet administration did not make the best of the country's vast labor resources, so that any change was a slow process. Pilot training was also a problem in a country whose people were agriculturally, not mechanically, minded. Russia was therefore destined to face the German Luftwaffe on unequal qualitative terms.

Japan

The Japanese were thrusting southward through Indochina to additional naval and air bases. This brought them within a short distance of Singapore and the Dutch East Indies. Concurrently, they were preparing five good divisions for use as an overseas expeditionary force.

In the Sino-Japanese conflict in mid-1940 Japan's naval air force used a new fighter whose impact startled military intelligence sources around the world. It was called the Zero, code-named Zeke. In just twenty-two attacks over a period of four months, 153 Zeros destroyed 160 Chinese aircraft with impunity.

3
1941

Year of Crisis

BRITAIN'S WARTIME LEADER, Winston S. Churchill, wrote in his postwar memoirs, "Looking back upon the unceasing tumult of the war, I cannot recall any period when its stresses and the onset of so many problems all at once or in rapid succession bore more directly on me and my colleagues than the first half of 1941."* The catalogue of that year's disasters began in the Mediterranean on 10 January with the German Luftwaffe's concentrated attack on the new British aircraft carrier *Illustrious*. She survived, but damage put her out of action for ten months. This superbly executed attack, which scored six direct hits, was conducted by thirty Stukas from Fliegerkorps X. On 11 January another Stuka attack sank the cruiser *Southampton*, and for the rest of the month Axis air forces concentrated on Malta, launching fifty-eight air attacks. During the next four months strikes came three or four times a day with only brief respites.

The greatest danger to Britain's ability to continue fighting was the U-boat scourge in the Atlantic, aided by the reconnaissance information of long-range Focke-Wulf 200 Kuriers. Britain required command of the ocean routes and free approach and entry to its ports to keep supplies of food, fuel, and materiel coming in.

In March the Mediterranean Fleet was reinforced by the arrival of the new *Illustrious*-class aircraft carrier *Formidable*, with her complement of Fulmars and Swordfish and ten of the new Albacore torpedo-bombers. All were soon in action; at the Battle of Matapan on 28 March three Italian heavy cruisers and two destroyers were sunk and a battleship damaged at the cost of one Swordfish and its crew. This result convinced Mussolini to convert two transatlantic liners into aircraft carriers.

*The Second World War, vol. 3 (London: Cassell, 1950), p. 3.

HMS Formidable *Entering the Straits of Gilbraltar to Reinforce the British Mediterranean Fleet (British Official Photograph)*

On 23 May the German battleship *Bismarck* and the heavy cruiser *Prinz Eugen* passed into the shipping-rich North Atlantic. On 24 May they were engaged by the British battleships *Hood* and *Prince of Wales*. The former was sunk, the latter damaged, and the German ships escaped. The Royal Navy mounted a major hunt with the new aircraft carrier *Victorious* and Force H's *Ark Royal*. On 27 May carrier-borne Swordfish achieved three torpedo hits and slowed the *Bismarck* sufficiently so that the gunfire and torpedoes of British warships could administer the coup de grâce.

On the same day the first catapult aircraft merchant (CAM) ship put to sea in an attempt to counter the Kurier menace over the Atlantic. Thirty-five ships were each fitted with a rocket catapult on which was mounted a high-performance Sea Hurricane fighter ready to intercept shadowing Kuriers. The first kill took place on 3 August, and by the end of 1941 the "Hurricats" had destroyed six long-range German aircraft.

On 22 June Germany invaded Russia with 1,700 aircraft in support, while Russia threw in 5,000 aircraft. To aid the stricken Soviet Union Britain began sending materiel to the northern ports of Murmansk and Archangel. The convoys to Russia were carrier escorted and in great danger because of the continuous summer daylight and the proximity of German air bases.

At the end of July the carriers *Furious* and *Victorious* sent fifty-three aircraft to strike the German-held ports of Kirkenes and Petsamo at the top of the North Cape, but opposition from defending fighters and antiaircraft fire was heavy, and sixteen were lost.

In early September the first operational escort carrier, HMS

CAM Ship with Hurricat (Imperial War Museum)

HMS Audacity

Audacity, sailed with a convoy bound for Gibraltar. This carrier, although a midget in size, was to have an overwhelming effect on the outcome of the Battle of the Atlantic. Her lend-lease Wildcat fighters were to dog the Kuriers and U-boats relentlessly during her short life, decisively proving that escort carriers were the best antidote to the deadly German combination.

On 13 November HMS *Ark Royal* was struck by a German submarine's torpedo and she sank next day, thus leaving the Royal Navy without a carrier in the Mediterranean for the first time since Italy entered the war.

On 5 December Fliegerkorps II was transferred from the Russian front to Sicily, bringing five groups of Ju 88A-4 torpedo-bombers, one of Ju 87 dive-bombers, one of Me 110 fighters, and four of Me 109F fighters—325 aircraft assigned the task of "neutralizing" Malta.

Mediterranean Theater

The Mediterranean air scenario had changed dramatically in favor of the Axis with the bolstering of the Italian Regia Aeronautica by the powerful Luftwaffe, which moved into Italian bases in large numbers

HMS Ark Royal *Sinking after a German Submarine Torpedoed Her (Imperial War Museum)*

as Hitler's strategy looked south and east. The new order of battle was as follows:

	Allied	Axis
Fighters:	Fairey Fulmar (FAA) Hawker Hurricane (RAF)	Messerschmitt 109F (Germany) Messerschmitt 110C (Germany) Reggiane 2000 (Italy)
Dive-Bombers:	Blackburn Skua (FAA)	Junkers 87B (Germany) Junkers 88A-4 (Germany)
Torpedo-Bombers:	Fairey Swordfish (FAA) Fairey Albacore (FAA)	Junkers 88A-4 (Germany) Savoia-Marchetti 79 (Italy)

The newcomers on the scene were the Albacore, Me 109F, Re 2000, and Ju 88A-4.

FAIREY ALBACORE

The Albacore, designed to a 1936 Admiralty specification, was ordered off the drawing board to replace the Swordfish. Surprisingly, it was another biplane, modernized with an all-metal monocoque fuselage and an enclosed cockpit for the three-man crew. It had hydraulically operated flaps on the lower wings, intended primarily for use as dive brakes, and carried ailerons on both top and bottom mainplanes. All

Fairey Albacore (Flight International)

movable control surfaces were fabric covered. The aircraft first flew
on 12 December 1938.

This large biplane was powered by a fourteen-cylinder, two-row,
sleeve-valve, air-cooled Bristol Taurus XII radial engine of 1,130 hp,
driving a three-bladed De Havilland variable-pitch propeller. The
engine was started by percussion cartridge impulse.

The first obvious change from the Swordfish was the pilot's view.
He sat forward of the wings and there was a downward slope to the
neatly cowled engine. This offered a good view forward, above, and
below. The next striking difference was the sleeve-valve engine, which
purred, unlike the raucous Pegasus of the old "Stringbag."

Takeoff in the Albacore was simple, with unstick occurring at
about 60 knots. The climb to 6,000 ft at 96 knots took about 8
minutes, a 30 percent improvement over the Swordfish. Cruising at
100 knots, the aircraft was slightly unstable longitudinally, with fairly
sensitive elevators, but its ailerons were heavy.

At 68 knots with flaps up and 66 knots with flaps down, the stall
was gentle and the nose drop straightforward. This gave an approach
speed of 75 knots for deck landing, which was dead easy.

With a maximum speed of 138 knots the Albacore was hardly in
the hot-rod class, but it improved on the Swordfish in range and
service ceiling, both of which almost doubled. Its armament consisted
of one .303 Browning machine gun in the starboard lower mainplane
and one Vickers "K" machine gun on a flexible mount in the rear

cockpit. The aircraft could carry three 500-lb bombs or one 18-in torpedo.

The Albacore was destined to have an operational life of only eighteen months, and during this time it served almost as much ashore as at sea. It conducted shore operations mostly at night and proved effective in both bombing and minelaying roles.

Assessment: The Albacore was an anachronism. Inevitably it would pay the penalty for pedestrian performance and maneuverability coupled with inadequate defensive armament.

Messerschmitt 109F

The Me 109F differed from previous models in a number of ways. First, it had the more powerful 1,300-hp Daimler-Benz 601E engine in a new symmetrical cowling. Modifications were also made to the supercharger and radiator intakes. Second, it had a fast-firing Mauser cannon passing through the airscrew hub, and two 7.92-mm MG17 machine guns in the fuselage top decking. Airframe modifications included rounded wingtips, a cantilevered tailplane, a smaller rudder, and a semiretractable tailwheel.

Top speed was increased to 391 mph at 20,000 ft, the rate of climb to 3,320 ft/min, service ceiling to 39,370 ft, and range to 440 miles.

Assessment: The Me 109F represented a significant advance over its predecessors with its increased performance at height and its better maneuverability and firepower. When it first appeared, it was almost certainly the best fighter in the world.

Reggiane 2000

The Re 2000 single-seat fighter was a low-wing monoplane of monocoque construction with stressed-skin covering. All the control surfaces were fabric covered. It had retractable main landing gear, and the tailwheel could be electrically retracted. In appearance it was reminiscent of a Seversky design.

Power was supplied by a Piaggio P.XI RC.40 radial air-cooled engine, rated at 1,000 hp at 13,000 ft and driving a three-bladed, constant-speed Piaggio D'Ascanio airscrew. The engine started by means of either an internal or external electrical power supply.

Takeoff was reasonably short, but retraction of the landing gear was slow. Rate of climb just exceeded 3,000 ft/min. Stability in the cruise was neutral around all three axes. With a wing loading of 25.62 lbs/sq. ft. and moderately light and effective controls, maneuverability was good. Maximum speed was 332 mph. The aircraft had a useful service ceiling of 37,720 ft and a range of 810 miles.

Reggiane 2000 (Peter M. Bowers's Collection)

Armament consisted of two fixed large-caliber machine guns in the fuselage, firing forward through the airscrew. Underwing bomb racks could be fitted.

Assessment: The Re 2000 was identical in performance to the Hawker Hurricane I, which made up Malta's fighter defense, but it lacked the latter's firepower. In the Mediterranean theater the Re 2000 was nevertheless a competent defense aircraft that would give a good account of itself in 1941.

JUNKERS 88A-4

The Ju 88 was designed to a 1935 specification for a high-speed bomber, and this it certainly was. However, it was adapted for a wide variety of additional roles, among which was torpedo dropping. By far the most important variant was the A-4, which had an increased wing span, a strengthened undercarriage, and the more powerful 1,340-hp Junkers Jumo 211J engines. It also had all-metal ailerons in place of the fabric-covered type, and provision was made for increased armor protection, especially for the pilot. Armament was increased to one 7.9-mm MG81 machine gun in the nose, one 13-mm MG131 firing forward, two MG81s in the rear of the cockpit, and an MG131 in the rear of the ventral gondola. Bomb load was four 1,100-lb bombs carried externally, or one 18-inch torpedo and ten 110-lb bombs, the latter carried internally.

There was something about the appearance of this midwing airplane suggesting that it was a thoroughbred. On clambering into the cockpit, my first impression was that accommodation for the four-

Junkers 88A-4 (U.S. Naval Institute)

man crew was cramped, although clearly this proximity made for
good morale in combat. The view from the greenhouse-style crew
compartment was good, but there was an awful lot of metal framework around the optically flat, transparent panels.

The Jumos were activated by electrically energized inertia starters. Takeoff was not made easy by the awkward position of the
throttle levers, set so low and far back that differential throttling was
difficult. A lockable tailwheel helped directional control in the initial
stages, but it was best to get the tail up for rudder control, and this
required considerable push force on the control column.

Once airborne the Ju 88A-4 handled beautifully, with the rudder
and ailerons light throughout the entire speed range. The elevator
was somewhat heavier, but automatic tail-incidence control assisted
any big moves. Rate of climb was 1,370 ft/min, cruising speed 230
mph at 17,000 ft with a top speed of 292 mph. Service ceiling was
27,000 ft and range, 1,112 miles.

This medium bomber was also designed for use as a dive-bomber.
It was fitted with an automatic dive/pullout mechanism initiated by
opening the slatted, wing-mounted dive brakes and completed by
retracting them.

Stalling speed with everything down was 92 mph with little warning and a sharp wing drop, so it was necessary not to let speed decay
too early in the landing approach, particularly in a single-engine
landing.

Assessment: The Ju 88A-4 was an aircraft that fulfilled multifarious roles and excelled in all of them. It had a turn of speed that could match some of the contemporary fighters, and from a pilot's viewpoint, it was a superb airplane to handle.

Fulmar Versus Messerschmitt 109F

The appearance of the Me 109F in the Mediterranean spelled danger for the Fleet Air Arm and RAF aircraft, for it was markedly superior to anything the Allies had in that theater. Certainly the Fulmar was no match for it in any performance aspect, although it could probably outturn the German plane. Both aircraft had good firepower, but the Fulmar presented a much bigger target. The Fulmar's only real hope was to catch the enemy unawares and get in a short burst when diving out of the sun; if it wasn't a first-time kill, the crew was in grave trouble.

   Verdict: The Fulmar was heavily outclassed by the Me 109F, and unless given the element of surprise it had little or no chance against this competent German fighter.

Fulmar Versus Reggiane 2000

The Italian fighter had an advantage in speed, a disadvantage in firepower. Both aircraft were almost equally maneuverable, with the Re 2000 quicker to roll but slower to accelerate in a dive. If the two aircraft got into a dogfight much would depend on individual pilot skill, with the odds slightly favoring the Re 2000. However, in a hit and run contest the odds decidedly favored the Fulmar.

   Verdict: Since both aircraft were used exclusively in the defensive role, their main chance of meeting was with the Fulmar acting as fighter escort. In such circumstances the Fulmar's role was to drive off the enemy rather than become involved in a dogfight. If, however, the Re 2000 attacked the bomber force, the Fulmar escort would probably find itself with a height advantage and so have a good chance of success.

Fulmar Versus Junkers 87B

The Ju 87B had little defense to offer against an eight-gun fighter like the Fulmar, which it could neither outpace nor outmaneuver. If the Fulmar made a diving attack from astern, flattening the dive angle as it came into range of the Ju 87B's rear gunner, this would prevent the latter from firing continuously, for he would want to avoid hitting his own tail.

   Verdict: The Fulmar should score an easy victory against the slow and vulnerable Ju 87B, provided it was not harassed by the Stuka's escort fighters.

Fulmar Versus Junkers 88A-4

The Ju 88A-4 was one of the outstanding aircraft of World War II and as a bomber had a speed comparable to that of contemporary fighters. It was also well armed and maneuverable for its size. The Fulmar would find it difficult to cope with the Ju 88A-4 in the bomber or dive-bomber role, particularly after it had got rid of its bomb load. The Ju 88A-4 was most vulnerable to head-on attack, but the Fulmar could only hope to make such a contact, and then only one pass would be possible because the Ju 88A-4 was actually faster than the fighter. In normal circumstances, a beam attack would stand the greatest chance of success. It would be best, if possible, to feint from one beam and rapidly switch to the other, as the upper rear gunner had to stow one gun before using the one on the opposite side. If an astern attack had to be made, it should be launched from slightly below the tailplane to avoid the enemy's defensive rear armament.

With the Ju 88A-4 in the torpedo-bomber role, the Fulmar had an easier task because of the limitation on the former's speed. In such case, a head-on attack would be best, with the Fulmar returning to a beam attack if necessary.

Verdict: The Fulmar would not find the Ju 88A-4 easy to tackle, because the bomber had a speed advantage over the fighter except when restricted by its external weapon load. The Ju 88A-4 was also endowed with a useful array of defensive armament that could pose a considerable threat to the Fulmar.

Skua Versus Reggiane 2000

The Italian fighter had the advantage in both speed and maneuverability over the Skua, whose only real defense lay in bringing its rear gun to bear on the attacker. There was always the tactic employed in Norway of getting close to the water and using the dive brakes to give an enemy attacking in a dive from astern an alarming closing speed; he would break off the attack prematurely and expose himself to the Skua's rear gun at close range. However, if caught with its bomb load the Skua was unlikely to escape destruction.

Verdict: Although not really a high-performance fighter, the Re 2000 had a significant edge over the pedestrian Skua, certainly enough to make the outcome heavily favor the Italian aircraft.

Skua Versus Junkers 88A-4

The Skua's only real chance of catching the Ju 88A-4 was when it had height to make a diving attack or when it attacked during a torpedo-drop run in. Of course, the Skua rear gunner could still attack on the breakaway.

Verdict: The Skua's main problem would be to catch the fleet-footed Ju 88A-4 and get into an attacking position. Even then its slow closing speed would make it vulnerable to the bomber's defensive fire.

Swordfish Versus Reggiane 2000

The Italian fighter was nimble enough to nail the Swordfish even in its most evasive mode, though there was always the risk of a lucky shot from the biplane's rear gunner. The Re 2000 was not heavily armed, but it was certainly potent enough to be lethal against an airplane covered in so much fabric.

Verdict: The Swordfish was virtually defenseless against any contemporary fighter, and the Re 2000 was no exception.

Albacore Versus Messerschmitt 109F

The Albacore was a large target that must have appeared like a gift from heaven to any fighter pilot. It was less able to defend itself even than its predecessor, the Swordfish, because it lacked the latter's maneuverability. The Me 109F was probably the highest-performance fighter encountered by the Albacore. Such an encounter was essentially "no contest," as evidenced by the massacre of the Albacore force sent to bomb Petsamo and Kirkenes.

Verdict: The Albacore was completely out of its operational depth in any daylight sortie, when it ran the extreme risk of fighter attack. Against a fighter of the caliber of the Me 109F, it had little or no chance of survival.

Albacore Versus Reggiane 2000

Although the Re 2000 did not belong to the same class as the Me 109F, from the standpoint of either performance or firepower, it had an easy prey in the lumbering Albacore. The latter could absorb more punishment than the Swordfish, and the Re 2000 had less firepower than the German fighter, so it could be argued that the Albacore's chance of survival was slightly better than that of the Swordfish. Such a hypothesis, however, is largely academic.

Verdict: The Albacore must be assessed as having an infinitesimally small chance of surviving an attack by the Re 2000, because the Italian fighter, with its limited firepower, might have to make more than one pass to finish off the job.

The Albacore was so vulnerable that it was even attacked by the Ju 88 in some instances. Such vulnerability led eventually to a policy of using it only at night or on antisubmarine duties. Its operational life was terminated after only eighteen months.

The North Atlantic

The action in this forbidding area of cold, grey, turbulent ocean ranged from the Strait of Gibraltar to the North Cape—an area infested with U-boats, Luftwaffe reconnaissance bombers, and Germany's marauding capital ships. Surviving an enemy action was often just the prelude to a numbing death in this ocean's waters.

Opposing each other in the air over this dreaded theater were planes from the Royal Navy's aircraft carriers, supported by shore-based RAF Coastal Command aircraft, and the Luftwaffe's long-range aircraft in France and Norway, supported by shorter-range attack bombers and fighters. Carrier operations are of particular interest.

The British carrier forces had been strengthened by the introduction of high-performance fighters, a timely event indeed, since Germany's reconnaissance-bomber force was formidable. The order of battle was as follows:

	British	*German*
Fighters:	Hawker Sea Hurricane	Messerschmitt 109F
	Grumman Wildcat II	Messerschmitt 110C
	Fairey Fulmar	
Torpedo-Bombers:	Fairey Swordfish	Junkers 88A-4
	Fairey Albacore	Heinkel 111H-6
Reconnaissance-Bombers:		Focke-Wulf Kurier

This maritime lineup brought new combatants into the war: the Sea Hurricane, Wildcat, He 111H-6, and Kurier. These four played a major part in my operational career, and again I am fortunate to have flown all the above listed as well as fringe participants in the Battle of the Atlantic, the Blohm and Voss (Bv) 138 and 222 included, which merit brief comment.

Hawker Sea Hurricane I

The Hurricane was designed to specification F.36/34 and first flew on 6 November 1935. The first-production Hurricane flew on 12 October 1937; it marked the beginning of Britain's buildup of air strength in preparation for war.

The aircraft was adapted for naval use as a result of the experience of the RAF squadron that landed its land-based Hurricanes on the carrier *Glorious* during the ill-fated Norwegian campaign of May 1940.

Two distinct lines of development for the Sea Hurricane were pursued simultaneously: one embraced the conventional operation of the fighter from carrier decks, and the other—to which greater urgency was attached—involved its launching from a simple rocket-driven catapult mounted on the forecastle of a converted merchant vessel.

The Sea Hurricane was a low-wing, single-seat fighter monoplane, the first such British airplane to be used aboard aircraft carriers of the Royal Navy. The Hurricane 1A was provided with catapult spools only and was specifically for CAM ships, but the 1B had both catapult spools and arrester hook. The wings and forward part of the fuselage were covered in metal, the latter part in fabric. All moveable flying controls were fabric covered.

The engine was the famous Merlin 2 or 3 of 1,030 hp, driving a three-bladed, constant-speed airscrew. It was started by internal or external electric battery. The Merlin coupled well with the Hurricane airframe, giving pleasing aerodynamic lines with a distinct impression of robustness. The view was reasonably good from the cockpit, except dead ahead.

Takeoff swing could be held easily on rudder until unstick occurred at 70 knots. Climb at 150 knots gave a rate of 2,000 ft/min with good all-round stability. While cruising, the Hurricane was again stable about all three axes. In a dive, the aircraft became tail-heavy, and it was important not to trim this out, otherwise difficulty might be experienced in recovery.

The all-up stall occurred at 68 knots, preceded by fore and aft instability before a sharp wing drop to the vertical attitude; care was necessary to avoid spin. The all-down stall at 57 knots exhibited similar characteristics.

Aerobatics were easy to execute in this maneuverable fighter, with its fairly good harmony of control throughout the speed range. The ailerons were the lightest control, the rudder the heaviest. Controls grew heavier with increases in speed but remained effective. Split trailing-edge flaps could be used for added maneuverability at virtually any speed, as their angle would adjust with the airflow.

As a deck-landing aircraft the Sea Hurricane left much to be desired, but then it had not been specifically designed for the task. Its harsh stalling characteristics and bouncy landing gear were its bad features, and the view in the approach at 70 knots was hardly ideal.

The armament of eight .303 Browning machine guns in the wings gave the airplane a powerful punch, but its performance was inferior to that of the RAF version. The top speed of 300 mph was some 30 mph slower, and the service ceiling of 30,000 ft was considerably below the 36,000 ft of the land version. Range was 450 miles.

Hawker Sea Hurricane (U.S. Naval Institute)

No Sea Hurricane was built from scratch as such, all being conversions of RAF builds. It was a stopgap in the Fleet Air Arm's armory, albeit a welcome addition.

Assessment: The Hurricane earned undying fame for itself in the Battle of Britain, but by the time it reached the Fleet Air Arm it was becoming seriously outclassed by contemporary enemy fighters. With a wing loading of 26.3 lb/sq. ft. and good controls it was a great dogfighter, and it had sufficient performance and firepower to deal effectively with contemporary enemy bombers.

In spite of being press-ganged into naval service, taking on tough duties with escort carriers protecting Russian convoys, the Hurricane adapted to its environment remarkably well and gave a good account of itself. Unfortunately, when it was ditched in the sea the consequences were lethal.

GRUMMAN F4F WILDCAT II

The Wildcat was a small, corpulent, single-seat shipboard fighter with a stubby midwing, squat landing gear, and a distinctly angular look about the wings and tail empennage. Among its features were two previously installed in British aircraft—0.5-in Colt-Browning machine guns and a sting-type arrester hook.

Before the end of 1939 a French order had been placed with Grumman for eighty-one F4F-3s to equip squadrons aboard the *Béarn* and the carriers *Joffre* and *Painlevé*, then under construction. Since the Twin Wasp, with the two-stage, two-speed supercharger specified for the U.S. Navy's F4F-3s, was not available for export, the French

Author Landing Grumman F4F Wildcat on HMS Illustrious

elected to power their fighters with the R-1820-G205A version of the Wright Cyclone; the latter had a single-stage, two-speed supercharger. These aircraft did not have wing folding for carrier stowage. With the fall of France the entire order was transferred to Britain, where the fighter was designated the Wildcat I.

The cockpit was roomy and, for British pilots, contained some unique features, including gun cocking handles, tailwheel lock, and toe brakes on the rudder pedals.

The 1,200-hp Wright Cyclone was a nine-cylinder, radial air-cooled engine driving a three-bladed, constant-speed Hamilton Standard Hydromatic airscrew. Activated by an inertia starter that could be energized manually or electrically, the engine emitted a deep, throaty roar as it came to life.

Takeoff was somewhat hazardous because the Wildcat was equipped with a small, solid, rubber wheel, which gave the aircraft a taildown attitude and caused the fuselage to blank the rudder. Directional control, even with the tailwheel locked, was dependent on judicious touches of the brake; if the brake was overapplied, the wingtip would dip alarmingly under the influence of the squashy landing gear. A crosswind could create a similar effect, and vicious swings were commonplace. Fortunately takeoff distance was short, although in the absence of automatic boost control one had to be careful not to give too much throttle.

After unstick the pilot had to work hard, cranking the landing gear with a hand lever on the starboard cockpit wall some twenty-nine times. This chore completed, the Wildcat could be pulled into its sensational initial climb of 3,300 ft/min. Not many aircraft could touch that figure.

In level flight the top speed was 265 knots (305 mph) at 15,000 ft and about 248 knots (285 mph) at sea level. The Wildcat displayed good stability but was also a maneuverable airplane with a good rate of roll. Plenty of stick handling was required on the part of the pilot to get the best out of it. With an innocuous all-up stall of 85 knots, the plane could be maneuvered to its limits with impunity. The all-round view was excellent for dogfighting.

In 1939 the British Purchasing Committee had placed a contract with Grumman for 100 F4F-3s with the fourteen-cylinder Pratt and Whitney S3C4-G version of the radial air-cooled Twin Wasp. It was 1,200 hp and used a single-stage, two-speed supercharger. The first ten of these Wildcat II aircraft had fixed wings, while the remainder had folding wings. For purposes of identification, the ten fixed-wing versions were called Wildcat IIIs. The Mk II and III also had the armament increased to six 0.50-in machine guns.

The first features I noticed with the Wildcat II were an improvement in forward view, resulting from a smaller diameter, the more tapered cowling of the Twin Wasp, and its purr, quieter than that of the Cyclone.

For deck landing the Wildcat was superlative. With an approach speed of 90 knots, it offered good forward vision and excellent slow-flying characteristics. Robust landing gear was fully capable of absorbing the most punishing vertical velocities, and the arrester hook was intelligently positioned. With an all-down stalling speed of 79 knots and good straightforward stalling characteristics, a powered approach to the deck could safely be made at 85 knots.

The Wildcat II was speedier, with a maximum of 286 knots (328 mph) at 19,500 ft and 252 knots (290 mph) at sea level. Service ceiling was the same for both models at 28,000 ft, as was the range of 1,150 miles. Ditching characteristics were excellent, and hydrostatically operated flotation bags were fitted in each wing.

Assessment: The Wildcat was a great asset to the Fleet Air Arm, bringing it to nearly the level of the fighter opposition. It was also an aircraft specifically designed for modern carrier operations, thereby setting new standards for British designers in that field.

Heinkel 111H-6 (U.S. Naval Institute)

The Wildcat was a potent fighter, with splendid maneuverability, good performance, heavy firepower, and excellent range and endurance. On top of this, it was a superb deck-landing aircraft.

HEINKEL 111H-6

This version was the first variant of the He 111H to be developed for torpedo carrying. Introduced late in 1941, it was powered by two Junkers Jumo 211F-1 engines of 1,400 hp, had six MG15 machine guns and a 20-mm MG FF cannon, and could carry two 1,686-lb LT F5b torpedoes externally. The latter, of course, affected performance and handling, but once they were dropped the He 111H-6 was similar in every way to the other H variants.

FOCKE-WULF 200 KURIER (CONDOR)

The Fw 200 Condor was designed by the great Kurt Tank in 1936 as an airliner for use by Lufthansa. It was a graceful, low-wing monoplane of all-metal construction except for the control surfaces, which were fabric covered. The first prototype made its debut flight on 27 July 1937. The third machine became Hitler's personal aircraft.

Late in 1938 the prototype, flying from Berlin to Tokyo, attracted much attention. The Japanese Naval Air Force ordered five civil transports and a single aircraft for reconnaissance duties. Although no Condors reached Japan, the order for the military variant resulted in the construction of a long-range armed reconnaissance version.

Just before Germany went to war, the chief of Air Staff, General Hans Jeschonnek, had ordered the establishment of a long-range anti-shipping squadron. The Condor was the only available choice of aircraft, but it required structural strengthening for its military role. The military version was named Kurier to distinguish it from the civil Condor.

The Fw 200C-3, which appeared during the summer of 1941, represented the first major modification of the aircraft. It had been structurally strengthened, and was powered by four 1,200-hp, nine-cylinder, air-cooled Bramo 323R-2 radial engines with two-speed superchargers. The engine was activated by electrically energized inertia starters.

The only Condor I flew was the Fw 200C-4/U1, which had been the personal transport of the notorious SS leader Heinrich Himmler and later of Grand Admiral Karl Dönitz. Although built as a passenger transport, it was fully armed, hence one can assume its flying characteristics were typical of the Fw 200C-3.

The cockpit layout was very much that of an airliner in concept and in the matter of view, which was somewhat restricted on either side by the heavy framework of the windscreen.

Takeoff was the most difficult aspect of the entire flight, as the Condor had a strong tendency to swing to port. The technique recommended by German pilots was to open the engines to half throttle only for about 300 meters, when the tail would begin to lift of its own accord. From this point on the throttles were progressively opened, and at the same time they were being manipulated differentially to counteract the swing until, after about a 700-meters run, the engines were at full power. The Condor then had to be allowed to fly itself off at 102 mph. If pulled off under that speed it veered sharply to starboard. With this recommended technique, the takeoff run with the aircraft in fully loaded condition was 900 meters.

After unstick, the landing gear retraction took 24 seconds, then the climb could be commenced at 155 mph. Stability on the climb was positive.

Maximum speed was 250 mph at 13,000 ft, some 25 mph faster than the production Fw 200C-3. The most economical cruising speed was 171 mph at 5,000 ft, which provided an endurance of 14 hours with normal safety reserves, or a range of about 2,400 miles.

In flight the Condor proved stable about all three axes, but any

Focke-Wulf 200 Kurier (Condor) (Imperial War Museum)

change of speed or power called for immediate trimming. It certainly turned more easily to port than to starboard on account of engine torque, but it was heavy to maneuver and its maximum permissible airspeed below 5,000 ft was 280 mph. All in all, this was the type of aircraft which, when attacked, had little option but to fly straight and level and give its heavy defensive armament a good platform for fighting off the attacker.

The Condor had an impressive array of all-weather equipment, including rubber pulse de-icers on the wings and tailplane, airscrew de-icing sprays, autopilot, and good internal heating.

The landing had to be carefully executed because if the Condor came down heavily and the rear spar failed, it could break the airplane's back. The approach speed was 102 mph, but this could be allowed to decay to 90 mph in the late stages with the aircraft wheeling. A three-pointer could be made at 80 mph, but that increased the risk of structural failure.

The most impressive thing about the military version of the Fw 200 was its range of armament. Indeed the Kurier must have been one of the most heavily armed aircraft of World War II. It had a 15-mm MG151 cannon in a hydraulically operated HDL 151 forward dorsal turret, one 13-mm MG131 machine gun with 500 rounds on a flexible mount in the aft dorsal position, two 13-mm MG131 machine guns with 300 rounds per gun firing from aft beam hatches, one 20-mm MG151 cannon on a flexible mounting with 500 rounds in the forward ventral position, and one 7.9-mm MG15 machine gun with 1,000 rounds in the aft ventral position. The normal bomb load was four 551-lb bombs for the offensive reconnaissance mission.

Assessment: The Kurier was a thoroughly effective long-range maritime reconnaissance bomber, but with the inherent shortcomings that were to be expected of a converted commercial airliner. A lack of armor and the placement of all fuel lines on the airplane's underside rendered it extremely vulnerable. To counter these weaknesses, the Kurier was armed to the teeth.

Sea Hurricane I Versus Messerschmitt 109F

The Me 109F had the edge over the Hurricane in every department except maneuverability, and therefore the initiative always lay with the German airplane. However, if the latter decided to indulge in a dogfight, the Hurricane would meet it on more equal terms. Any attempt by the Me 109F to follow the Hurricane in steep turns and the 109F's slats would snatch open, causing lateral twitching and ruining the pilot's chances of accurately sighting his guns.

Verdict: A good Hurricane pilot could hold his own against the Me 109F in a dogfight, but the initiative to mix it or break it off lay with the German. Therefore the odds favored the Me 109F.

Sea Hurricane I Versus Messerschmitt 110C

For speed these two fighters were on a par at low level, but the Hurricane was much more maneuverable. Its best chance of success was a beam attack on the German aircraft, turning to quarter with the point of aim behind the pilot's cockpit. An astern attack could be quite effective if made somewhat flat to limit the rear gunner's field of fire. A head-on attack would be inadvisable because of the Me 110C's heavy nose armament. The twin's best evasive tactic would be to use its superior acceleration in the dive.

Verdict: The Me 110C should not deliberately mix it with the Hurricane; the latter was a splendid dogfighter, which the twin fighter certainly was not.

Sea Hurricane I Versus Junkers 88A-4

Here the situation was similar to the previous one, except that the Ju 88A-4 was better armed for rear defense. Consequently a head-on or beam attack would be the best tactic for the Hurricane. With almost the maneuverability of a fighter, the Ju 88A-4 could make things difficult for the Hurricane, but the outcome was weighted in the latter's favor, provided it kept out of the astern cone of the bomber's fire.

Verdict: The Hurricane had a good edge over the Ju 88A-4, but not as much as it had over the Me 110C.

Sea Hurricane I Versus Heinkel 111H-6

The Hurricane performed significantly better than the bomber. Moreover, the fighter's excellent maneuverability would allow it to pick its spot much as it chose. The He 111H-6 was very vulnerable during its torpedo-drop run in, when its speed was restricted and its lower guns could not be brought to bear on the Hurricane.

Verdict: The He 111H-6 had little chance of winning a contest with the Hurricane, and virtually none at all if caught in a torpedo attack.

Sea Hurricane I Versus Kurier

The Kurier was a formidable opponent on account of its heavy armament, but it had an Achilles heel—a weak spine. The eight guns of the Hurricane could hammer that soft spot in a beam attack. On the other hand, there were no blind spots in the defensive armament of the Kurier, so an attack was high risk.

Verdict: The odds in such a combat favored the maneuverable Hurricane, but not so heavily that it was not at severe risk against the Kurier's flying arsenal.

Wildcat Versus Messerschmitt 109F

The Wildcat, although faster and more maneuverable than the Sea Hurricane, was still some 60 mph slower than the German fighter. The lower the altitude the less the odds favored the Me 109F. The Wildcat also had a heavier punch to deliver.

Verdict: As a dogfighter the Wildcat was superior to the Me 109F, but the initiative always lay with the German because of superior performance. At low altitudes the Me 109F had the edge over the Wildcat, but not by much.

Wildcat Versus Messerschmitt 110C

The Me 110C, with its inferior performance, would find it difficult to escape the Wildcat's attentions. A beam or flat astern attack by the powerfully armed Wildcat was likely to meet with success, the German forced to rely on the rear gunner for survival.

Verdict: The Me 110C would be unlikely to survive an encounter with a Wildcat, and only a lucky hit could stop the latter.

Wildcat Versus Junkers 88A-4

The odds in such a combat would be pretty evenly balanced. The Wildcat had a speed advantage, but defensively the Ju 88 was well armed. The most effective attack would be head on to the German aircraft; a flat trajectory would prevent his dorsal gun from being brought to bear. The Wildcat would have to break off with a tight 180-degree diving turn to regain position for another head-on or beam attack.

Verdict: In single combat the Ju 88 would be a tough opponent to overcome, but its greenhouse cockpit made the crew vulnerable to a well executed head-on attack by the Wildcat.

Wildcat Versus Heinkel 111H-6

The He 111H-6 would be no match for the agile Wildcat, with its considerable advantage in speed and its heavy firepower. The encounter would be particularly lethal if the bomber was caught during a torpedo run in.

Verdict: The Wildcat should find the He 111 easy prey, especially when it was carrying a torpedo.

Wildcat Versus Kurier

The Wildcat had two trump cards to play against this flying armory. It could use its maneuverability to attack from the beam and concentrate its considerable firepower on the weak point just forward of the tail, or it could use its speed advantage for a head-on attack against the crew. The head-on attack trajectory had to be flat to keep the forward dorsal turret gun from depressing beyond its limit and the forward ventral cannon from elevating beyond its limit. Closing speed was high, and it was critical that the pilot judge the breakoff point to avoid collision. Preferably, he would break upward to avoid negative "g" and again to keep the break shallow, giving the defensive guns a rapidly changing deflection with minimum sighting time.

Verdict: The Kurier was a big but not an easy target for fighters because of its lack of blind spots. However, the Wildcat's speed and firepower allowed it to launch a devastating head-on attack through the one blind area. For the fighter, attack from any other sector would be a very high risk.

Fulmar Versus Messerschmitt 110C

In this encounter the Fulmar had a speed disadvantage and not much of a maneuverability advantage. Its options were limited, if indeed it could even come to grips with the Me 110C, whose rear gunner could cause problems.

Verdict: The initiative lying with the Me 110C, the odds of its success against the ponderous Fulmar were about three to one.

Fulmar Versus Heinkel 111H-6

There being little difference in performance between these two aircraft, the Fulmar's maneuverability and firepower should be the decisive factors. If the Fulmar attacked the He 111H-6 from astern while the latter was making its torpedo drop run in, his efforts would be well rewarded.

Verdict: The He 111H-6 should be a comparatively easy kill for the Fulmar, which would run only a small risk from the German's defensive armament.

Fulmar Versus Kurier

Lacking the speed to exploit a head-on attack, the Fulmar would be forced into a beam or astern attack. Since the fighter presented a fairly big target, any attack against the Kurier would be very high risk, although the Fulmar had the firepower to deliver a lethal blow if it could get into close firing range.

Verdict: The odds of success in this encounter would be equal.

Against the Odds

In 1941 Britain's war machine was pushed to the limit, nowhere more so than in the Royal Navy's Fleet Air Arm, which was fighting in the Mediterranean, in the North and South Atlantic, in the Arctic Ocean, and ashore in Malta, Crete, and North Africa. In the majority of aerial conflicts involving naval aircraft the enemy had numerical superiority. The losses nonetheless make interesting comparison.

On 10 January 1941 the carrier *Illustrious* was heavily attacked by Stuka dive-bombers and SM 79 torpedo-bombers off Malta. Her Fulmar squadron shot down five Ju 87s and two SM 79s without loss.

On 8 May 1941 Fulmar squadrons from HMS *Formidable* fought a severe battle while escorting a vital convoy carrying tanks and aircraft to the Western Desert. The Fulmars accounted for three Ju 87s, three He 111Hs, two SM 79s, and a Ju 88, losing only one fighter in the process.

Over the North Atlantic the situation dictated odds of a very different nature. U-boat wolf packs directed by long-range reconnaissance Kurier aircraft were hunting slow convoys lightly escorted by corvettes and destroyers. The enemy success rate was high until the escort aircraft carrier appeared on the scene with its patrolling fighters. The first such operational escort carrier had an explosive impact on the Battle of the Atlantic; its six tiny Wildcats destroyed five of the large German marauders, and only one fighter was lost. Despite the loss of the carrier itself to a U-boat, Grand Admiral Dönitz wrote in his war diary, "In HG 76 convoy the worst feature, from our point of view, was the presence of the aircraft carrier *Audacity*. The year 1941 came to an end in an atmosphere of worry for the U-boat command." From this point on, the escort carrier was to play an increasingly important role in World War II.

The Rising Sun in the Pacific

In the fall of 1941 Japanese carrier strength consisted of five carrier divisions—nine carriers with a total of 474 aircraft. This powerful aerial armada was made up of 114 Mitsubishi Zeke 22 (A6M Zero) and 43 Claude fighters, 135 Aichi D3A Val dive-bombers, and 182

Nakajima B5N Kate torpedo-bombers. All of these types were involved in the attack on the U.S. Fleet at Pearl Harbor, when six Japanese carriers launched 350 aircraft.

MITSUBISHI ZEKE 22 (A6M ZERO)

The Zeke 22 single-seat fighter, which made its first flight on 1 April 1939, was a monoplane with low wings of equal taper and rounded tips, which in some models could be folded up for carrier stowage. The designer, Jiro Horikoshi, had made extensive use of extra super duralumin to lighten the airframe. Consequently, the stressed-skin fuselage was of extremely thin gauge, while the wings and tail unit were of only slightly heavier gauge. There were split flaps between the ailerons and the fuselage. The elevators and rudder were fabric covered, and although the elevators had controllable trim tabs, the rudder trim tab was only adjustable on the ground.

This beautiful airplane was similar in appearance to the German Focke-Wulf 190, and both were outstanding fighters. The Zeke had wide track landing gear and a well laid-out cockpit, from which a good view was obtained round the neatly cowled, 1,115-hp engine, a fourteen-cylinder, air-cooled radial Nakajima Sakae 21. The absence of bulletproof glass in the windscreen enhanced the view.

The most astonishing features of the Zeke were a lack of armor in the pilot's seat and three non-self-sealing fuel tanks, one in the fuselage forward of the cockpit, one in each inner wing. The tanks had a total capacity of 130 imperial gals (156 U.S.). This was all part of the design philosophy employed by the American-trained Horikoshi; he wanted to keep the Zeke's weight to a minimum and obtain the fighter maneuverability demanded by Japan's Naval Air Staff. According to traditional Japanese thinking, attack is the best form of defense, and it certainly paid great dividends in the Chinese conflict.

Apart from the folding wingtips, a special naval characteristic was the deck arrester hook, which lay flush with the fuselage, just forward of the partly retractable tailwheel. Each wing had two watertight compartments, and there was a canvas bag in the rear fuselage for flotation.

The cockpit layout was neat, with only two unusual features. There was no canopy emergency release, which seemed in keeping with the kamikaze mentality of the Japanese. Secondly, there was a flotation valve which was normally kept open but which, during emergency ditching, was closed by the pilot to trap air at atmospheric pressure.

Takeoff acceleration was lively and the run short. The undercarriage was retracted hydraulically, not particularly quickly, but once it was up rate of climb improved to 4,000 ft/min.

Mitsubishi A6M2 Zero (National Archives)

The stability of the Zeke was neutral around all three axes, the sign of a good fighter. The controls were all light and beautifully harmonized, but a moderate rate of roll kept maneuverability short of excellence. There were also considerable directional trim changes with power and speed, so that a rather sensitive rudder had to be constantly used. Since the stall of the Zeke was gentle, the high maneuverability margin could be utilized to the full.

As a deck-landing aircraft the Zeke was impressive, with a surprisingly good view, effective lateral control, a responsive throttle, and resilient landing gear. Landing speed was 65 knots.

The Zeke had a top speed of 296 knots (341 mph), but its acceleration in the dive was slower than expected. The most outstanding performance feature was its superb range of 1,385 nm (1,595 statute miles).

Armament was two 12.7-mm machine guns in the engine cowling, synchronized to fire through the airscrew, and two 20-mm cannon in the wings.

Assessment: The Zeke was possibly the world's outstanding fighter at low and medium altitudes in 1941, and it was excellently suited to the demanding aircraft carrier environment, a combination that qualifies it as one of the greatest naval fighters of all time. The

Aichi D3A1 Val 11 (U.S. Navy)

aircraft's obvious weakness was an inability to absorb punishment from heavy-caliber guns, but it did not expect to reckon with many of these.

AICHI D3A1 VAL 11

The Val two-seat dive-bomber formed the major part of the force attacking Pearl Harbor. This low-wing monoplane had fixed landing gear, and the tips of the elliptical wings folded up for carrier stowage. Single slat-type dive-brakes were attached under the main spar. A deck arrester hook was fitted forward of the tailwheel.

The Val was powered by a 1,045-hp Mitsubishi Kinsei 44, a fourteen-cylinder, air-cooled radial engine. Fuel capacity was 206 imperial gals (247.5 U.S.).

The handling characteristics of the Val were good, especially in regard to maneuverability. The airplane was steady in the dive and, with its fixed landing gear and dive brakes, slow to accelerate, so there was ample time to line up on the target and make any necessary corrections.

The Val's top speed was 210 knots (241 mph), and it had a range of 1,085 nm (1,250 statute miles). Armament was two 7.7-mm synchronized machine guns over the engine and one 7.7-mm flexible machine gun in the rear cockpit. One 1,050-lb bomb, carried under the fuselage, was swung down and forward on arms before release.

The Val was suited to the role of carrier aircraft because it was simple to land.

Assessment: The Val was slightly superior in performance and

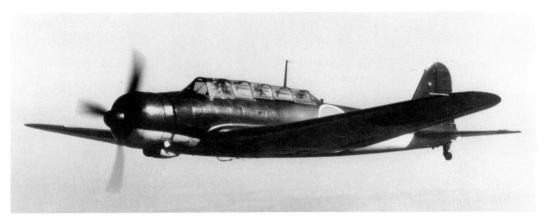

Nakajima B5N2 Kate 12 (Smithsonian Institution)

considerably superior in handling to its German counterpart, the Stuka, and not far short of it in dive-bombing efficiency. However, the Val carried only about half of the Stuka's bomb load.

NAKAJIMA B5N1 KATE 12

The Kate two/three-seat torpedo-bomber was the aircraft that led the devastating attack on Pearl Harbor. It was a low-wing monoplane with retractable landing gear and a fuselage of metal monocoque structure. It had clean lines. The crew sat in tandem under a continuous raised canopy.

The Kate was originally fitted with a 700-hp, nine-cylinder, Nakajima Hikari radial engine in 1937, but with this it was under-powered. A new 985-hp engine, the fourteen-cylinder, air-cooled radial Nakajima Sakae 11, was later used as a replacement.

The Kate exhibited good stability and this, combined with adequate maneuverability, made it an effective bombing platform. It had a docile stall and thus could be flown to its maneuver limits with impunity. It was also endowed with good deck-landing qualities, though a long nose somewhat impaired the forward view.

Maximum speed was 193 knots (222 mph), range, 1,060 nm (1,220 statute miles). Armament was the same as for the Val, and it could carry either one 18-in torpedo of 1,764 lbs or a bomb load of 1,100 lbs.

Assessment: The Kate was a thoroughly competent torpedo-bomber which, when covered by Zeke fighters, would be a devastating attacker.

Pearl Harbor

This attack was a masterpiece of planned surprise, brilliant execution, and staggeringly successful results. It is interesting to analyze the composition of the attacking forces and their comparative effectiveness.

The first wave of 183 planes was made up of 43 Zekes; 51 Val dive-bombers, each carrying a 551-lb bomb; 48 Kate bombers armed with torpedoes; and another 49 carrying 1,760-lb armor-piercing bombs (actually, 16-in naval shells fitted with fins). The second wave of 167 planes comprised 35 Zekes; 78 Vals, each with a 551-lb bomb; and 54 Kates, each carrying a 551-lb and six 132-lb bombs. Thirty-nine Zekes remained with the Japanese carrier force for air defense.

The appalling damage these aircraft inflicted amounted to four battleships sunk, three damaged, and one beached, as previously mentioned, along with three destroyers and a minelayer sunk, two cruisers and a repair ship crippled, and several other ships slightly damaged. A total of 188 American aircraft were destroyed, many more disabled, and 2,335 officers and enlisted men were killed.

Japanese losses came to a mere fifty-five men and twenty-nine aircraft—nine Zekes, fifteen Vals, and five Kates in the actual attack. An additional Kate had to ditch before reaching its carrier. These losses were attributable primarily to antiaircraft fire.

It is difficult to draw conclusions about the relative lethality of bombs and torpedoes, and to compare the effectiveness of dive-bombing, torpedo-bombing, and low-level bombing, because the targets were static and the defenses unprepared. However, an analysis of direct hits in relation to weapons launched shows an equal distribution of torpedoes and bombs.

Japanese losses amounted to 8.5 percent of the attacking force, rather high in view of the element of surprise and the environment of total air superiority involved, but the attacks were carried home with grim determination, and in the final analysis, the results more than justified the losses.

Further Allied Setbacks

December 1941 was a month of unabated disasters for the Allies in the Indian Ocean as well. Attacks by land-based bombers resulted in the loss of the battleships *Repulse* and *Prince of Wales* off Malaysia on the tenth. Thirty-five torpedo-bombers and eight medium-level bombers attacked the *Repulse*, the Japanese claiming eighteen torpedo hits and one direct 550-lb bomb hit. The *Prince of Wales*, attacked by fifteen torpedo-bombers and eight medium-level bombers, suffered eight torpedo hits and one direct 1,100-lb bomb hit. The battleships had no fighter protection. Japanese losses amounted to three aircraft and twenty-one aircrew.

On 23 December the U.S.-held island of Wake fell to a Japanese invasion force supported by carrier aircraft. This event removed a valuable strategic platform for American forces in the Pacific.

North Africa

The Western Desert seemed to offer little of worth to justify bloody battle, but under its hot sands lay oil and in its Atlas Mountains, mineral wealth. It was also the key to the Nile Valley and the strategic Suez Canal.

In mid-1941, after initial British successes against the Italian desert forces, there arrived on the scene the formidable German General Rommel. The ensuing period of furious fighting involved some Fleet Air Arm planes, which had been put ashore to supplement the RAF's dwindling resources being used in support of the army.

The duties of the Swordfish and Albacores were mainly nighttime bombing and minelaying raids on harbors and convoys, conducted to cut off the enemy's supplies. Secondary duties included dive-bombing attacks on desert airfields, panzer concentrations, and ammunition dumps. Hurricanes and Wildcats, participating in fighter sweeps and acting as escorts to RAF bombers, were particularly successful against German Ju 87s. The fighters also protected Allied convoys and scored a number of kills on torpedo-carrying SM 79s.

Wildcat Versus Junkers 87

The superiority of the Wildcat in every department of performance, handling, and armament would have made its task against the Stuka a simple one. There simply would not have been an escape route for the German.

Verdict: There could only be one outcome to such a combat— swift victory for the Wildcat.

Wildcat Versus Savoia-Marchetti 79

The Wildcat again held all the aces, particularly bringing its weighty firepower against a wooden opponent. But if the SM 79 was at its most vulnerable during a torpedo attack, so was the attacking Wildcat, which could only break upward, thereby exposing its underbelly to the bomber's light defensive armament.

Verdict: The odds heavily favored the Wildcat over the lightly armed wooden bomber.

4

1942

Year of Mixed Fortunes

AFTER PEARL HARBOR and Wake Island the U.S. Navy decided to move the carrier *Yorktown* from the East Coast to the Pacific to join the *Enterprise, Lexington,* and *Saratoga.* This force of four aircraft carriers was cut back to three on 11 January 1942, when the *Saratoga* was torpedoed by a Japanese submarine. She had to limp back to the United States for repairs that were to take five months.

The first stage in the U.S. Navy's planned offensive was to raid the Marshalls. The *Enterprise* launched the first air attacks on 1 February against the northern islands, while the *Yorktown* hit the southern atolls. These strikes, while they inflicted relatively little damage, succeeded in blooding the air groups. In this first aerial confrontation with the Japanese the *Enterprise* lost five SBD Dauntless dive-bombers, four to antiaircraft fire and one to a Claude fighter, but destroyed four Claudes, three Betty bombers in the air, and several of the latter on the ground. The *Yorktown* fared worse: she lost seven bombers, and her only victory was a four-engine flying boat shot down by Wildcats.

Meanwhile, in Europe, there was a spectacular incident on 12 February involving the German battle cruisers *Scharnhorst* and *Gneisenau* and the cruiser *Prinz Eugen.* They escaped from Brest and made a dash through the English Channel unscathed, in spite of the attentions of Dover batteries, motor torpedo boats, and a heroic torpedo attack by six Fleet Air Arm Swordfish, all of which were lost. Further waves of bombers and torpedo-bombers, as well as a torpedo attack launched by five destroyers, failed to stop the German ships with their powerful destroyer and air escort. They reached the safety of their home port on 13 February.

This Allied setback was dwarfed by the significance of events on

USS Saratoga (U.S. *Naval Institute*)

the other side of the world. On 15 February Singapore surrendered to the invading Japanese force. On 19 February Admiral Nagumo, with a four-carrier force, launched an air attack on Port Darwin to sever Allied communications between Australia and Java in preparation for the invasion of the latter. The Japanese force of 188 planes sank almost a dozen ships, destroyed eighteen aircraft, and blasted the airfield out of operation.

On 20 February the carrier *Lexington*, headed to Rabaul with a task force to stop the Japanese advance down the Bismarck Archipelago, was detected by three Mavis flying boats. Two were shot down by Wildcats, but the third escaped and shortly afterward eighteen Kate bombers swept in to attack. Wildcats destroyed sixteen Kates, another was shot down by antiaircraft fire. Despite a resounding victory, the element of surprise had been lost and the Rabaul raid was called off. During this action Lieutenant E. O'Hare became the U.S. Navy's first war ace, scoring five kills.

On 24 February the USS *Enterprise* made a raid on Wake Island, destroying three flying boats in exchange for two Dauntless dive-bombers. On 4 March *Enterprise* aircraft struck Marcus Island, and one Dauntless and one Wildcat were lost. These were morale-boosting offensives; there was not much on either island.

All the American raids in the Pacific had been single-carrier actions to date, but now that policy changed. The first two-carrier operation against Japanese shipping took place on the northern coast of New Guinea on 10 March, when the *Lexington* and the *Yorktown* launched eighteen Wildcats, sixty Dauntless dive-bombers, and

Kawanishi Mavis 23 (U.S. Navy)

twenty-five TBD Devastator torpedo-bombers. The air strike met with virtually no resistance, yet achieved only moderate success. One Dauntless was lost and one enemy float biplane shot down.

This operation and those in the previous month revealed a tactical difference between Japanese and American carrier doctrine. The Japanese navy used battleship and cruiser floatplanes or shore-based flying boats for reconnaissance, thus preserving maximum strike capability in the carriers, while the U.S. Navy devoted a quarter of its carrier air strength to reconnaissance.

On the morning of 5 April eighty Japanese dive-bombers, from a battle fleet including five aircraft carriers commanded by Admiral Nagumo of Pearl Harbor fame, attacked Colombo in Ceylon. It was the first action in which British and Japanese aircraft opposed each other. At midday a further dive-bombing attack sank the British cruisers *Dorsetshire* and *Cornwall*.

Early in 1942, two squadrons of twenty-four Fulmars had been sent from the Middle East to defend Ceylon and augment three RAF Hurricane squadrons stationed there. At the time of the Japanese attack on Colombo there were sixty fighters on the island.

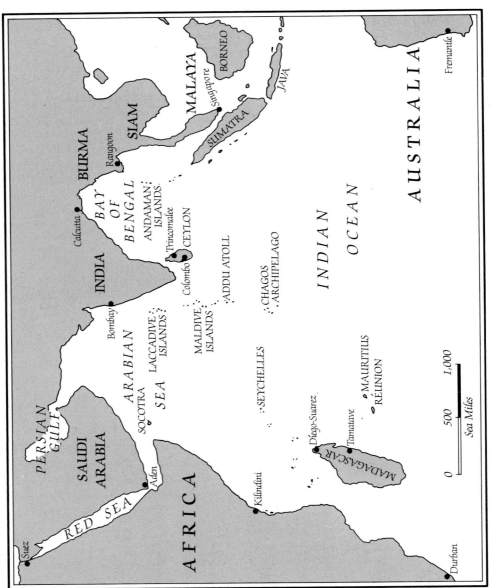

The Indian Ocean

HMS Cornwall *Sinking in the Indian Ocean after Attack by Japanese Vals, 5 April 1942 (Imperial War Museum)*

The attack force was composed of thirty-six Zekes, thirty-six Val dive-bombers, and fifty-three Kate attack bombers. The defenses had been alerted on the evening of 4 April by a Catalina, which sighted the Japanese battle fleet and managed to make a radio report before being shot down by a Zeke. Thus forty-two fighters opposed the Japanese attackers. When combat was joined, the Zekes shot down nineteen opposing fighters, many of them Fulmars, and the bombers destroyed six Swordfish on the ground. The Japanese lost one fighter and six dive-bombers.

As the Colombo raid continued, Admiral Nagumo received a report from one of his reconnaissance aircraft of two enemy ships 300 nm southwest of Colombo. He immediately launched eighty Val dive-bombers, which annihilated the warships, a couple of British cruisers.

Following the Colombo attack, Nagumo's force regrouped and moved eastward, planning to raid Trincomalee on 9 April. Again a Catalina sighted the battle fleet and reported its position. On 9 April 129 Japanese carrier aircraft—38 Zekes, 36 Vals, and 55 Kates—struck Trincomalee and were opposed by 23 fighters. Of these, eight Hurricanes and three Fulmars were shot down by the Zekes. Japanese losses amounted to one Zeke, four Vals, and one Kate.

Before the Trincomalee raid, nine Bristol Blenheim light bombers had taken off to attack the Japanese aircraft carriers. This daring assault met with no success. Five Blenheims were destroyed, at a cost of four Zekes.

Meanwhile, Nagumo's reconnaissance planes were seeking the warships that had been missing in Trincomalee harbor. They found the destroyer *Vampire* and the aircraft carrier *Hermes*, which had left her aircraft on Ceylon and was virtually defenseless. Nagumo launched eighty-five Vals escorted by nine Zekes. These dispatched the enemy ships with devastating accuracy within fifteen minutes.

The Ceylon episode heavily underlined the supremacy of the Zero in the Far East and the almost total dependence of the Japanese navy on this outstanding fighter for the success of its carrier attack force. Without the cover of escorting Zeros, dive- and torpedo-bombers, although effective in their roles, would be highly vulnerable to enemy fighters.

Fulmar Versus Zeke 22

The specification that produced the Fulmar was based on a Naval Staff concept of passive defense, in direct contrast to the Japanese philosophy of defense through attack. The result was a pedestrian two-seat airplane of limited performance and fighting capability. The Zeke, on the other hand, was a superbly agile single-seat fighter of world-beating class.

There is no advantage one could give the Fulmar over the Zeke except in the matter of absorbing punishment, which in this case is somewhat academic.

Verdict: This would be a totally one-sided combat, the initiative always lying with the Zeke and the outcome a foregone conclusion.

Fulmar Versus Val 1

The Fulmar had a slight speed advantage over the Val but would not be able to outmaneuver the dive-bomber. The Fulmar did, however, have one trump card to play—its superior acceleration in the dive. If it could catch the Val in a committed dive, it should be able to overtake it rapidly and deliver an eight-gun punch for the kill.

Verdict: The Fulmar would have a reasonable chance of downing the Val in single combat, assuming that it caught the dive-bomber without its usual escort of Zekes.

Fulmar Versus Kate

The Kate was significantly slower than the Fulmar and of comparable maneuverability, so the initiative should always be with the fighter, especially if the Kate was carrying its weapon load. The Japanese bomber was poorly armed and would be easy prey in single combat.

Verdict: The Fulmar would deal easily and effectively with the Kate, again assuming that it was without its covering Zeros.

Invasion of Madagascar

Although Madagascar, the world's largest island, is separated from Ceylon by the breadth of the Indian Ocean, there was now the fear that the Japanese might have ideas of using it as a base from which to hold sway over those waters. Or perhaps the Vichy French, who controlled the island, might commit some act of betrayal. Thus the Allies decided to secure control of the invaluable harbor of Diego Suarez.

So as not to complicate the operation, the Free French were excluded. It was also diplomatically preferable not to compromise U.S. relations with Vichy France, so the expedition was to be all British. The United States would send naval reinforcements to sustain the strength of the British Home Fleet, from which units would have to be withdrawn.

The Operation Ironclad assault force, assembled at Durban, South Africa, included a battleship, the aircraft carriers *Illustrious* and *Indomitable,* two cruisers, eleven destroyers, some smaller ships, and fifteen assault ships. On 5 May the invasion opened from the east. Diego Suarez fell on the seventh. The main ships departed after putting an occupation force of men and aircraft ashore that would undertake the laborious task of moving slowly south through the jungle. The takeover was completed by 5 November.

During the Diego Suarez phase of the operation there was air resistance from the Vichy air force, which flew Morane-Saulnier 406 fighters and Potez 63 bombers against Wildcats covering the assault troops. Four MS 406s and three Potez bombers were shot down by Wildcats from the *Illustrious* in exchange for one British fighter. Sea Hurricanes from the *Indomitable* destroyed three more Moranes on the ground.

Battle of the Coral Sea

By the middle of April 1942 the Japanese had already reached the geographical limits set in their prewar plans. The incredible speed of their success made the Tokyo government pause to consider whether it was wiser to pursue the original policy of consolidation or continue expansion. It adopted the latter course, setting its sights on the western Aleutians, Midway, Samoa, Fiji, New Caledonia, and Port Moresby, in southern New Guinea. At the end of April the Japanese high command began their new strategic plan with the capture of

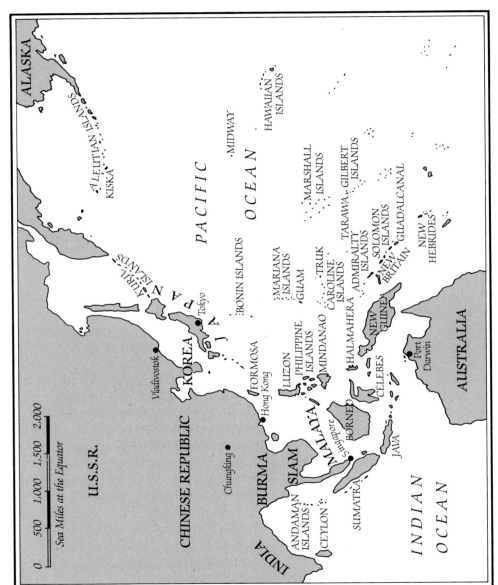

The Pacific Theater

U.S.S.R.

ALASKA

ALEUTIAN ISLANDS
KISKA

KURIL ISLANDS

CHINESE REPUBLIC

Chungking

Vladivostok

KOREA

JAPAN
Tokyo

PACIFIC OCEAN

MIDWAY

HAWAIIAN ISLANDS

BONIN ISLANDS

MARIANA ISLANDS
GUAM

MARSHALL ISLANDS

FORMOSA
Hong Kong

LUZON
PHILIPPINE ISLANDS
MINDANAO

TRUK
CAROLINE ISLANDS

TARAWA GILBERT ISLANDS

ADMIRALTY ISLANDS
SOLOMON ISLANDS
GUADALCANAL

NEW HEBRIDES

BURMA
SIAM
MALAYA
Singapore
BORNEO

HALMAHERA
CELEBES

NEW BRITAIN
NEW GUINEA

INDIA
ANDAMAN ISLANDS
CEYLON
SUMATRA

JAVA

Port Darwin

AUSTRALIA

INDIAN OCEAN

Sea Miles at the Equator
0   500   1,000   1,500   2,000

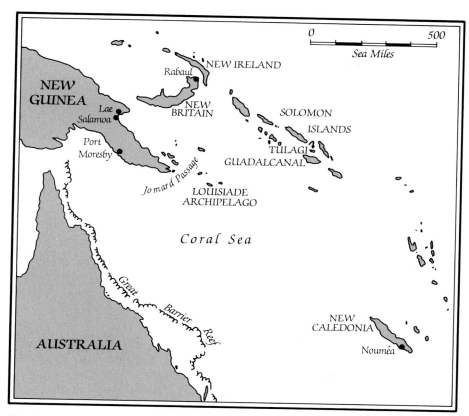

The Coral Sea

Port Moresby. At this time American aircraft carriers were widely dispersed on various missions, including the spectacular Doolittle air attack on Tokyo conducted by sixteen B-25 Mitchell bombers.

For Operation MO, as the Japanese called their offensive against the British-administered Solomon islands and southeastern New Guinea, seventy ships were mustered. This included two large carriers, the *Shokaku* and the *Zuikaku*, with 126 aircraft, and the small carrier *Shoho* with 21.

American intelligence had alerted the U.S. Navy that a Japanese invasion force would enter the Coral Sea in early May. Thus the carriers *Lexington* and *Yorktown* were in the western Coral Sea on 1 May with 143 aircraft. On 3 May the *Yorktown* headed north toward Tulagi. On 4 May several air strikes were made against Japanese ships off Tulagi, but with little success.

On the morning of 5 May the two carriers rejoined each other, while that night the two large Japanese carriers entered the Coral

A B-25 Mitchell Bomber Taking Off from the Deck of the USS Hornet *for the Doolittle Raid on Tokyo (National Archives)*

Sea. The *Shoho* was heading south toward them. Thus was the scene set for the first naval battle fought entirely by carrier aircraft.

After false sighting reports on 7 May, the Japanese launched a seventy-eight-plane strike against an American destroyer and oiler, both of which were sunk. The American carriers flew off a ninety-three-plane strike intended for the two large enemy carriers. Instead they found the *Shoho* and her cruiser destroyer escort. The strike force of eighteen Wildcats, fifty-three Dauntless, and twenty-two Devastators overwhelmed the small carrier. Receiving thirteen bomb and seven torpedo hits, she sank within minutes and lost three-quarters of her crew. Most of the *Shoho*'s Zekes were on convoy patrol, so American losses amounted to only three aircraft.

Now the odds had evened up for a showdown between the large carriers. The two U.S. ships had forty-four Wildcats, seventy-four Dauntless, and twenty-five Devastators, while the two Japanese ships carried forty-two Zekes, forty-two Vals, and forty-two Kates. Therefore, the U.S. Navy possessed a slight superiority in aircraft numbers, a slight inferiority in quality.

In late afternoon of 7 May the Japanese flew off twelve Vals and fifteen Kates to search for and attack the U.S. carriers, but the mission failed. On their return flight they ran into the U.S. Wildcats. Eight Kates, one Val, and two Wildcats were lost. Night had fallen

The Japanese Light Carrier Shoho *Being Hit by One of Seven Torpedoes in the Coral Sea (U.S. Navy)*

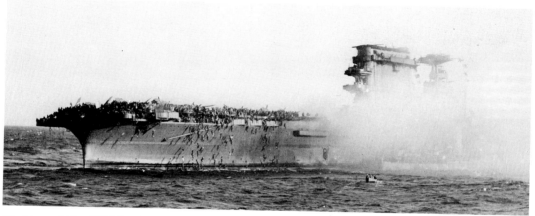

Sinking of the USS Lexington *(U.S. Navy)*

and a further eleven Japanese planes were ditched—a severe blow to the Japanese carrier force.

On the morning of 8 May the two opposing carrier groups launched air strikes against each other almost simultaneously. Sixty-nine Japanese aircraft gained two torpedo and five bomb hits on the *Lexington* and one bomb hit on the *Yorktown*. An hour after the attack, damage to the *Lexington* caused a huge internal explosion, and the crippled carrier had to be sunk by her escort. The American strike force of eighty-two aircraft obtained three bomb hits on the *Shokaku*, damaging her so that she could not launch or recover aircraft. The *Zuikaku* escaped in a rain squall.

Japanese losses amounted to thirty combat aircraft, another thirteen operational planes, and several that were jettisoned from the *Zuikaku* to make space for the *Shokaku*'s planes. American losses were thirty-three aircraft in combat and thirty-six that went down with the *Lexington*.

The Japanese could claim a tactical victory because they lost fewer ships and aircraft than the Americans. The long-term results, however, were different. The Battle of the Coral Sea was a strategic Allied victory, for it forced the Japanese to postpone their advance toward Port Moresby. The carrier battle marked the limit of Japan's expansion toward Australia. Perhaps most important of all, the Japanese had been deprived of a significant number of their most experienced naval aircrew and the use of the *Shokaku* for six weeks.

Douglas SBD-3 Dauntless

The Dauntless was the true workhorse of the U.S. Navy's Pacific War. Indeed, it was the only American aircraft to participate in all five engagements fought exclusively between carriers. It was exactly what it looked like, a decidedly prewar airplane of obsolescent design. This two-seat, low-wing scout dive-bomber was of oval alclad monocoque structure with flush-riveted skin. Nonfolding wings had fabric-covered ailerons with slots ahead of them, near the leading edge. Perforated, hydraulically operated metal dive brakes were fitted above and below the trailing edges of the outer wings and below the trailing edge only of the center section beneath the fuselage. Rudder and elevators were fabric covered. The main landing gear was retractable, and there was an arrester hook fitted under the fuselage, forward of the fixed tailwheel.

Power was supplied by a 1,000-hp Wright Cyclone R-1820-52, a nine-cylinder, radial air-cooled engine driving a full-feathering Hamilton Standard airscrew. Fuel was contained in two self-sealing tanks in the center section, each with a capacity of 62.5 imperial gals (75 U.S.), and two tanks in the outer wing panels that could hold 45.75 imperial gals (55 U.S.).

The cockpit was commodious. It offered a relatively good view for takeoff, which was somewhat lumbering, the airplane being underpowered. It climbed sluggishly, at a rate of about 1,000 ft/min when carrying a 1,000-lb bomb. The cockpit was noisy and drafty during the climb, and there were signs of lateral instability.

The Dauntless cruised at a sedate 120 knots (138 mph), and its controls were light and responsive unless it was heavily laden. The stall at maximum weight was 65 knots (75 mph) and very gentle. The bomber had a vicious "g" stall, particularly off a tight lefthand turn, when it would snap without warning and enter a spin if corrective action was not taken immediately.

As a dive-bomber the Dauntless had two major faults. First,

Douglas SBD-3 Dauntless (U.S. Navy)

deployment of the dive brakes was slow, and it was therefore necessary to activate them before half rolling into a dive. Second, the
telescopic sight and the windscreen tended to fog over if sudden
temperature changes were experienced in the dive.

Acceleration was slow, and an angle of 70 to 75 degrees was
normally obtained before the release height of 1,500 ft. If a tactical
getaway was to be made, manual release of the bombs had to be
followed immediately, before pullout, by retraction of the dive brakes.

Among the best features of the Dauntless were its landing characteristics. The view for deck landing was good, the controls were
crisp and effective, and the flaps were draggy enough to give a defi-
nite deceleration when the pilot cut engine power. The landing gear
could be faulted for being a little bouncy.

Armament consisted of two 0.5-in machine guns synchronized to fire through the airscrew, and twin 0.3-in, rear-firing machine guns, belt fed and flexible, with 2,000 rounds per gun. One 1,000-lb bomb was carried on a swinging cradle under the fuselage, or alternatively, one 500-lb bomb plus two 100-lb bombs could be carried on racks mounted under the roots of the outer wing sections.

Maximum speed was 214 knots (246 mph), and range was 1,172 nm with a single 500-lb bomb. For scouting, range was increased to 1,468 nm, and because of the endurance involved, the pilot was provided with a Sperry autopilot. These range figures make no allowance for reserves, which could be considerable, for rendezvous or landing after a multiaircraft strike.

Assessment: The Dauntless was a rugged and reliable airplane with mediocre performance because it was underpowered. It seemed vulnerable to fighters and yet gave a good account of itself in the Pacific. Its loss rate in that theater is reputed to have been lower than that of any other U.S. Navy shipboard airplane. This I find hard to believe, considering that the Zeke was its opposition.

As a dive-bomber it was effective. I rate it below the Ju 87, above the Skua, and probably on a par with the Val. It would have benefited by improved sighting arrangements.

Douglas TBD-1 Devastator

The Devastator was a low-wing, three-seat torpedo-bomber with an oval metal fuselage containing a compartment for semi-internal stowage of the torpedo or bombs. This gave the airplane its somewhat pregnant look and made the engine look small. The wings, which could be folded up at points midway between the roots and the tips, had split flaps on the inner sections. Of 1934 design, the Devastator was the first all-metal monoplane carrier aircraft in the U.S. Navy.

It had a Pratt and Whitney Twin Wasp Junior SB4G, an 825-hp, fourteen-cylinder, air-cooled radial engine driving a Hamilton Standard controllable-pitch airscrew.

The airplane had a takeoff similar to that of the SBD, but its rate of climb was only 720 ft/min. It exhibited good stability characteristics, though the controls were heavy and rather unresponsive. Certainly the Devastator would not enjoy meeting a nimble fighter. With a good view, adequate control response at low speeds, and plenty of flap drag for a positive touchdown, it was easy to deck-land.

The performance of the Devastator was poor. It had a top speed of 180 knots (207 mph) and a range of 855 nm. The service ceiling was only 19,700 ft. Armament consisted of a synchronized, forward-firing 0.3-in machine gun and a flexible gun of the same caliber in the rear cockpit. The plane could carry a 21-in torpedo or 1,000-lb bomb. When it was acting as a torpedo-bomber, only the pilot and

Douglas TBD-1 Devastator (U.S. Navy)

rear gunner rode; when it was a bomber, a bombardier-navigator occupied the middle cockpit before taking up a prone position, below the pilot and just aft of the engine, for bomb aiming and release.

Assessment: The Devastator was an obsolescent design plagued by unreliable torpedoes. It was highly vulnerable to fighter attack because of its poor performance and poor defensive armament. It was significantly inferior to its Japanese counterpart, the Kate.

SBD-3 Dauntless Versus Zeke

The Dauntless would find itself totally outclassed by the redoubtable Zeke, which would be able to deal with it summarily in any phase of flight. The slow operation of its dive brakes made the Dauntless particularly vulnerable at the start and termination of a dive-bombing attack. The only hope of survival was a lucky hit by the rear gunner.

Verdict: From this one-sided affair the Zeke would likely emerge victorious.

TBD-1 Devastator Versus Zeke

Without any viable form of defense and because of poor maneuverability and climb performance, the Devastator would be particularly vulnerable if caught climbing away from a torpedo attack.

Verdict: The Devastator would be a sitting duck for the Zeke.

Dauntless Versus Val 11

In this clash the maneuverability limitations of the Dauntless would undoubtedly be exploited by the more agile Val, and since there was little speed difference between the two aircraft, the Dauntless could only hope for a surprise chance to bring its heavier armament to bear on the enemy.

Verdict: With the Val's agility, it would gain ascendancy easily in this contest.

Dauntless Versus Kate

The Dauntless, without its weapon load, should be able to deal effectively with the Kate if it caught the Japanese plane on a torpedo run in. With the Kate on a bombing run the Dauntless, unless it possessed a height advantage, would not have the performance to ensure a kill.

Verdict: The Dauntless had a reasonably good chance of success against the Kate on a descending, weapon-dropping run.

The Battle of Midway

An advance into the Coral Sea was only phase one of Japan's expansionist policy, and in spite of what it regarded as a temporary setback in the southern area, the fateful decision was made to undertake phase two with an offensive against Midway. As with the Battle of

Carrier	Fighters	Dive-Bombers	Torpedo-Bombers
Akagi	18 A6M2 Zeke 22	18 D3A1 Val 11	18 B5N1 Kate 12
Kaga	18 A6M2 Zeke 22	18 D3A1 Val 11	27 B5N1 Kate 12
Hiryu	18 A6M2 Zeke 22	18 D3A1 Val 11	18 B5N1 Kate 12
Soryu	18 A6M2 Zeke 22	18 D3A1 Val 11	18 B5N1 Kate 12
TOTAL	72	72	81
Enterprise	27 F4F-4 Wildcat	38 SBD-3 Dauntless	14 TBD-1 Devastator
Hornet	27 F4F-4 Wildcat	37 SBD-3 Dauntless	15 TBD-1 Devastator
Yorktown	27 F4F-4 Wildcat	37 SBD-3 Dauntless	13 TBD-1 Devastator
TOTAL	81	112	42

Consolidated PBY Catalina (U.S. Navy)

the Coral Sea, the stage was set for a major carrier force confrontation. The Japanese held the advantage in number of carriers but not of aircraft.

American aircraft numbers were in fact modified by the loss of two Wildcats, one Dauntless, and one Devastator through accidents en route to the battle area. The Dauntless and the Devastator were replaced, thus reducing total American carrier aircraft strength to 233. Japanese air strength amounted to 225 aircraft.

The Japanese had on board the *Soryu* two experimental models of the new Yokosuka D4Y-2 Judy 11, a two-seat dive-bomber powered by the 1,180-hp Aichi Atsuta 21 engine, the Japanese version of the German Daimler-Benz 601A. With a speed of 312 knots (360 mph), the Judy could outpace the Wildcat and so was to be used in the reconnaissance role.

Also on board the four Japanese carriers were twenty-one Zekes being ferried to a base on Midway. They were kept intact for that purpose and not used in the battle.

On Midway itself were 106 American aircraft, comprising 17 Boeing B-17 Flying Fortresses; 4 Martin B-26 Marauder medium bombers operated by the army air force; and 7 F4F-3 Wildcats, 21 F2A-3 Buffalo, 16 SBD-2 Dauntless, and 17 Vought-Sikorsky SB2U-3 Vindicators, all operated by the marines. The United States also had thirty Catalina flying boats and six brand-new Avenger torpedo-bombers assigned to the *Hornet*. These, however, arrived at Pearl Harbor after the carrier had sailed.

The Battle of Midway began on 4 June with a dawn strike launched by 108 Japanese carrier aircraft—36 Kates and an equal number of Vals, all carrying bombs, with 36 Zekes providing escort cover. An additional 9 Zekes from the *Kaga* formed a combat air patrol over the task force. Nine more Zekes were combat ready on the deck of the *Akagi*. There was also a plan to send out two search planes from the carriers, one from the battleship, and four from the cruisers; the cruiser aircraft were delayed for a vital half hour owing to technical problems. The small search force was to seek out any U.S. warships in the area.

The first alert of enemy strike planes came from a patrolling Catalina, and shortly afterward Midway radar picked the force up when it was 93 miles away. Twenty Buffalo and six Wildcats rushed to intercept and were met head on by the Zekes, which destroyed fifteen planes and severely damaged seven in exchange for two of their own. The Japanese bombers remained intact.

Midway suffered a considerable amount of damage from the strike, but its airfield could still be used. At this stage the Japanese lost four Kates, a Val, and two Zekes to antiaircraft fire. Meanwhile the six Avengers, which had flown to Midway from Pearl, and four Marauders, each carrying a torpedo, were ordered to attack the Japanese carriers after they had been sighted by a Catalina. The defending Zekes shot down five Avengers, two Marauders, and badly damaged the other attackers.

The next attack was launched by Midway's sixteen Dauntless dive-bombers against the *Hiryu*. Again the defending Zekes shot down eight aircraft and severely damaged another six. Then followed an attack by eleven obsolescent Vindicator dive-bombers, four of which fell to the Zekes. Thus nineteen American planes were lost and nine severely damaged for no apparent gain. In fact, however, these attacks had occupied the Zekes, which had been earmarked to escort the second strike against Midway.

The task force commanders in the Battle of Midway had analyzed the Battle of the Coral Sea, and it remained to be seen who had learned the best tactical lessons. Each made a decision vitally affecting the course of battle. Vice Admiral Nagumo opted for a second strike against Midway. He had to rearm his torpedo bombers with bombs and recover the first returning strike, which tied up two of his carrier decks for one critical hour. Rear Admiral Fletcher, commanding the U.S. Carrier Striking Force, decided not to commit all his strike planes to an initial attack against the Japanese carriers. He split his two task forces while awaiting the return and recovery of ten Dauntless scout planes to the *Yorktown*. Rear Admiral Spruance,

Vought-Sikorsky SB2U-3 Vindicator (National Archives)

in charge of the two-carrier group, planned to attack the Japanese carriers before they could launch a second strike against Midway.

The *Enterprise* and the *Hornet* flew off sixty-eight Dauntless, twenty-nine Devastators, and twenty Wildcats. Eighteen Wildcats were held over the carriers for combat air patrol, while another eighteen remained combat ready on deck. The 117-plane strike departed in four waves.

The first wave of thirty-five Dauntless and ten Wildcats from the *Hornet* failed to find the enemy carriers. Two Dauntless and all ten Wildcats had to ditch for lack of fuel. The *Hornet*'s fifteen Devastators found the Japanese carrier force and, in the subsequent attack, were lost. They were followed by the *Enterprise*'s fourteen Devastators, of which ten were downed. Yet another attack force arrived, twelve Devastators and six Wildcats from Admiral Fletcher's *Yorktown*. Once more all the Devastators were overcome, together with one Wildcat; the other five American fighters were badly damaged. The tally for these four attacks were thirty-seven Devastators destroyed for no torpedo hits.

Suicidal attacks by American torpedo-bombers had drawn the Japanese fighters low, leaving the sky clear for the Dauntless dive-bombers that had followed the Devastators. They were able to attack virtually unopposed. Thirty-three Dauntless from the *Enterprise* achieved two direct hits and one near miss on the *Akagi,* and four direct hits and five near misses on the *Kaga,* while seventeen Dauntless from the *Yorktown* scored three direct hits on the *Soryu.* Because the deck of every Japanese carrier was cluttered with aircraft rearming and refueling, all were vulnerable and all succumbed.

U.S. losses, including ditchings, amounted to sixty-eight planes: fourteen Wildcats, seventeen Dauntless, and thirty-seven Devastators.

The *Hiryu,* separated from the other three Japanese carriers, flew off six Zekes and eighteen Vals in a counterattack. They found the *Yorktown* and ran into its combat air patrol. Six Vals got through and made three direct hits on the carrier. Three Zekes and thirteen Vals were lost in this attack.

The depleted *Hiryu* flew off a second strike of six Zekes and ten Kates. These met twelve Wildcats from the *Yorktown* but managed nonetheless to achieve two torpedo hits. Meanwhile, the *Enterprise* dispatched twenty-four Dauntless. They attacked the *Hiryu,* scoring four direct hits and four near misses and losing, in the process, three dive-bombers, one to ditching.

On the evening of 4 June the *Soryu* and the *Kaga* sank, and next day the crippled *Akagi* and *Hiryu* were torpedoed by their own destroyer escorts. The *Yorktown* sank on the morning of 7 June after being hit by two torpedoes fired from a Japanese submarine, which also sank an escorting destroyer.

On 5 June a Catalina sighted two Japanese cruisers. A strike of six Dauntless and six Vindicators was launched from Midway, which resulted in nothing but the loss of a Vindicator. On 6 June the two undamaged U.S. carriers flew a 112-aircraft strike against the cruisers, sinking one and badly damaging the other.

The balance of losses in the Battle of Midway was as follows: Japan, 4 fleet carriers, a heavy cruiser, another heavy cruiser badly damaged, and 250 carrier aircraft; the United States, 1 aircraft carrier,

The Japanese Carrier Akagi *(U.S. Navy)*

The Japanese Carrier Hiryu, Crippled after an Attack by Dauntless Dive-Bombers. (U.S. Navy)

1 destroyer, 109 carrier planes, and some 40 Midway-based aircraft. Casualties were heavy on the Japanese side; the loss of many experienced pilots and mechanics was a particularly grave blow to Japanese naval aviation.

Thus Midway closed with a resounding American victory. It marked the turning point in the Pacific war and heralded an Allied switch to the offensive.

Sinking of the USS Yorktown *(National Archives)*

Grumman TBF-1 Avenger

The Avenger, designed to a 1939 specification for a three-crew torpedo-bomber to replace the aging Devastator, made its first flight on
1 August 1941. It was a corpulent, midwing airplane very much in
the Grumman style, with angular wings and tail, a long greenhouse
cockpit fairing into a dorsal gun turret, and a ventral gun position aft
of the large internal bomb bay. The wings folded hydraulically and,
as they moved backward, turned to lie flat along each side of the
fuselage. There was a sting-type arrester hook, and the tailwheel was
fully retractable.

The TBF-1 Avenger was powered by a 1,700-hp Wright Cyclone
R-2600-8, a fourteen-cylinder, radial air-cooled engine with a two-
speed supercharger and driving a three-blade, constant-speed Hamilton Hydromatic airscrew. There were three main fuel tanks carrying
a total of 275 imperial gals (330 U.S.), which gave a range of 960 nm
(1,105 statute miles) at 191 knots (215 mph). The engine was started
by an electrically energized inertia starter.

On entering the cockpit I was impressed by its roominess and
comfort, and the view was acceptable, despite the bulky engine and
not inconsiderable ground angle. Care was required in taxiing in a
crosswind, when the large keel surface of the Avenger made it advisable to lock the tailwheel.

The shortest takeoff was achieved with a 10-degree flap setting,
though this was seldom used because of the severe nose-down trim
changes that occurred when the flaps were raised. The throttle had
to be regulated, for there was no automatic boost control. The climb,
made at 115 knots, gave a rate of about 1,000 ft/min. Service ceiling
was 22,600 ft.

While cruising the Avenger was stable about all axes, but controls
were heavy at every speed. The stall was abrupt and came without

Grumman TBF Avenger (U.S. Navy)

warning, except that the elevator grew heavy. The all-up stall occurred at 76 knots, the all-down at 68 knots.

The Avenger's diving characteristics clearly ruled it out as a dive-bomber. The heavy controls permitted a maximum diving speed of 285 knots. Landing gear could be lowered at speeds up to 200 knots and used as a dive brake, while the weapons-bay doors could be opened at maximum diving speed. None of this changed the fact that the aircraft's maneuverability was inadequate for the dive-bombing role.

In the shallow dive required for torpedo-dropping, the aircraft stabilized almost immediately to produce a steady launching platform. The evasive breakaway after a torpedo drop called for two hands and a heavy foot load on the rudder pedals.

The Avenger made carrier deck landing about as easy as that difficult art is likely to be. It offered a good view with the cowl gills closed and remained superbly steady at an approach speed of 78 knots. The huge sting-type arrester hook was ready to convert the most ill-judged landing attempt into a safe arrival, and the landing gear was able to absorb vertical velocities of up to 16 ft/sec.

The Avenger's maximum speed was 223 knots (257 mph) at 12,000 ft and 216 knots (249 mph) at sea level. Its defensive armament consisted of one forward-firing 0.3-in machine gun in the engine cowling, synchronized to fire through the airscrew, one 0.5-in machine gun with 400 rounds in the power-operated dorsal turret, and one 0.3-in machine gun with 500 rounds firing aft from the ventral position. Weapon load was one 22-in torpedo or 2,000 lbs of bombs. Loaded weight with one torpedo was 16,412 lbs.

Assessment: The Avenger was a new dimension in shipboard bomber design, with its enclosed weapons bay and all-round defensive armament. It was 50 mph faster than its predecessor but still slow by fighter standards, evidence that its designers had heeded the adage, "If you're slow you're bound to go, unless you have the might to fight."

The Avenger was a ponderous airplane, certainly out of court as a dive-bomber, and even as a torpedo-bomber it would be vulnerable during breakaway. It would only be effective if operating in an environment of air superiority or under cover of darkness.

TBF-1 Avenger Versus Zeke 22

These two aircraft were unevenly matched in maneuverability; the initiative lay totally with the Zeke. With its speed advantage the Japanese fighter could afford to attack and reattack if necessary from the forward sector, thereby avoiding the Avenger's reasonably well-defended tail. Alternatively, a low quarter attack should keep the Zeke out of harm's way and present it with a large target area.

Verdict: The Avenger would have a considerably better chance of survival against the Zeke than its predecessor did, but the odds still heavily favored the fighter.

Zeke 22 Versus F4F-4 Wildcat

The role of the fighter was to prove crucial in the Battle of Midway, where 32 percent of American aircraft were Wildcats and 37 percent of embarked Japanese planes were Zekes. Japan's numerical superiority was offset by the radar equipment fitted in the American carriers. Therefore examining the single-combat capabilities of the opposing fighters is of great interest.

The Japanese fighter was superior to the Wildcat in speed and climb at all altitudes above 1,000 ft, and was the better of the two in both service ceiling and range. In a dive the Wildcat and the Zeke were virtually equal, but the turning circle of the latter was much smaller by reason of its lower wing loading and, consequently, its lower stalling speed. Therefore it was foolhardy for the Wildcat to dogfight with the Zeke. However, with two-plane units the American pilots could take full advantage of the Wildcat's virtues, such as its superior firepower and structural integrity.

Verdict: In single combat, the Wildcat was outclassed by the Zeke but could handle it by assiduously avoiding dogfights and sticking to tactical two-plane formations.

Zeke 22 Versus F2A-3 Buffalo

The little Buffalo could almost match the Zeke for maneuverability but was badly outclassed in performance and inferior in firepower. Thus it had little hope of besting the Japanese fighter. In a dogfight the initiative would rest entirely with the Zeke, which could mix it or break off at will.

Verdict: The Buffalo was in a fighter class below the Zeke and, as such, stood little or no chance of survival in single combat against such a strong opponent.

Invasion of the Aleutians

Compared to the Battle of Midway the simultaneous action in the Aleutians was a mild affair, even though it involved four Japanese carriers. Initially, only the light fleet carriers *Junyo* and *Ryujo* closed on Dutch Harbor, carrying thirty-two Zekes, twenty-four Vals, and twenty Kates. On 3 June the first strike was flown off. Bad weather, which plagued the operation throughout, meant that only six Zekes and six Kates reached Dutch Harbor, but they inflicted considerable damage. The fighters shot down two Catalinas and destroyed another on the water. One Zeke was lost in the action. A second strike had to be abandoned because of the weather, but not before one Japanese cruiser's floatplane was shot down.

On 4 June a thirty-two plane Japanese strike flown against Dutch Harbor inflicted heavy damage. On the return flight four Zekes and four Vals were bounced by eight P-40 Warhawk fighters; two Zekes and two Vals were shot down, resulting in the loss of two Warhawks. Another Zeke failed to return to its parent ship. During the strike several Flying Fortresses attacked the Japanese carriers to no avail, and one was shot down by the combat air patrol of Zekes.

The two-carrier force was now joined by the light carrier *Zuiho* and the fleet carrier *Zuikaku*, but there were no further carrier operations. On 7 June the Japanese made unopposed landings on the islands of Kiska and Attu.

The Mediterranean

General Rommel's counteroffensive in North Africa, begun on 21 January, again highlighted the strategic value of Malta for attacks on Axis supply convoys between Italy and North Africa. Fighters were needed to protect the base from which the attacking ships and bombers would operate. The USS *Wasp* made two vital ferry runs in mid-April and early May to reinforce the island with over ninety Spitfires.

The British Carriers Victorious, Indomitable, *and* Eagle *Operating Albacores and Sea Hurricanes in Operation Pedestal (Imperial War Museum)*

This duty was then taken over by HMS *Eagle* and *Argus*. The Sea Hurricanes from the *Eagle* shot down six Italian attackers on 14 June.

Events in North Africa took a critical turn on 21 June when Tobruk fell to Rommel. With the resupply of Malta critical, particularly after two June convoys were mauled, a major convoy effort was planned for August. Meanwhile, in July, the desert Wildcats enjoyed their last victories over two SM 79s before moving to Mombasa in East Africa for antisubmarine patrol.

Operation Pedestal was to depend on four British carriers, the *Eagle, Furious, Indomitable,* and *Victorious.* To protect the convoy of fourteen merchant ships three carriers would operate seventy-two fighters—Fulmars, Sea Hurricanes and Wildcats—and twenty-eight torpedo-bombers. The *Furious* would carry thirty-eight Spitfires to be flown off by RAF pilots directly to Malta.

The forty-one warships assembled to defend the convoy were opposed by over two hundred German and almost four hundred Italian aircraft as well as motor torpedo boats and submarines. A gigantic battle was unavoidable within the confines of the Mediterranean.

The force steamed past Gibraltar on 10 August. Next day the attack started. A German U-boat hit the carrier *Eagle* with four torpedoes, and she sank in eight minutes. The *Furious* flew off her Spitfires and returned to Gibraltar. The two remaining carriers had sixty fighters and twenty-eight torpedo bombers.

On 11 August a Sea Hurricane shot down a Ju 88 shadower. The first Allied air attack followed that evening. Because of the fading light it failed.

Three Italian SM 79s shadowed the convoy during the night. At dawn one was shot down by a Fulmar. Meanwhile, the force braced itself for the inevitable onslaught.

The first Axis attack of 12 August was launched by twenty aircraft, which were repulsed by the carrier fighters without receiving damage. The second attack of seventy aircraft sank only one merchant ship. About one hundred aircraft, mainly German dive-bombers, came in the third wave, this time with more determination. Three direct hits and two near misses put the *Indomitable*'s flight deck out of action. A destroyer was also torpedoed and had to be sunk. That evening the carriers left the convoy to the protection of a cruiser-destroyer screen as it entered the Sicilian narrows, where the larger ships had no space to maneuver in defense.

The combat tally for these attacks was as follows: Sea Hurricanes (three squadrons)—five Ju 87s, seven Ju 88s, one Me 109, one Me 110, five SM 79s, one SM 84, one Macchi C.202 fighter, one Reggiane 2000, and one Reggiane 2001; Wildcats (one squadron)—five Cant Z.1007 fighters and one C.202 fighter; Fulmars (one squadron)—one Z.1007. Thus in three days of attacks the carrier aircraft scored thirty-nine victories in exchange for twenty-five fighters, including those lost when the nineteen-year-old carrier *Eagle* was sunk.

In the Sicilian narrows on 12 August Italian submarines sank one light cruiser and damaged two others, along with a tanker. On 13 August Italian torpedo boats sank the last cruiser in the screen and four merchantmen. Enemy aircraft sank four more merchantmen, so that only five eventually arrived at Malta, and of these three were damaged. The result, however, was the reinforcement of Malta with thirty-seven Spitfires and enough vital supplies to allow the island to defend itself and survive.

The furious air activity of 12 August had brought some new Italian aircraft to the scene: Re 2001 and Macchi C.202 fighters, and SM 84 and Cant Z.1007 torpedo-bombers.

REGGIANE 2001 AND MACCHI C.202

The Re 2001 and C.202 had been developed from the Re 2000 and C.200 when designers converted them from radial to in-line engines. Both aircraft used the twelve-cylinder, inverted-V, liquid-cooled Daimler-Benz DB 601 engine of 1,150 hp. As before, the two aircraft resembled one another, but the Re 2001 had a top speed of 348 mph, some 20 mph more than the C.202. Both were similarly armed, with two 12.7-mm machine guns synchronized to fire through the airscrew and two 7.7-mm machine guns in the wings.

SAVOIA-MARCHETTI 84

The SM 84 differed from the SM 79 in being fitted with a cantilevered tail unit with twin fins and rudders. The upper gun blister was replaced by a turret, and the ventral portion aft of the torpedo compartment was improved in shape. Performance remained the same as that of the SM 79.

CANT Z.1007

The Z.1007 was a midwing torpedo-bomber that generally looked like an enlarged version of the SM 84. Of all-wood structure, it had fabric-covered control surfaces. The Z.1007 was powered by three Piaggio P.XI RC.40 radial air-cooled engines of 1,000 hp, driving three-bladed, controllable-pitch Alfa-Romeo airscrews.

The crew arrangement for such a large airplane was unusual.

Macchi C.202 (Flight International)

Two pilots sat in tandem with a rotatable turret over the second pilot. Normal crew size was five, including two gunners and a bomb-aimer/ radio operator.

The Z.1007 was a ponderous aircraft in flight with heavy controls and rocklike stability. Performance was generally superior to that of the SM 79: a top speed of 280 mph and a service ceiling of 26,500 ft. Range was, however, less, at 800 statute miles.

Armament consisted of one 12.7-mm machine gun in a dorsal turret, one of similar caliber under the fuselage, and two 7.7-mm guns on lateral mountings. Two 1,000-lb torpedoes or 2,600 lbs of bombs could be carried.

Assessment: The Z.1007 was of the same class as the SM 79, with marginally better speed and defensive armament. Its size made it an easier target. It was as vulnerable to fighters as the SM 79.

Fulmar Versus Macchi C.202

The C.202, 75 mph faster than the Fulmar, was also very maneuverable. The British fighter's best hope was to lure the Italian into a dogfight and outturn him, jockeying into position to unleash its eight guns. The initiative, however, lay with the Italian.

Verdict: The Fulmar's chances against the nimble C.202 were much less than even.

Fulmar Versus Reggiane 2001

The Re 2001 had an even greater margin of performance superiority than the C.202, so the odds favored the Italian even more in this conflict.

Verdict: The Re 2001 should have no great problem outfighting the ponderous Fulmar.

Sea Hurricane Versus Macchi C.202

The Italian fighter possessed a speed advantage, but it was not critical, especially as the British fighter was more maneuverable and had the heavier firepower. A dogfight would slightly favor the Hurricane.

Verdict: This would be a finely balanced affair, the outcome depending primarily on pilot skill.

Sea Hurricane Versus Reggiane 2001

The Re 2001 resembled the Hurricane but had a significant speed advantage and was equally maneuverable. It lacked the firepower of the British fighter. Overall, the Italian aircraft was better endowed.

Verdict: With its performance superiority, the Re 2001 should be able to assert its will in this encounter.

Wildcat Versus Macchi C.202 or Reggiane 2001

In either combat situation the Wildcat would fare the way the Hurricane would against the same enemy, except that the Wildcat was capable of absorbing more punishment than the Hurricane.

Fulmar, Sea Hurricane, or Wildcat Versus Z.1007

Any of the British fighters should be able to deal with the Italian bomber almost as effectively as with the SM 79. The Z.1007 was big, wooden, relatively slow, not well defended, and quite vulnerable during a torpedo drop run-in.

The Battle of the Eastern Solomons

While the fight for Malta's survival was taking place in the Mediterranean, U.S. carriers in the Pacific were in action again. At Midway Japan and the United States had learned the value of fighter strength; by now both had increased fighter ratio to 41 percent of the carrier aircraft complement.

America, now buoyed by the victory of Midway, was ready to strike back and recover Allied territory lost to Japan. A decision was made to open the offensive in the southwest area of the Solomon-Bismarck Sea. The first targets were the islands of Tulagi, where the Japanese had established a seaplane base, and Guadalcanal, where they were constructing an airfield.

The U.S. assault, which began on 7 August, involved the carriers *Enterprise* (thirty-six Wildcats, thirty-six Dauntless, fifteen Avengers), *Saratoga* (thirty-four Wildcats, thirty-seven Dauntless, sixteen Avengers), and *Wasp* (twenty-nine Wildcats, thirty Dauntless, ten Avengers). The *Enterprise* and the *Saratoga* sent forty-four planes against Guadalcanal to soften it up for the impending marine assault. Meanwhile, the *Wasp*'s fifteen fighters and fifteen dive-bombers destroyed the seaplane base at Tulagi together with nineteen floatplanes and two four-engined flying boats.

In retaliation, twenty-seven Japanese Betty bombers escorted by eighteen Zekes launched an attack from Rabaul against the invasion force. This was followed by a second wave of sixteen Vals. In these strikes the Japanese lost fourteen bombers and two fighters, while American losses numbered eleven Wildcats, one Dauntless, and a damaged destroyer. On 8 August twenty-six Betty bombers made a torpedo attack, sinking a transport and severely damaging a destroyer at a cost of seventeen aircraft.

Both islands had fallen to the U.S. marines by the end of 8 August. Work was immediately begun to complete the airstrip on

The Japanese Light Aircraft Carrier Ryujo, *a Casualty of the Battle of the Solomons (U.S. Naval Institute)*

Guadalcanal. It was ready on the twelfth and had received its planes by the twentieth, ferried to the area by the escort carrier *Long Island.*

The Japanese made a determined effort to retake Guadalcanal, sending a large amphibious force supported by the two fleet carriers *Shokaku* and *Zuikaku* and the light carrier *Ryujo.* These ships brought with them a total of 168 combat aircraft, including sixty-nine Zekes, forty-one Vals, and fifty-seven Kates. The *Shokaku* carried one scout plane.

The Americans had kept their three carriers in the area with 256 aircraft. Once again a major carrier confrontation, featuring the former antagonists Vice Admirals Nagumo and Fletcher, was imminent.

The Japanese split their force, putting the *Ryujo* in the lead. On the morning of 24 August she launched fifteen fighters and six bombers to attack the airfield on Guadalcanal. They were joined by twenty Rabaul-based Betty bombers. Marine Wildcats met this strike and shot down about half the carrier force and five Bettys, losing ten of their own in the process.

In the afternoon thirty Dauntless and five Avengers from the *Saratoga* overwhelmed the *Ryujo,* scoring ten direct bomb hits and two torpedo hits. The Japanese carrier sank that night. While this attack was taking place, the *Shokaku* and the *Zuikaku* launched nineteen Zekes and fifty-four Vals. These flew against the *Enterprise* and *Saratoga,* which had put up a defending force of fifty-three Wildcats. The Japanese dive-bombers scored three direct hits on the *Enterprise,* inflicting severe damage.

American losses resulting from the eastern Solomons carrier battle amounted to seventeen planes and the badly damaged *Enterprise,* while the Japanese lost the *Ryujo,* fifty-six carrier-based aircraft, two

Sinking of the USS Wasp (U.S. Navy)

flying boats, three land-based bombers, a destroyer, and a transport. But the action was not quite over. On 31 August the *Saratoga* was torpedoed by a Japanese submarine and put out of action. On 15 September a fatal torpedo struck the *Wasp*, which was carrying forty-six planes. An American battleship and destroyer were badly damaged the same day.

The *Hornet*, now the only Allied aircraft carrier in the Pacific, continued to operate intermittently in support of Guadalcanal. On 16 October she mounted an air strike against a Japanese seaplane base on Santa Isabel Island, destroying twelve aircraft, and attacked Japanese troop positions on Guadalcanal. On the same day the hastily repaired *Enterprise* left Pearl Harbor for the southwest Pacific.

MITSUBISHI G4M1 BETTY 11

The Betty was a naval land-based, midwing, medium-attack torpedo bomber of aluminum alloy construction with fabric-covered control

A Japanese Dive-Bomber Scores a Direct Hit on the Flight Deck of the USS Enterprise (U.S. Navy)

surfaces. It normally carried a crew of seven, comprising two pilots, a navigator/bomb-aimer, and four gunners.

The aircraft was powered by two 1,440-hp, fourteen-cylinder, radial air-cooled Mitsubishi Kasei 15 engines with two-speed superchargers. They drove four-blade, constant-speed Mitsubishi-Hamilton airscrews.

This cigar-shaped airplane performed well with a top speed of 276 mph at 15,090 ft, a rate of climb of 1,000 ft/min, and a superb range of 2,200 miles.

Armament was one 7.7-mm machine gun in an electrically operated ball mount in the nose; one 20-mm cannon in the upper turret; two 7.7-mm guns in side ports, one on each side of the fuselage aft of the wings; and one 20-mm cannon in the tail. The open bomb bay beneath the wings' center section could accommodate one 1,760-lb torpedo or 4,840 lbs of bombs.

Assessment: The Betty 11 appeared to have the attributes neces-

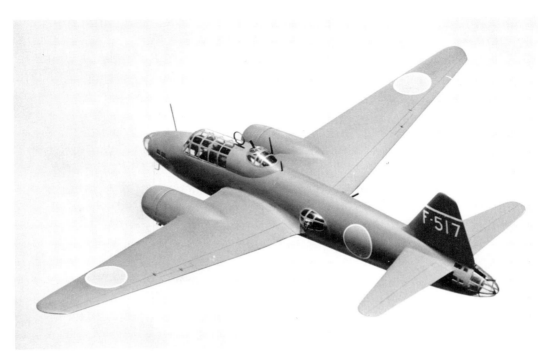

Mitsubishi G4M1 Betty (U.S. Navy)

sary for effective action, but it had the same Achilles heel as the Zeke, an inability to absorb punishment. It carried a lot of fuel and no self-sealing fuel tanks.

Wildcat Versus Betty 11

The rugged but sprightly little Wildcat had the speed and maneuverability to attack flat on the quarter, so that minimum defensive armament could be brought to bear against it. Its own target would be the five fuel tanks in each wing of the Betty, highly vulnerable to the Wildcat's lethal firepower.

   Verdict: If flown tactically to avoid the bomber's upper rear cone of fire, the Wildcat should find the Betty a fragile target.

Battle of the Santa Cruz Islands

The Japanese, incensed at the occupation of Guadalcanal, determined to make another major effort at recapturing it. They assembled a powerful task force that included the fleet carriers *Shokaku* and *Zuikaku*, the medium carrier *Junyo*, and the light carrier *Zuiho*. The carriers' complement was 212 aircraft—eighty-seven Zekes, sixty-eight Vals, and fifty-seven Kates.

The American opposition, revolving around the carriers *Enterprise* and *Hornet,* assembled off the unoccupied Santa Cruz islands to intercept any enemy forces approaching Guadalcanal. The carriers had on board seventy Wildcats, seventy-two Dauntless, and twenty-nine Avengers.

On 25 October a Catalina sighted two carriers, whereupon the *Enterprise* flew off a forty-one-plane search. The effort was fruitless, resulting in the loss of seven aircraft to ditching.

On 26 October the *Enterprise* mounted another attack/search with sixteen Dauntless. The *Zuiho,* hit by two 500-lb bombs, received flight-deck damage. The dive-bombers also accounted for five Zekes without loss to themselves, a significant episode indicating that the diminishing number of experienced fighter pilots was now beginning to take its toll on the Japanese.

Earlier, the *Zuiho, Shokaku,* and *Zuikaku* had flown off a sixty-two plane strike. Almost simultaneously the American carriers had launched a seventy-three-plane strike. When these two groups passed each other, nine Zekes broke away and shot down three Wildcats and three Avengers. Five of the nine Japanese planes emerged unscathed.

The Japanese strike force found the *Hornet* and hurled a mass of bombs and torpedoes at her, scoring many hits. A number of pilots flew their damaged planes into the carrier on suicide attacks. Japanese combat losses in this devastating assault totaled twenty-one planes. Thirteen were ditched on the return passage.

The American strike force achieved a similar success against the *Shokaku,* which was forced to withdraw from battle. Her departure was a particular loss, she being the first and only Japanese carrier fitted with radar. This attack cost the Americans fourteen planes.

Before being hit, the *Shokaku* had flown off her contribution to the second forty-four-plane strike against the *Enterprise,* which received two direct bomb hits and a near miss. Japanese aircraft losses were twenty in combat, four from ditching. A third strike by twenty-nine planes from the *Junyo* further damaged the *Enterprise* and some of her escorts. Nine of the Japanese planes were shot down, two ditched.

The fourth Japanese strike of the day came from a small group of fifteen planes launched from the *Junyo* against the crippled *Hornet,* which the heavy cruiser *Northampton* had taken under tow. She was a soft target for the bombs and torpedoes that pelted her, but the raid deprived the Japanese of six planes, two by ditching. The *Junyo* scraped together yet a fifth strike of ten planes to battle the ship, and this time another bomb hit. The *Hornet* was reluctant to die. Heavily torpedoed by her own destroyer escort and left to her

The USS Hornet *under Attack by Japanese Dive- and Torpedo-Bombers (U.S. Navy)*

fate, she then faced Japanese surface forces. Two enemy destroyers administered the death blow with torpedoes, and finally, in the early hours of 27 October, the *Hornet* slid under the waves.

Santa Cruz was the fourth major carrier battle of the war and a tactical victory for the Japanese, but like the Battle of the Coral Sea, it was a strategic victory for the United States. The Japanese emerged with two carriers heavily damaged and ninety aircraft gone, the United States with a carrier, a battleship, and two destroyers heavily damaged, and a carrier, a destroyer, and seventy-four aircraft gone. Japanese reinforcement of troops on Guadalcanal had been thwarted, and once more the ranks of experienced carrier pilots had been heavily depleted—two setbacks that would prove irreversible, despite continued Japanese efforts.

The Tide Turns in Europe

While the Battle of Midway was a turning point in the Pacific, the Battle of Alamein in the North African desert was a watershed event for Europe. The defeat of Field Marshal Rommel's Axis troops on 6 November was summed up by Prime Minister Winston Churchill in

The USS Hornet *Survives a Dive-Bombing Attack during the Battle of the Santa Cruz Islands (U.S. Navy)*

later years when he said, "Before Alamein we never had a victory. After Alamein we never had a defeat."*

Now the first steps could be taken toward total victory in Europe. Operation Torch, the Anglo-American occupation of French northwest Africa, had been agreed on in July 1942. The expeditionary force of 650 ships carrying 70,000 troops sailed from Britain and the United States in late October.

Three separate Allied task forces were involved in the operation. The Western Naval Task Force of 102 U.S. ships included the carrier *Ranger,* with fifty-four F4F Wildcats, eighteen Dauntless, and one Avenger, as well as the three escort carriers *Sangamon, Santee,* and *Suwannee,* with fifty-seven Wildcats, eighteen Dauntless, and twenty-

*The Second World War, vol. 4 (London: Cassell), p. 541.

six Avengers. A fourth escort carrier, the USS *Chenango*, ferried seventy-eight P-40F Warhawk fighters for army use after the local airfield was captured. The Western Naval Task Force was to land troops in the Casablanca area.

The Center Naval Task Force, which was to attack Oran, had three aircraft carriers in support. Veteran carrier HMS *Furious* brought twenty-seven Seafire IIC fighters, eight Albacores, and one Fulmar for reconnaissance duty, while two escort carriers, HMS *Biter* and *Dasher*, had a combined complement of thirty Sea Hurricanes and three Swordfish.

The Eastern Naval Task Force was to seize Algiers. It included an old carrier, HMS *Argus*, with twelve Seafire IICs, and escort carrier HMS *Avenger*, with twelve Sea Hurricanes and three Swordfish.

In addition, Force H (fleet carriers HMS *Formidable*, carrying twenty-four Wildcats, six Seafire IICs, and six Albacores, and HMS *Victorious*, eleven Wildcats, six Fulmars, twenty-one Albacores, and nine Swordfish) was to take up position in the Mediterranean and protect the invasion against interference from French or Italian warships.

A critical unknown in Operation Torch was whether Vichy French forces would oppose the landings. They possessed about 170 aircraft in the Casablanca area, 213 in Algeria, and 105 in Tunisia, and they might well call in German and Italian air support.

For this operation all British Fleet Air Arm aircraft carried U.S. star markings, the French being less likely to resist an American than a British invasion.

Early on 8 November the landings began on all three fronts. Up to that point the expeditionary force had been undetected, although a Wildcat from the *Formidable* had shot down a French Potez at 10,000 ft over Force H on 7 November.

The heaviest air resistance was met around Oran, when Albacores bombing the La Senia airfield, escorted by Seafires and Sea Hurricanes, were intercepted by French D 520s. Two of the French planes were shot down by Seafires, five by Sea Hurricanes, without loss to the British fighters. Four Albacores were shot down, but not before destroying forty-seven aircraft on the airfield and shooting down a D 520. French authorities at Oran capitulated on 10 November.

Albacores made a number of bombing sorties against hard targets around the port of Algiers, but otherwise a solitary raid by Ju 88s against Force H was the only activity. In the next three days the *Formidable*'s Wildcats shot down an He 111, a Ju 88 in Italian markings, and an SM 84. Algiers itself ceased opposition on the afternoon of 8 November.

The *Ranger*'s Wildcats strafed French airfields in the Casablanca area, destroying twenty-one aircraft. There was also an aerial skirmish between a squadron of Wildcats and sixteen French fighters. Half the French force was shot down in exchange for four Wildcats.

On 9 November Dauntless dive-bombers from the *Ranger* hit targets in Casablanca's port, and on 10 November nine of them sank the battleship *Jean Bart* in the harbor's shallow water, having hit her with two 1,000-lb bombs. On the same day aircraft from the *Suwannee* sank a French submarine. All French resistance ceased at Casablanca on 11 November.

U.S. carriers in the Western Task Force lost forty-four planes in the four-day assault, most for operational reasons. A large number of inexperienced pilots had embarked for Operation Torch.

The British carriers also suffered their share of operational losses. The new Seafires had trouble deck-landing, among other deficiencies. Lack of wing folding meant they could only be hangared in the two old carriers fitted with T-shaped elevators. Those embarked in the large fleet carriers were permanently parked on the flight deck, exposed to the elements and the enemy. Moreover, their initial rate of climb and low-altitude speed left something to be desired, and of course it was at low altitude that most carrier combats took place.

As French resistance collapsed, fighters were flown to the captured airfields from Gibraltar. The escort carrier *Archer* arrived off Casablanca with thirty-five Warhawk fighters, which were flown off to Port Lyautey airfield by the U.S. Army Air Force.

As a postscript to Operation Torch, the *Avenger* was torpedoed by a German U-boat on 15 November and blew up with the loss of virtually her entire crew. The Axis reacted to the North African landings by occupying Vichy France on 14 November and scuttling its fleet in Toulon.

SUPERMARINE SEAFIRE IIC

The Seafire was born of desperation. The Royal Navy found its Sea Hurricane and Wildcat fighters beginning to succumb to the high-performance fighters appearing on the European scene. The best Allied fighter in late 1941 was the Spitfire V, to which the Admiralty turned its attention. Performance the Spitfire certainly had, but its robustness for shipboard operations was very much in question.

Carrier trials with a hooked Spitfire in late 1941 were so encouraging that the Admiralty decided to convert 250 such planes for naval use—48 Spitfire VBs, the rest being new-production VCs. After navalization these would become Seafire IBs and IICs, respectively. The former were used for training only, while the latter entered operational units in mid-1942. Wings on these early models were nonfolding.

The Seafire, aesthetically the most elegant fighter ever to grace a carrier deck, was a low-wing, single-seat monoplane of all-metal construction with fabric-covered control surfaces. It was powered by a 1,470-hp Rolls-Royce Merlin 45, a twelve-cylinder, liquid-cooled V engine driving a three-bladed, constant-speed Rotol airscrew. The engine was started by internal or external electrical battery. Two fuel tanks in the fuselage had a total capacity of 85 imperial gals (102 U.S.).

The Seafire's cockpit was a fairly tight fit for anyone of above-average size, but not claustrophobic like the Me 109's. The view on the ground was poor because of the long nose ahead, but in the air the vision for fighting was only impaired to the rear; by way of compensation, a rear-view mirror was positioned on top of the windscreen frame.

Takeoff was reasonably short, but there was a powerful swing to port that required a lot of counteracting rudder. One had to be careful not to raise the tail too much to improve view ahead, as clearance from the ground to the airscrew tip was limited when the aircraft was horizontal. Once the Seafire was airborne, its landing gear retracted smartly and the initial rate of climb was 2,950 ft/min.

The stability of the Seafire was marginal, the mark of a good day fighter, and harmony of control was excellent. All the controls were light and effective, although the ailerons tended to grow heavy above 400 mph. Rate of roll was good, not outstanding. The aircraft had a superb turning circle, and since its stall was docile this maneuverability could be exploited to the full without fear of drastic consequences from a high "g" stall.

The Seafire had a top speed of 315 knots (365 mph) at 21,500 ft, a service ceiling of 32,000 ft, and a range of 427 nm (493 statute miles).

Armament was eight 0.303 machine guns in the wings. A bomb rack capable of carrying a 250-lb bomb could be fitted between the legs of the landing gear.

It was in the critical area of deck landing that the Seafire had significant shortcomings. The view on the approach was poor. Speed control was difficult because the airplane was underflapped and too clean aerodynamically. Furthermore, landing gear had too high a rebound ratio and was not robust enough to withstand the high vertical velocities of deck landing.

In September 1942, as a young test pilot, I was given a "pierhead jump" to the escort carrier *Biter* to assess the suitability of the Seafire for operation from small ships. The British navy wanted to blood the

Seafire in the forthcoming Operation Torch and operate it from two old carriers, as the elevators in British fleet carriers could not accommodate the nonfolding fighter. Trials were successful, and the Seafire went off to war.

Assessment: The Seafire's performance fell below that of the land-based Spitfire because navalization incurred the penalties of increased weight and drag. Never designed for shipboard use, the Seafire was difficult to deck-land, and it acted like a submarine when ditched. In spite of this, it was the fastest shipboard fighter in the world at the time of Operation Torch. A great airplane to fly and fight, it boosted the morale of the Royal Navy's Fleet Air Arm pilots.

DEWOITINE 520

A new opponent appeared in the North African operation in the form of the Vichy French D 520, a fighter similar to the British Spitfire in appearance but very inferior in performance. This low-wing, single-seat fighter had the pilot seated aft of the trailing edge of the wings and the cockpit almost faired into the fin. It was powered by a 910-hp, 12 Y liquid-cooled Hispano-Suiza engine driving a three-bladed Ratier propeller.

The D 520, marginally stable, was sensitive directionally to changes of power and snaked badly in turbulent air, thus making it difficult to aim accurately. Though maneuverable, it had an abrupt stall that came without warning, and this inhibited pilots, who were afraid to push it to its maneuver margins; a high-speed stall could occur without warning and rapidly develop into a spin from which recovery could be difficult. Deliberate spinning of the D 520 was forbidden. Acceleration in the dive was very good with a limiting speed of 360 mph.

The landing characteristics of the D 520 presented considerable difficulty after touchdown, for the aircraft's ground attitude tended to blank rudder effectiveness; any attempt at directional control by use of the slow-acting pneumatic brakes could set up an uncontrollable swing and collapse the wide-track-landing gear or tip the aircraft on its nose.

Maximum speed was only 288 mph, but initial rate of climb was high at almost 4,000 ft/min. Armament consisted of four 7.5-mm machine guns in the wings with 675 rounds per gun, and one 20-mm Hispano-Suiza cannon with 60 rounds, firing through the airscrew spinner.

Assessment: The D 520 was a good-looking airplane with several bad handling characteristics. It was underpowered, as its lowspeed clearly indicated, but had a surprisingly good initial rate of climb.The plane was also underarmed by contemporary fighter

Dewoitine 520 (Pilot Press)

standards: its single cannon was provided with a small ammunition load.

Sea Hurricane Versus Dewoitine 520

The British fighter, superior in every department of combat effectiveness except rate of climb, was also stronger in firepower.

Verdict: The Hurricane should have a clear enough margin of all-round superiority to ensure victory over the French fighter.

Seafire IIC Versus Dewoitine 520

The Seafire was markedly superior to the D 520 in every aspect except rate of climb, and in a dogfight there was little the French fighter could do except try and climb out of trouble.

Verdict: The Seafire could run rings round the D 520, which should be a sure kill.

Wildcat Versus Dewoitine 520

The D 520 had the ability to outdive and outclimb the Wildcat but not to outmaneuver or outgun it. The odds therefore favored the American fighter, although it lacked the initiative to open or close combat. Provided the Wildcat could get into a dogfight with the D 520, it would have the upper hand.

Verdict: This would be a combat situation largely dictated by tactics, but whatever the methods used, the outcome should be 10 to 30 percent on the side of the Wildcat.

Albacore Versus Dewoitine 520

This would seem to be a no-hope situation for the biplane. It would, however, have a slim chance hugging the surface and using its good turning circle to try and lure the 520 pilot into following. In the heat of battle, this tactic could prove fatal to the French fighter because of its lethal high "g" stalling characteristics.

Verdict: The Albacore would have little or no chance against the D 520 if caught in transit to a target. A slim chance of survival would be had against a D 520 pilot who was not willing to play the cat and mouse game at very low level.

The Continuing Struggle for Guadalcanal

The Japanese, still grimly determined to retake Guadalcanal, mounted a major operation starting on 12 November. It was supported by the aircraft carriers *Hiyo* and *Junyo,* providing distant cover 150 miles north of Guadalcanal. Meanwhile, the U.S. garrison was being continuously reinforced by the carrier *Enterprise* well to the south of the island. She staged her attack aircraft through the island airstrip. The combined strength of carrier and land-based marine aircraft succeeded in finishing off the Japanese battleship *Hiei,* sinking a heavy cruiser and several transports as well as damaging two light cruisers and other transports. The *Enterprise* withdrew from the area on 14 November, having smashed the twelve-ship Japanese troop convoy.

During the aerial battles of this operation, each side lost about twenty-five aircraft. A significant statistic was the high proportion of Zekes the Japanese lost, at least three falling to Dauntless rear gunners. Once again, the outcome pointed to the heavy dent that had been put in the ranks of Japanese fighter pilots.

The Arctic Convoys

Convoys carrying equipment from Britain to the Russian ports of Archangel and Murmansk starting in the winter of 1941 were not seriously molested for the first four or five months. Then, in March 1942, U-boats and German aircraft operating from northern Norway began to concentrate their efforts against this maritime supply line.

The enemy buildup culminated in the disastrous P.Q. 17 convoy attack on 4 July when twenty-three out of thirty-four merchantmen were sunk. The Russian convoys were suspended till September, and a revised scheme of defense involving the use of escort carriers was brought into play. The first such convoy with air cover was P.Q. 18, supported by HMS *Avenger* carrying twelve Sea Hurricanes for fighter protection. The enemy attack began on 12 September, with He 111Hs and Ju 88s dropping torpedoes and bombs all day and restricting themselves to high- and low-level bombing the next day. Thirty-five out of an attacking force of one hundred fell to antiaircraft and fighter defenses. The Sea Hurricanes claimed eight aircraft for the loss of four of their own, three of whose pilots were saved. Twelve out of thirty-nine merchantmen were sunk.

Because of commitments to Operation Torch the Russian convoys were again suspended until December 1942. Late in that month P.Q. 19 sailed in two parts, each with an escort of destroyers. Since air support was not available, the Home Fleet gave cover. The Germans had taken such an aerial beating from P.Q. 18 that they decided to use surface warships to attack the convoy. On 31 December a surface action took place in the Barents Sea involving the German heavy cruiser *Hipper*. This resulted in the loss of one British destroyer and one merchant ship slightly damaged.

Role of the Fighter

By the end of 1942, the halfway point in the war, it was clear that future conflicts would be dominated by aerial strengths. The combatant who enjoyed air superiority over the battle area had a huge advantage, even if his ground strength was inferior. Air superiority depended on the right balance of numbers and quality. The enemy could be allowed a certain numerical advantage if this was countered by superior quality. The key, of course, was the fighter airplane, without which the enemy air force could not be challenged and one's own attack force could not be protected. Possession of fighter strength could also wear down the enemy's morale and deplete his pilot replacement program.

German victories on the European mainland, British success in the Battle of Britain, Japanese achievements in the Indian Ocean, and the Anglo-American invasion of North Africa were all decided by the performance of outstanding fighter aircraft. And the determined aggression of American carrier planes at Coral Sea, Midway, and Santa Cruz resulted in the critical attrition of experienced Japanese pilots.

5
1943

The Corner Turned

By the end of 1942 the Allies had got their first foothold in enemy-occupied territory in the Far East and North Africa, while the Russians were stemming the tide of invasion at Stalingrad. On 31 January 1943 German forces in that city capitulated, and the enemy onslaught would soon be halted.

The year 1942 had been one of sustained combat activity for aircraft carriers. The first half of 1943 saw a relative lull in carrier battle if not in operations.

The Atlantic

Everything happening in the various World War II theaters depended on the outcome of the ongoing Battle of the Atlantic. Until the end of 1942 German U-boats sank ships faster than the Allies could build them, and the lifeline from the United States to Europe was in continuous danger of being severed. In March 1943 escort carriers released from combat operations were made available for work in the mid-Atlantic. They carried a few fighters for protection and a preponderance of antisubmarine attack bombers such as the Avenger and Swordfish, the latter armed with rocket projectiles. These "Woolworth" carriers were so successful in killing U-boats that the balance of the battle began to turn in April 1943.

The 60-lb rocket projectile, of which the Swordfish II carried eight under the wings, proved a particularly potent weapon. This armament combined with ASV radar was extremely effective in antisubmarine warfare. The Swordfish II had the improved Pegasus 30 engine, no more powerful than its predecessor but easier to maintain in the rugged environment of the mid-Atlantic.

MAC with Two Swordfish on the Flight Deck (Imperial War Museum)

But a few escort carriers were not enough to keep the Atlantic situation under control. They had to be reinforced, and at this timely juncture the MAC (merchant aircraft carrier), a British innovation, appeared. The MAC replaced the CAM ship. It was a converted bulk carrier with a flight deck, and its mercantile status as a cargo ship or tanker had been preserved. Six grain carriers with an elevator and small hangar and thirteen tankers with a deck park were converted.

Each MAC carried four Swordfish, and the possibility of operating Wildcats from its deck was considered. I had flown Wildcats from the even smaller flight deck of HMS *Audacity* and was serving as a pilot in the Royal Navy's service trials unit, so I was given the job of carrying out landing trials on the *Amastra*, a MAC tanker. There were no problems, but in fact Wildcats were not embarked on MACs because the Kuriers had largely vanished from the Atlantic scene.

The Pacific

After the Battle of Santa Cruz American progress up the Solomon archipelago toward Rabaul could be supported by land-based aircraft from Guadalcanal. Thus U.S. carriers withdrew from the area.

On 12 February twelve marine F4U-1 Corsairs arrived at Guadalcanal. These single-engine fighters and the twin-engine Lockheed P-38 Lightnings, which had entered service in the Far East in the fall of 1942, represented a significant advance in performance over their predecessors. They would be better equipped to combat the ubiquitous Zeke.

The Chance-Vought F4U-1 Corsair

In essence, the Corsair was built to meet the need for the smallest airframe that could be coupled with the largest and most powerful radial engine under development. The huge propeller that was to absorb this power needed an excessively acute fuselage ground angle to provide proper ground clearance for the propeller tips. The solution was an inverted gull wing, which not only gave the required clearance but also kept the landing gear to a manageable length. As a bonus, the wing minimized drag by offering a right-angle junction between wing and fuselage, eliminating the wetted area of the large fairing that would otherwise have been needed. The outer wings folded up for carrier stowage. All control surfaces were fabric covered.

The Corsair's first flight on 29 May 1940 revealed handling problems. Among many modifications introduced was the relocation of the cockpit 3 ft farther aft, to make room for a large fuel tank in the center fuselage, as near the center of gravity as possible to obviate excessive trim changes as fuel was consumed. This change made the already poor view ahead worse.

My first sight of the Corsair gave me an impression of rugged strength rather than aerodynamic refinement. On entering the cockpit I found it inordinately spacious, tailor made for a tall pilot. Indeed, the principal Corsair project pilot was 6 ft 4 in tall. The view on the ground was only reasonable in an upward direction.

The power plant was the mighty Pratt and Whitney R-2800-8 Double Wasp. It was an eighteen-cylinder, two-stage, two-speed, supercharged air-cooled radial engine of 2,000 hp, and it drove a 13-ft 4-in constant-speed, three-bladed Hamilton Standard propeller. Fuel capacity was 300 imperial gals (361 U.S.), and the maximum loaded weight was 13,846 lbs. The engine was started by the percussion cartridge method.

The lack of forward view meant taxiing with the tailwheel un-

Chance-Vought F4U-1 Corsair (U.S. Navy)

locked, a condition in which the airplane was directionally unstable
so that a lot of braking action was required. Takeoff acceleration was
good, with the airplane exhibiting no tendency to swing if the tailwheel was locked and the rudder correctly trimmed. Unstick was
rapid.

The climb at 125 knots was made at an initial rate of 2,400 ft/
min with the intercooler shutters fully open. The cowl gills were only
half open, otherwise there was some buffet. The climb was disappointing in light of the power available, but this was a heavy aircraft
for a single-seat fighter.

Cruising speed was 218 knots (251 mph) and stability was positive—too much so for fighter agility. Harmony of control was poor,
the elevators being heavy and the ailerons moderately light, enabling
the airplane to be rolled to its maximum rate even at fairly high
diving speeds. Acceleration was quite dramatic; a clean Corsair could
reach a maximum of 342 knots (394 mph) at its critical altitude of
24,000 ft. This owed much to the technical innovation of spot weld-
ing in the skin covering, reducing surface friction to a minimum. The
flaps could be lowered 20 degrees to assist maneuvering at speeds up
to 200 knots. It was recommended that the airplane not be held
inverted for more than three seconds.

Stalling characteristics were very poor. The pilot received little warning other than that afforded by a light on the instrument panel that was operated by the breakdown of airflow over the center section. At the stall, the right wing dropped sharply and an incipient spin developed if the control column was not moved smartly forward. At about 11,500 lbs, all-up stall occurred at 90 knots (103.5 mph), all-down at 76 knots (87.5 mph) with the warning light coming on at 80 knots (92 mph).

Acceleration while diving was excellent up to the limiting speed of 400 knots (460 mph) below 10,000 ft. The landing gear could be extended to serve as a dive brake by using the dive-brake control so that the tailwheel remained retracted. The limiting speed in this condition was 350 knots (403 mph). Any attempt to exceed these speeds produced pronounced elevator buffeting.

As a deck-landing aircraft the Corsair left so much to be desired that the U.S. Navy handed it over to the marines for shore duty. The problems it presented for shipboard use were the terrible view, sluggish aileron and elevator control on the approach, a propensity to torque stalling, and bouncy landing gear that reacted to the heavy dropping of the aircraft's nose as the throttle was cut. Even when landing ashore the Corsair, despite its tailwheel lock, was plagued by directional instability.

Armament consisted of six wing-mounted 0.5-in machine guns, some early-production models having only four such guns fitted. The four inboard guns were supplied with 400 rounds apiece, the two outboard guns 375 rounds each. No other weapons were carried in the first models.

With a service ceiling of 37,100 ft and a range of 1,070 miles (930 nm), the Corsair was well suited to Pacific operations. With a drop tank holding 145 imperial gals (175 U.S.), range increased to 1,735 miles (1,506 nm).

Assessment: The Corsair was a mixture of the good, the mediocre, and the bad. It had excellent acceleration, speed, and firepower, and was rugged in construction, but its slow-speed characteristics left much to be desired. Maneuverability was mediocre from the point of view of dogfighting, but it had a good rate of roll that could be used to advantage defensively. In summary, as a fighter the Corsair was a formidable aircraft to introduce into the Pacific theater, but as a shipboard aircraft it had serious shortcomings.

F4U-1 Corsair Versus Zeke 32

As Corsairs were arriving in the Pacific, the Japanese were bringing the Zeke 32 into operation. This was similar to the Zeke 22 but had the folding wingtips removed, leaving clipped ends for improved lateral control. Speed had increased to 348 mph, but it carried less fuel, which reduced range to 1,100 miles (955 nm).

The Corsair would be ill advised to mix with the Zeke in a dogfight, for if the U.S. plane attempted to outturn the Japanese fighter, it would almost certainly flick out of the turn and find itself momentarily defenseless or in a spin. Hit-and-run tactics by the American fighter should pay handsome dividends because of its superior acceleration and its heavy firepower. If caught unawares by the Zeke, the Corsair could accelerate in a dive and then use its higher rate of roll to evade any attempt to follow it.

Verdict: The Corsair's superior speed, acceleration, and rate of roll as well as its powerful firepower should ensure its victory over the Zeke as long as it did not engage in a dogfight and retained the initiative to determine the course of action. The American fighter's robust construction was another point in its favor.

The Corsair first encountered the Zeke on 14 February 1943. Marine Corps F4U-1s were escorting a force of PB4Y Privateers on a strike against enemy shipping in the Kahili area of Bougainville when they were intercepted by a large formation of Zekes. The Japanese lost four fighters while shooting down a top cover of four Lightnings, two Warhawks, two Privateers, and two Corsairs. The F4U's inauspicious debut taught the marine pilots a severe lesson in tactics that was not wasted on them. In fact, the aircraft would go on to establish an enviable 11.3:1 kill-to-loss ratio and be flown by the Marine Corps' two top aces, Gregory Boyington and Joseph Foss.

Operation Avalanche

The victory in Tunis on 13 May effectively ended the war in North Africa and allowed the Allies to turn their attention toward their main objective—the European mainland. Operation Husky was launched to conquer Sicily. The first steps were taken in mid-June with the bombardment and subsequent capture of the islands south of Sicily. The invasion of Sicily itself started on 10 July and was completed by 17 August. The British fleet aircraft carriers *Formidable* and *Indomitable* operated with Force H to the east of Sicily to prevent the still powerful Italian surface fleet from interfering with the landings.

The ninety-seven aircraft aboard the carriers did not see much action during this attack, nor did their presence stop a lone Italian torpedo plane from scoring a hit on the *Indomitable* in the early-morning darkness of 16 July. The damage was not critical, but the eventual departure of that carrier for repairs just before Operation Avalanche was of considerable significance; it had just been completed with an enlarged forward lift and was carrying forty Seafires, the largest fighter complement embarked by a British carrier up to that time.

In the interim Mussolini fell from power, being arrested on 25 July by order of the king of Italy. This political event firmed Allied resolve to invade the Italian mainland in a two-pronged attack, through the Strait of Messina into the toe of Italy and through the Bay of Naples at Salerno. Since the latter was too far from Sicily for effective fighter cover, aircraft carriers were to provide air support.

The Royal Navy replaced the damaged *Indomitable* with the *Illustrious* for the Salerno assault. In addition, it provided the Support Carrier Force, four escort carriers—the *Attacker, Battler, Hunter, Stalker*—and the small fleet carrier *Unicorn.* Force H was to provide air cover for the support force, which was to keep thirty-five fighters continuously over the assault area during daylight.

On 3 September the British army crossed the Strait of Messina and Italy surrendered unconditionally, but this only stiffened German resistance in the country. The Salerno assault started on 9 September. German opposition set the schedule back two days, and the Support Carrier Force could not withdraw until 12 September. When the local airfield at Montecorvino was taken it was inoperable, so a temporary landing ground was flattened in the dust of a tomato plantation at Paestum. Twenty-six Seafires were flown there before the carriers departed.

The aircraft carried by the Support Carrier Force were mainly Seafire LIICs and Wildcat IVs and Vs, augmented over the battlefield by Lightnings, Mustangs, and Spitfires flown from airfields in Sicily. The Spitfires could only remain for twenty minutes at most.

The Seafire LIIC had been developed because Seafire IBs flying from the old carrier *Furious* in Operation Train had failed to overhaul Ju 88s shadowing the force in which the carrier was included. The German bomber, moreover, had proved capable of outdistancing the Spitfire IICs with some ease. As a result of these frustrating encounters, the Merlin 32 engine was installed in the Seafire. This aircraft differed from the Merlin 45 or 46 in having a cropped supercharger impeller and a maximum output of 1,640 hp at 3,000 ft, an increase of 430 hp. Full advantage of the increase was taken by means of a four-bladed propeller, which replaced the standard three-blader. A percussion-cartridge starting system was also introduced.

The result was electrifying—a dramatic reduction in takeoff distance, an initial climb up to 6,000 ft at 4,600 ft/min, and superb acceleration. Maximum speeds at low altitude were now 291 knots (335 mph) at 6,000 ft and 274 knots (316 mph) at sea level. To improve lateral control a few Seafire LIICs had their span reduced, which increased the rate of roll and brought maximum speed up by 4.5 knots (5 mph). This, however, lengthened the takeoff run and reduced service ceiling, so the clipped version was normally only used on fleet carriers.

I was indirectly involved in the preparations for Operation Avalanche when I carried out a series of trials to ascertain the minimum acceptable wind speed at which a Seafire could be operated from an escort carrier. Thus, on 3 August I completed ten low-wind-speed landings aboard HMS *Fencer,* and on 11 August twenty similar landings aboard HMS *Tracker,* rounding these off on 14 August with another five landings, all without any problems other than a burst tire.

For Avalanche, nine squadrons and two flights of Seafire LIICs totaling 106 aircraft were carried in the four escort carriers and the *Unicorn.* The weather was calm, and the carriers were operating at wind speeds hardly exceeding their own speed of about 18 knots. This, coupled with lack of experience on the part of many pilots, yielded an unexpectedly high incidence of deck-landing accidents. Forty-two Seafires were either damaged beyond repair or destroyed, and Seafire availability had dropped by 38 percent on the second day. On D-day plus 2 the small carriers had only thirty-nine serviceable Seafires.

During the three and a half days of carrier-based flying by the Support Carrier Force, two enemy aircraft were shot down and four damaged, but no Seafire was lost through enemy action. The opposition consisted mainly of Fw 190A-4 fighter-bombers, because the other fighter types had been pulled back to Germany for defense against Allied bombers. One Wildcat from Force H shot down a Cant Z.506B snooper.

On the day the Salerno assault began the Italian Fleet surrendered to the Allies, and control of the Mediterranean, except for the Aegean Sea where German aircraft still held their grip, was now secure.

The deck-landing fiasco at Salerno resulted in my involvement in another set of trials to alleviate the problem with the Seafire. These started on 30 September with a series of fifteen landings using arrester wires on a dummy deck ashore. Photographs were taken of each stage of each landing. Analysis of the photos led to some hook-strengthening modifications.

THE WILDCAT IV

The Wildcat IV, which the Royal Navy had received under lend-lease, was the Fleet Air Arm equivalent of the U.S. Navy's F4F-4 and differed from the earlier models in having six 0.5-in machine guns in the wings. It had a 1,200-hp Twin Wasp R-1830-86, which gave it a maximum speed of 286.5 knots (330 mph) at 19,500 ft and 252 knots (290 mph) at sea level. The Wildcat V, the model built by the Eastern Aircraft division of General Motors, was the British equivalent of the American FM-1. These Wildcats were embarked in fleet carriers for Avalanche.

FOCKE-WULF 190A-4

Germany's famed Fw 190 fighter was first deployed to Italy on 18 June 1943 and fought in the invasion of Sicily in the fighter-bomber role. It was equally active in the defense against the Salerno assault.

This superb creation of the great German aircraft designer Kurt Tank was a departure from the Luftwaffe staff's preference for in-line-engine fighters. It looked as if the Daimler-Benz series of liquid-cooled engines would be in short supply, and so Tank's proposal to use the new radial air-cooled BMW engine was accepted. The bulky radial engine blended beautifully into the contours of the new fighter, and as an exercise in the mating of compactness with functional elegance the single-seat, low-wing design was a masterpiece.

The Fw 190 sat high on the ground, but in the somewhat narrow cockpit the forward view was reasonably good in spite of a semireclining armored seat and obtrusive nose. The cockpit layout was decent, and the ingenious *Kommandogerät*, a sort of "brain box," relieved the pilot of the job of controlling airscrew pitch, mixture, boost, and rpm. The fuselage was an all-metal monocoque structure, and all control surfaces were fabric covered. The split trailing-edge flaps were electrically operated, as was the landing gear. The tailwheel could be retracted partway by a cable connected to the starboard oleo leg.

The aircraft was powered by a 1,600-hp, fourteen-cylinder, super-charged BMW 801D with induced fan cooling and fuel injection. The engine drove a three-blade VDM airscrew and was activated by an electrically energized inertia starter. Fuel capacity was 115.5 imperial gals (138.5 U.S.) in two self-sealing fuselage tanks, plus 25.3 imperial gals (30.5 U.S.) in an optional rear fuselage tank.

Taxiing was easy; the plane had good wheelbrakes and a self-centering tailwheel, which was locked for takeoff by moving the control column to an aft position. Using 10 degrees of flap, and showing a tendency to swing to port that was easily corrected by rudder, the Fw 190 had an unstick speed of 112 mph.

At 160 mph climb rate was 3,150 ft/min, and like all good fighters the aircraft had only marginal stability. A remarkable aspect was the lack of retrimming required for various stages of flight.

Decidedly, the most impressive feature of the German fighter was its beautifully light ailerons and its extremely high rate of roll.

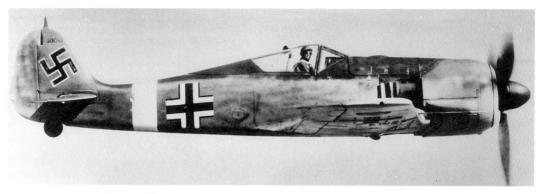

Focke-Wulf 190A-4

The ailerons maintained their lightness from the stall up to 400 mph, although they grew heavy above that speed. The elevators proved to be heavy at all speeds, particularly above 350 mph, when they became heavy enough to impose a tactical restriction on the fighter during pullout from low-level dives. Heaviness was accentuated because of the nose-down pitch when the aircraft was at high speed trimmed for low speed. The critical point at which the change in trim occurred was around 220 mph, and it could be easily gauged in turns. At lower speeds the Fw 190 had a tendency to tighten up the turn, but backward pressure on the stick was necessary above 220 mph.

At low speeds rudder control proved positive and effective, and I found it satisfactory at high speeds as well; the rudder was seldom needed for any normal maneuver. It was when the three controls were taken together rather than in isolation that the Fw 190 performed its magic as a fighter: it had superb control harmony. At a normal cruise of 330 mph at 8,000 ft, stability was excellent directionally, bad laterally, and neutral longitudinally. It was not at all easy to fly on instruments, but of course the airplane had been conceived solely as a clear-weather day fighter.

Stalling speed in clean configuration was 127 mph. The stall came suddenly and virtually without warning, the port wing dropping so violently that the aircraft almost inverted itself. This proved to be the fighter's Achilles heel, for if it was pulled into a "g" stall in a tight turn, it would flick into the opposite bank and, unless the pilot had his wits about him, into an incipient spin. The stall in landing configuration was quite different, there being intense prestall buffeting before the starboard wing dropped comparatively gently at 120 mph.

Approach speed for the terminal phase of landing was 125 mph. View on the approach was decidedly poor, because the attitude with power on was rather flat and, to avoid the risk of exhaust fumes entering the cockpit, the canopy had to remain closed. Anything less than a perfect three-pointer produced a reaction from the nonresilient landing gear. The landing run was short and the brakes could be applied harshly without fear of nosing over.

The maximum speed of the A-4 model was 394 mph, with a service ceiling of 37,403 ft and a range of 500 miles. Armament was two 13-mm or 7.9-mm engine-mounted machine guns synchronized to fire through the airscrew, and four 20-mm wing cannon.

A specialized version designated the Fw 190A-4/U8 was developed as a fighter-bomber and used at Salerno. It could carry tanks with a capacity of 66 imperial gals (80 U.S.) or 550-lb bombs under the wings, as well as one 1,100-lb bomb under the fuselage. The outer-wing cannon and engine-mounted machine guns were removed, as were the inner doors on the landing gear. The inner-wing cannon were harmonized at 220 yards instead of the usual 490. The pilot was well protected from frontal attack by the engine and the sharply sloping 50-mm armor-glass windscreen, and from the rear by his shaped, 8-mm, armored seat back, 13-mm head and shoulder armor, plus small 8-mm plates disposed above and below the seat back and on each side. Speed at sea level was 310 mph.

Assessment: When the Fw 190A-1 entered service in July 1941, it was the most advanced fighter in the world. The A-4 model appearing a year later maintained that status for a while. It was a technically superb airplane, a good dogfighter, and a good gun platform with magnificent performance—in short, an outstanding combat aircraft.

Wildcat IV Versus Focke-Wulf 190A-4 and A-4/U8

The only superiority that could be claimed by the Wildcat was its ability to outturn the German fighter, but turning doesn't win battles. In every other department the Fw 190 was in command. Even in the fighter-bomber role the German faced minimal danger, and he could always jettison his bombs in an emergency to defend himself.

Verdict: The superiority of the Fw 190A-4 and A-4/U8 was so comprehensive that the Wildcat had little or no chance to do anything more than perhaps harry the German enough to make him jettison his bombs prematurely.

Seafire LIIC Versus Focke-Wulf 190A-4 and A-4/U8

The Seafire was no real match for the Fw 190A-4, because like the Wildcat its only trump card was its better turning circle. (It did perform well enough to make a fight of it in a low-altitude encounter.) The British fighter was a threat, however, to the loaded fighter-bomber version, the Fw 190A-4/U8, because the latter had to operate at low level, where the Seafire was marginally faster, exhibited better zoom climb and acceleration in the dive, and had greater firepower.

Even after dropping its bombs the Fw 190A-4/U8 had a fight on its hands, because it would find it difficult at low level to exploit its usual tactic against Spitfires of maneuvering in the vertical plane (the Spitfire preferred the horizontal).

Verdict: In the type of scenario at Salerno the Seafire had a fair chance of success against the Fw 190A-4/U8, which would find the British fighter's low-altitude performance a distinct threat.

The Pacific Initiative Passes to America

By mid-June 1943 nine fast carriers were commissioned into the U.S. Fleet—the fleet carriers *Essex, Yorktown,* and *Lexington,* and the light fleet carriers *Bunker Hill, Independence, Princeton, Belleau Wood, Cowpens,* and *Monterey.* At the same time a significant new shipboard fighter, the Grumman F6F Hellcat, became available to join the Avengers and Dauntlesses aboard the new carriers.

With the renewed strength of new carriers and fighters, the Americans started systematically to gnaw away at the outer ring of Japan's island defenses. Marcus Island was attacked on 1 September by six strikes flown from the carriers *Essex, Yorktown,* and *Independence.* These caused heavy damage to ground installations at a cost of three Hellcats and one Avenger.

On 18 and 19 September the *Lexington, Princeton,* and *Belleau Wood* launched seven attacks against the Gilbert islands, losing four planes. The tempo was then stepped up, with a six-carrier-force attack on Wake Island on 5 and 6 October. Twelve planes were lost in combat and fourteen in operations. The Hellcat achieved its first Zeke kills on 5 October.

These attacks were the preliminaries to a U.S. invasion of the Gilberts on 20 November supported by six fleet and five light carriers. This task force was split into four groups, ranging from the Marshall islands in the north to the Solomons in the south, where the earlier American invasion force was still progressing northward. On 5 November the *Saratoga* and the *Princeton* attacked the major Japanese base at Rabaul with fifty-two Hellcats, twenty-two Dauntless, and twenty-three Avengers. Heavy damage was inflicted on the Japanese cruisers in the harbor, and some twenty-five Japanese planes were shot down for the loss of five Hellcats, three Dauntless, and two Avengers.

This first attack on Rabaul was to be followed by a second, launched from a five-carrier task force. One of these carriers, the *Bunker Hill,* carried thirty-three of the new SB2C-1 Helldivers, which were to replace the aging Dauntless.

The second attack by the five-carrier American task force—split into two groups—was made on Rabaul on 11 November. It met strong opposition from some seventy fighters, but only seven planes were lost. An estimated twenty-four enemy aircraft were destroyed. Before a second strike could be launched, the three-carrier U.S. group was attacked by some 120 Zeke fighters and Val, Kate, and Betty bombers. The *Bunker Hill, Essex,* and *Independence* flew off their fighters, reinforced by shore-based aircraft, some of which had previously landed aboard and refueled, and in the ensuing battle thirty-eight Japanese aircraft were lost at a cost of eleven U.S. carrier planes. The shore-based element included twenty-four Corsairs and twelve Hellcats. The Corsairs distinguished themselves by shooting down an entire group of fourteen Kate torpedo planes and then landed safely on the *Bunker Hill* and *Essex* to refuel.

The Corsairs involved in this action were fitted with full plexi-glass cockpit canopies, which supplanted the confining bird-cage canopy with its restricted width at the apex. Other improvements were the elimination of cutouts for aft vision behind the headrest and the raising of the seat by about seven inches.

The Helldiver, blooded in an environment of air superiority, did not suffer unduly, nor did it particularly distinguish itself at Rabaul.

Japanese aircraft based on Rabaul included those of Carrier Division 1 (*Shokaku, Zuikaku, Zuiho*). The two U.S. carrier raids severely depleted the only combat-ready carrier squadrons available to the Japanese.

On 20 November, when the American invasion of the Gilberts was launched, the Japanese had less than fifty intact aircraft in the entire Gilberts-Marshalls area. The U.S. Carrier Task Force of six fleet and five light carriers had seven hundred aircraft aboard, to which could be added another two hundred on the eight smaller escort carriers supporting the amphibious forces.

The Japanese launched torpedo-bomber attacks against the U.S. carriers and managed to score one hit on the *Independence,* losing nine aircraft in the process. Japan's major success was the sinking of the escort carrier *Liscome Bay* with her twenty aircraft; she was torpedoed by a submarine early on the morning of 24 November.

By the end of November U.S. fast carriers had left the Gilberts area to move north to the Marshall islands. They struck on 4 December and destroyed sixty-five Japanese aircraft, mostly on the ground, for the price of five carrier planes. The *Lexington,* retiring from the area, suffered a hit that night from an attacking torpedo-bomber.

Thus the year 1943 ended on a high note for the Allies in the Pacific. They had breached the ring of Japan's outer defenses and were now preparing to drive on toward the Japanese homeland.

The Japanese Carrier Zuiho *(U.S. Navy)*

GRUMMAN F6F-3 HELLCAT

This single-seat fighter was designed not just to replace the Wildcat but also to provide a backup for the Corsair program in case it ran into trouble, which it showed every sign of doing during its development. The speed with which the design progressed from prototype to production was the result of a prodigious effort crowned with success.

The Hellcat was unmistakably from the same stable as the Wildcat and Avenger, having the characteristic Grumman corpulence and angularity. While not beautiful, it was rugged. It looked big and indeed had the largest wing applied to any U.S. wartime-production single-seat fighter.

The first flight, on 26 June 1942, was four days short of the

Grumman F6F-3 Hellcat (U.S. Naval Institute)

anniversary of the award of the prototype contract and three weeks after the decisive Battle of Midway. The tempo continued with the first flight of the first-production Hellcat on 3 October. Some eighteen months later, ten thousand had been produced.

The fuselage was an all-metal monocoque structure with flush-riveted aluminum-alloy skin. The low midwing was mounted at the minimum angle of incidence to reduce level flight drag, and a negative thrust line was adopted for the engine to attain the comparatively large angle of attack required for takeoff. All control surfaces were fabric covered.

The Hellcat was powered by the magnificent eighteen-cylinder Pratt and Whitney R-2800 Double Wasp, a two-stage, two-speed, supercharged, air-cooled radial engine driving a three-bladed Hamilton Standard airscrew. It was protected by a substantial deflection plate built into the underside of the cowling. The oil cooler and tank were protected, and all internal fuel tanks were self-sealing. The main tanks, side by side in the center section, each held 73 imperial gals (87.5 U.S.), and there was a contoured reserve tank holding 62 imperial gals (74.5 U.S.) immediately aft and beneath the pilot's seat. The engine was started with a percussion cartridge.

With a maximum overload weight of 13,221 lbs, the Hellcat was certainly a lot of airplane. It had a capacious cockpit, from which the view on the ground was not unreasonable because of a humped-back profile (the pilot was perched at the highest point) and the downward curve of the nose cowling.

Takeoff with the tailwheel locked was straightforward, although the noise with the canopy open was deafening. For short takeoffs 20 degrees of flap was normally applied, and unstick occurred at

70 knots (80.5 mph). The wheels retracted rapidly. At a climb speed of 130 knots (150 mph) the initial rate was 3,650 ft/min, and it remained good up to 20,000 ft. The supercharger gave the Hellcat a service ceiling of 35,500 ft, but the aircraft was distinctly sluggish above 32,000.

At the normal cruise speed of 190 knots (219 mph) the fighter was stable about all axes, but there were marked changes of lateral and directional trim with changes of speed and power. The controls were reasonably light and effective but grew heavy at high speeds, particularly the ailerons. In a dive there was heavy engine vibration at high rpm, and the aircraft had to be trimmed into the dive as speed built up and the tail became heavy.

The stall occurred with little warning and either wing could drop, but recovery was straightforward and easy. Stalling speeds varied from as low as 58 knots (67 mph) in the landing configuration to 80 knots (92 mph) in clean configuration with combat load. In steep turns pronounced buffeting of the tail surfaces heralded a stall, and unless the backward pressure on the control column was eased, the aircraft would flick out of the turn. Subsequent recovery was quick and easy.

As a deck-landing aircraft the Hellcat was as steady as a rock at 80 knots (92 mph), with precise attitude and speed control. View, though not good, was certainly acceptable. It was best not to cut the throttle too early for touchdown, otherwise the heavy nose would drop and could cause a bounce. The sturdy landing gear had good shock absorption.

Armament was six 0.5-in Colt-Browning machine guns in the wings with 400 rounds apiece. The Hellcat was versatile as a weapon carrier; models following the F6F-3 could carry bombs, drop tanks, or rockets.

Assessment: The Hellcat was a first-class fighter, and although not outstanding in performance compared with land-based fighters, it was superb in the environment of the Pacific, where its performance, maneuverability, firepower, and ability to absorb punishment would give it supremacy over the much-dreaded Zeke. It was unquestionably the most important Allied shipboard fighter of World War II.

F6F-3 Hellcat Versus Zeke 32

The contrast between these two magnificent fighters could hardly have been greater—the big and heavy Hellcat and the nimble, featherweight Zeke. They were, of course, products of totally different design philosophies. The American airplane was the faster of the two in level flight at all altitudes, and above 10,000 ft could almost match the climb rate of the Japanese fighter, while its altitude capabilities were markedly superior.

The weight of the Hellcat gave it greater acceleration in a dive but placed it at a disadvantage in a dogfight, where its maneuverability was no match for the supremely agile Zeke at low speeds. At higher speeds the controls of the Japanese fighter stiffened up, and the turn rate disparity was dramatically reduced.

The Hellcat had to use its assets to advantage. If it got on the tail of the Zeke, it could usually stay with the latter in the first 70 to 80 degrees of an evasive turn, enough to get in a burst of powerful armament against the fragile enemy before breaking away. If the Zeke surprised the Hellcat, the American fighter could usually accelerate out of trouble, and its robustness might allow it to survive a burst of fire from Japanese guns.

Verdict: Provided it used hit-and-run tactics and did not mix it with the Zeke, the Hellcat should succeed in destroying its ill-protected opponent with heavy firepower.

Curtiss SB2C-1 Helldiver

The Helldiver was designed to a 1938 U.S. Navy specification for a carrier-based dive-bomber with a substantial internal fuel capacity and an integral weapons bay. The prototype made its first flight on 18 December 1940, exhibiting poor stability and low-speed handling characteristics. Subsequent modifications included lengthening the forward fuselage and considerably enlarging the tail surfaces, as well as providing increased protection and armament. All these changes had a dramatic effect on weight and performance.

The Helldiver was a low midwing design whose dominant physical characteristic was the inordinate size of the wing and tail surfaces compared with the fuselage. The latter was an oval-section, alluminum-alloy, semimonocoque structure with a smooth, flush-riveted Alclad skin. The trailing edges of the wings inboard of the ailerons were occupied by split-plain flaps, which opened both upward and downward to serve as dive brakes. Hydraulic locks for the upper portions permitted the lower flaps to operate in orthodox fashion for landing. These flaps caused tremendous tail buffet when serving as dive brakes. Slats mechanically linked with landing gear extended from the outer third of the wings' leading edges to aid lateral control at low speeds. The wings folded up for carrier stowage. The weapon bay on the underside of the fuselage was equipped with hydraulically operated doors.

The Helldiver was powered by a fourteen-cylinder, 1,700-hp Wright R-2600-8 Cyclone 14, a radial air-cooled engine. It drove a three-blade, constant-speed Curtiss Electric propeller and was started

Curtiss SB2C-1 Helldiver Taking Off from the USS Bunker Hill, *June 1944* (U.S. Navy)

by an electrically energized inertia starter. A self-sealing fuel tank of 87 imperial gals (105 U.S.) was housed between the spars of the center section on each side, and there was a fuselage fuel tank of 91.5 imperial gals (110 U.S.) immediately behind the pilot.

The cockpit was the usual large office so beloved of the Americans, and the layout was a random mess showing little sign of constructive planning. The pilot was provided with an armor-glass windscreen and back armor. There was noticeable friction in all three control circuits, especially the elevator.

Taxiing was unpleasant owing to the combination of poor forward view, particularly with the cowl gills open, and weathercocking tendencies in a crosswind. Takeoff was straightforward, except that the view over the nose with the cowl gills half open was rather poor until the tail was raised. This required a firm push on the control column to overcome friction in the control circuit. There appeared to be little or no aileron control response until a speed of at least 90 knots (103.5 mph) had been reached. Rate of climb at 130 knots (150 mph) was 1,620 ft/min; two 1,000-lb bombs reduced that to 1,270 ft/min. Stability on the climb was marginal longitudinally and positive laterally.

In a level-flight cruise at 190 knots (219 mph), instability characteristics persisted and harmony of control was spoiled by the heavy elevator. In turbulent air the plane wallowed about continuously, and it was terrible to fly on instruments. Not surprisingly, an autopilot was fitted.

Maximum speed at sea level was 220 knots (253 mph) and 240 knots (276 mph) at critical altitude. Maximum range was 964 nm (1,110 statute miles), and service ceiling was 24,200 ft. In effect, then, the Helldiver's performance did not improve on that of the SBD-5 Dauntless, except for a marginal increase in speed.

A clean stall occurred at 77 knots (88.5 mph) with no warning whatsoever, but it was mild, no more than a gentle nose drop. The all-down stall at 66 knots (76 mph) was difficult to achieve unless the aircraft was trimmed well back and the control column was pulled right back. This induced heavy elevator buffeting, followed by a sharp wing drop.

In unbraked dives up to 320 knots (368 mph) there was no buffeting and the Helldiver was easy to hold on target. Constant rudder trimming was necessary above 280 knots (320.5 mph), and corrections to line by aileron turns were hard work. In a braked dive there was constant tail buffeting, although no adverse effects on control resulted from the use of the split flaps. The pullout gave fairly high forces and set up extra buffet. The flaps, normally retracted at 180 knots (207 mph) after recovery, gave a slight nose-up trim change.

For landing, the gear was lowered at 100 knots (115 mph), the leading-edge slats extending simultaneously. Poor aileron control was already in evidence. At 95 knots (109 mph) the flaps were lowered. The first third of flap travel was accompanied by a violent nose-up change of trim; this was canceled by the nose-down trim change that resulted from the remaining two-thirds of flap travel. At the deck-landing approach speed of 80 knots (92 mph) the ailerons were sluggish, the elevator fairly heavy but effective, the rudder light and effective. The view was poor, and power had to be held on virtually till touchdown to prevent the nose from dropping heavily. The probability of a bounce was low owing to the delightfully soft landing gear. One dangerous feature was the balked landing, when the application of engine power gave a nose-up trim change that could not be held without retrimming rapidly.

The armament was one 20-mm cannon with 400 rounds in each wing and two 0.3-in machine guns on a flexible mounting with 2,000 rounds for rear defense. Two 1,000-lb bombs could be carried internally in the bomb bay. Provision was made for a torpedo as well.

Assessment: The Helldiver was an airplane riddled with handling faults. It was a mediocre dive-bomber and a poor deck-landing aircraft, with a performance that barely bettered that of its predecessor. It was nicknamed The Beast, an epithet it fully merited. In its main role as a dive-bomber it was less effective than the Dauntless it replaced.

SB2C-1 *Helldiver Versus Zeke 32*

The Helldiver would find it virtually impossible to evade the attentions of an attacking Zeke. However, if the Japanese risked a head-on attack it could get a nasty surprise from the wing cannon of the dive-bomber. An attack from any other sector against such a comparatively large target would leave the Helldiver with little or no chance of survival.

Verdict: The Helldiver would be a sitting duck against the Zeke.

The Allied Fight in Europe

The Allies, driving north from Sicily, ran into a barrier of strong resistance at the Gustav Line, a great fortified system in the rocky mountains south of Rome. This barrier still stood firm as the year closed.

In Russia, during the last six months of 1943, the Germans were driven back some two hundred miles to the Black Sea. In the air about twenty-five hundred German aircraft were opposed by at least twice as many Russian planes whose efficiency had been much improved. The Il-2 Sturmovik assault bomber was one model, of which more were produced than any other aircraft in the world.

By the end of 1943 the Finnish war was in its third year, and the Brewster Buffalo fighters were still enjoying considerable success. Nonetheless, from March 1943 the Germans had to make Me 109Gs available to the Ilmavoimat to help match the steadily improving quality of Soviet fighters and pilots, and because of a shortage of spares there was a constant struggle to keep the Buffalo airworthy. One of the stopgap solutions was to fit the aircraft with captured Soviet M-63 engines, these being license-built versions of the Cyclone and therefore comparable in size and performance.

The Finns were ferocious fighters, claiming 446 victories with their Buffalo. One aircraft alone was reputed to have scored forty-one victories, though not all with the same pilot. If true, this would be a world record.

6

1944

Victory in Sight

THE RELENTLESS TEMPO of the American assault continued unabated into 1944. On New Year's Day the U.S. carriers *Bunker Hill* and *Monterey* staged a strike against Kavieng, New Ireland, just north of Rabaul. Thirty Japanese fighters opposed the attackers, but the Americans shot down at least fourteen of the enemy at a cost of only three carrier planes. A further strike on 4 January gave the Americans a few more kills without incurring loss.

The invasion of the Marshalls, Operation Flintlock, was delayed because U.S. land-based aircraft in the Gilberts could not gain control of the skies. The distances involved were too vast. This situation changed with the reappearance of the U.S. Navy's Fast Carrier Task Force. Reinforced by the USS *Langley*, it had a strength of six fleet carriers and six light carriers with a complement of seven hundred aircraft in four groups. Four of the carriers carried special night-fighter detachments for the first time in naval aviation history. The *Enterprise* and the *Intrepid* each had three F4U-2 Corsairs fitted with radomes on their right wings and thus armed with only five machine guns. The *Bunker Hill* and the *Yorktown* both carried four F6F-3N Hellcats with radar housings on their right wings.

Operation Flintlock opened on 29 January with strikes against Kwajalein. In the next three days all 150 Japanese planes on the archipelago were destroyed, compared with forty-nine U.S. carrier planes and forty-eight aircrew, about half of these due to operational accidents.

From Kwajalein the task force moved to Eniwetok atoll, 350 miles closer to Japan. Covering the Eniwetok invasion, three of the fast carrier groups attacked Truk, in the Caroline Islands, on

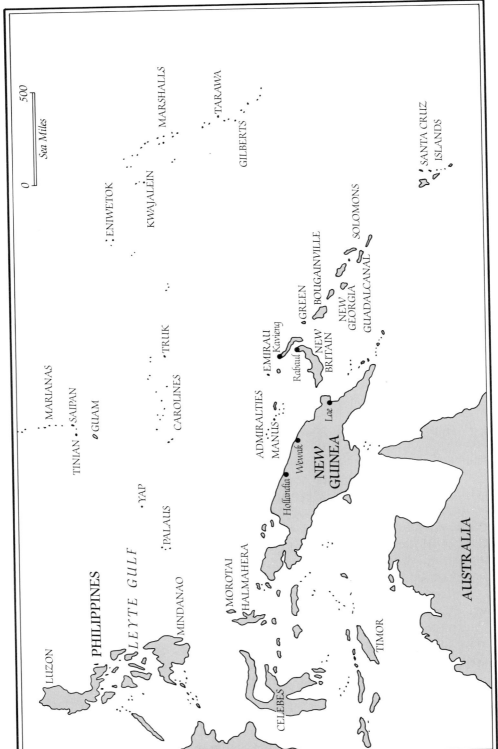

The Southwest Pacific

Kawanishi Emily 22, Which Replaced the Earlier Mavis as Japan's Main Reconnaissance Flying Boat (U.S. Navy)

17 February. This heavily fortified, Japanese-occupied atoll lay 670 miles southwest of Eniwetok and had 365 aircraft on its airstrips.

The goal of the first strike against Truk, made by seventy carrier fighters, was to knock out air opposition over the atoll. It proved highly successful, more than thirty Japanese aircraft being shot down and forty destroyed on the ground by Hellcats. Hellcats and Avengers sustained the tempo of the attack for the next thirty hours, destroying 125 Japanese aircraft, damaging a similar number, and sinking thirty ships. The only successful retaliation came at night when a Kate bomber hit the carrier *Intrepid* with a torpedo, jamming her rudder and causing a number of casualties.

With its large complement of fighters, the Fast Carrier Task Force heralded a change in U.S. Navy carrier aviation tactics. Now the Americans sought to saturate their opposition, gaining air superiority by force of numbers.

The next target for the Fast Carrier Task Force was the Marianas, just 1,500 miles from Japan. The strength of enemy forces there was relatively unknown, so the operation was to be largely for reconnaissance. As it happened, a number of planes from the Japanese navy's Third Carrier Fleet had lately arrived, including Zeke 52s and Judy bombers.*

In their reconnaissance probe of the Marianas, the two U.S. carrier groups were sighted some 420 miles east of Saipan and attacked unsuccessfully on the night of 21 February. Early the following morning thirty-five Betty and five Judy bombers, escorted by Zekes, continued the attack. The Americans had to rely heavily on radar-controlled antiaircraft fire because the night-fighter Hellcats proved unsuccessful, as they had in the Marshalls. The Japanese suffered heavily, losing twenty-three Bettys, two Judys, and six Zekes without damaging any U.S. ships.

The carriers retaliated with a dawn strike on Saipan, Tinian, and Guam. They accounted for 168 Japanese aircraft on the ground, losing five Hellcats and one Avenger in the air. Above all, the raid produced excellent photographs of the Marianas.

The next operation for the Fast Carrier Task Force was a series of strikes on the Carolines. The Palau islands, at the western end of the Carolines, took the brunt of the attack on 30 March. Three squadrons of Avengers laid seventy-eight mines in the passages of the main harbor, whereupon thirty-six trapped Japanese ships were destroyed by dive- and torpedo-bombers. In the day and a half of strikes, 157 enemy aircraft were destroyed in exchange for 25 American planes.

The Fast Carrier Task Force moved on to the New Guinea area and on 21 April began four days of attacks on Japanese bases. Twenty-one U.S. carrier aircraft were lost. The next stop was Truk again, and in two days of strikes task force planes destroyed fifty-nine Japanese aircraft in the air and thirty-four on the ground, losing twenty-seven of their own in combat and nine for operational reasons.

Yokosuka D4Y-3 Judy 33

The earlier, experimental D4Y-2 Judy 11 had appeared briefly at the Battle of Midway, fitted with a 1,380-hp Aichi Atsuta 31 engine, the Japanese version of the Daimler-Benz 601E. Maintenance problems and the slow production of the water-cooled Atsutas had resulted in a change to an air-cooled engine.

The Judy was a low midwing, two-seat naval dive-bomber or reconnaissance monoplane, designed for shipboard operations as a replacement for the well-tried Val. The fuselage was an oval-section, all-metal structure with a flush-riveted, smooth-metal skin. The wings

*The Zeke 52 had wings of the same span as the Zeke 32, but with rounded, not clipped tips. Performance was the same, but firepower had been improved by the fitting of two 13.2-mm machine guns in the fuselage, which replaced the 7.7 caliber.

had Fowler-type flaps, and dive brakes hinged to the rear spar ahead of the flaps. The brakes, raised in recess when the flaps were lowered, created a slot effect. All controls were fabric covered. The landing gear and arrester hook were retractable.

Model 33 was powered by a 1,400-hp, fourteen-cylinder, radial air-cooled Mitsubishi Kinsei 62. It drove a three-bladed, constant-speed Mitsubishi Hamilton airscrew. There were four wing fuel tanks and one fuselage tank.

The aircraft is reported to have had good stability and control characteristics, but it did not have the maneuverability of its predecessor. Apparently it was an effective dive-bomber and a fairly easy airplane to deck-land.

Maximum speed was 290 knots (355 mph) at 18,500 ft, and initial rate of climb was 2,500 ft/min with a service ceiling of 30,000 ft. Range was 1,037 nm (1,200 statute miles). There were two forward-firing 7.7-mm machine guns in the fuselage and one 7.7-mm gun on a flexible mounting in the rear cockpit. The plane had an internal bomb bay with displacement gear for a 1,100-lb bomb, and one 132-lb bomb could be carried under each wing.

Assessment: Judy 33 was the counterpart of the Helldiver. It was 47 knots (54 mph) faster and had superior all-round performance, but was less well armed and carried a lighter weapon load. As a dive-bomber the Judy was more effective in delivery and had a better chance of survival against contemporary fighters. In short, the Japanese airplane was a thoroughly competent dive-bomber.

D4Y-3 Judy 33 Versus F6F-3 Hellcat

With the Hellcat almost 50 knots (57 mph) faster, it would always have the initiative. Nevertheless, the Judy had sufficient performance and maneuverability to make the fighter work for a kill. En route to its target the Judy was most vulnerable, but in the attack mode the aircraft would be more difficult to deal with because of the steepness of its braked dive. Having dropped its bomb, the Judy's best chance of survival would be to retract the dive brakes and limit the pullout to a 30-degree dive toward the surface; it could then seek to escape at full throttle and low level to limit the Hellcat's attack envelope.

Verdict: The Judy had about as much chance of survival against the Hellcat as the Helldiver had against the Zeke—minimal.

Allied Return to the Indian Ocean

After being driven out of the eastern Indian Ocean by Japanese carrier forces in April 1942, the Royal Navy returned quietly in October 1943 with the escort carrier *Battler*, equipped with Swordfish and Seafires, in the antisubmarine role. Early in 1944 she was rein-

Yokosuka D4Y-2 Judy 22 (Smithsonian Institution)

forced by the escort carriers *Begum, Shah,* and *Ameer,* carrying Avengers, and the fighter escort carrier *Atheling.* In undertaking its convoy protection duties this force was extremely successful—not a ship was lost.

The Eastern Fleet, as it was called, was strengthened by the fleet carrier *Illustrious.* She carried a complement of lend-lease F4U-1A Corsairs (Corsair IIs, as they were known in the Royal Navy) and the new Fairey Barracuda II bombers.* The loan of the USS *Saratoga,* which joined the force on 27 March, further augmented fleet strength, operating F6F-3 Hellcats, Avengers, and Dauntless aircraft.

U.S. Marine Corps Corsairs had destroyed an impressive total of 584 Japanese aircraft by the end of 1943. However, the U.S. Navy had still not cleared the F4U for shipboard use. Oddly enough the Royal Navy was not quite so fastidious, approving it for carrier operations some nine months before the Americans.

A period of training was necessary to make operating between the two big carriers possible, for there were considerable differences between British and American deck-landing techniques and procedures. Although by this time the Royal Navy had adopted the U.S. Navy's methods in the interests of standardization, British pilots were still finding the change difficult to cope with.

The new Allied Eastern Fleet took up the offensive on 19 April with a strike against the Japanese-occupied port of Sabang, on the northwest tip of Sumatra. Eighty-three carrier aircraft destroyed twenty-four aircraft on the ground as well as three of the four large oil storage tanks, and heavily damaged the docks, losing one Hellcat

*The Corsair II received certain modifications to make it suitable for operations aboard British carriers. Its wing span had been reduced by 16 in to accommodate below-deck hangars, and it had landing gear with long-stroke oleo legs. There was also provision for 2,000 lbs of bombs or long-range tanks holding up to 471 imperial gals (565 U.S.).

in the process. Three Kate torpedo-bombers launched a counter-attack on the carriers and were shot down by a combat air patrol of Hellcats.

On 17 May eighty-five aircraft made a second strike against the aviation fuel store at Surabaya, on the eastern side of Java. Moderately successful against the target, they also managed to destroy twenty-three aircraft on the ground and in the air. One of the *Saratoga*'s Avengers was lost. Now the Japanese realized they were in the middle of a carrier pincer movement.

Neutralizing the *Tirpitz* Threat

The German battle cruiser *Tirpitz*, operating in Norwegian waters, had been a constant threat to Arctic convoys traveling from Britain to Russia. After being heavily damaged by midget submarine attack in September 1943 in Altenfiord, she was moved for repairs to Kaafiord, on the northern tip of Norway, where the steep sides of the fiord would protect her from torpedo attack by air.

The Admiralty, anxious when repairs to the *Tirpitz* neared completion, assembled a carrier force of two fleet and four escort carriers for Operation Tungsten. The fleet carriers *Victorious* and *Furious* would each carry a striking force of twenty-one Barracuda IIs, the first escorted by twenty F6F-3 Hellcats and twenty FM-1 Wildcat Vs, the second by twenty-one Corsair IIs and twenty Wildcat Vs. The escort would certainly be needed if surprise was not achieved, in which case stern opposition from German Me 109s and Fw 190s could be expected. The Barracuda had already been operational with Force H during the Salerno landings, but its first action was the attack on the *Tirpitz*.

Launched on 3 April 1944, the attack achieved almost complete surprise, allowing the first wave of dive-bombing Barracudas to score a number of direct hits. The second wave, which had to dive through the smoke of the explosions from the first, met a box barrage of antiaircraft fire but pressed the attack home. A total of fourteen direct hits was obtained with 500- and 1,600-lb bombs, killing 122 of the *Tirpitz*'s crew and starting a great fire amidships. Two Barracudas and a Hellcat were lost in the action, while another Barracuda had crashed on takeoff. The *Tirpitz* was disabled for three months.

No enemy fighter opposition was met, but it was known that some Me 109G-6s and Fw 190A-4s were assigned to protect the battle-cruiser. The Corsairs flew top cover for the strike force, with the Hellcats as close escort and the Wildcats forming a low screen. The element of surprise was complete in this action, but was unlikely to be repeated in subsequent attacks. In any event, the potential opposition was formidable.

British carriers made further attempts to attack the *Tirpitz* in

Fairey Barracuda II (Peter M. Bowers's Collection)

April and May but were thwarted by bad weather. On 8 May Hellcats from the carrier *Emperor* downed two Me 109s and a Fw 190.

FAIREY BARRACUDA II

Design work on the Barracuda began in 1937, and the aircraft made its first flight on 7 December 1940. The first all-metal monoplane torpedo-bomber for carrier-borne duties ever built in Great Britain, it was intended as a replacement for the Albacore biplane. Because the British aircraft industry concentrated on achieving maximum output of a few selected aircraft at this critical juncture, the Barracuda's progress toward series production was delayed for almost two years, and first-production aircraft did not fly until 18 May 1942.

The Barracuda was a shoulder-high wing monoplane carrying a crew of three, and although primarily a torpedo-bomber, it could also be used as a dive-bomber. An unusual feature was the Youngman flaps, suspended below and staggered back from the trailing edge of the wing. Giving a biplane effect in cruising flight, they could be lowered differentially for takeoff and landing and raised to a negative angle for retarding speed in a dive. Wing folding was complicated by the flaps. The tailplane was mounted near the top of the fin and braced by a single strut on each side. All controls were fabric covered, and all the landing gear except for the tailwheel was retractable.

The Barracuda I, of which only thirty were built, mainly for training, was powered by a 1,260-hp liquid-cooled Rolls-Royce Merlin 30 driving a three-blade airscrew. The Mk II had the uprated 1,640-hp Merlin 32, which drove a four-blade Rotol airscrew. Self-sealing fuel tanks in the center section carried 226 imperial gals (271 U.S.) with provision for an additional 116 (140) in a crutch tank. The Mk I Barracuda was hopelessly underpowered.

Takeoff with 20 degrees of flap setting was simple if uninspiring, but the view was good and the rudder effective for directional control. After unstick there were some seconds to admire the ingenuity of the mechanical link that raised the inverted L-shaped landing gear.

After this monstrous piece of gangling iron had been stowed away, the crew could relax while climbing to 5,000 ft, which took six minutes.

Once the aircraft was cruising at 160 knots (185 mph), the Barracuda was pleasantly maneuverable, being particularly light on the ailerons. It displayed a mild sign of rudder overbalance. Surprisingly, the aircraft accelerated well in the dive, and the dive flaps provided good deceleration if a steep angle was required. Stability was positive about all axes, and the aircraft flew well on instruments.

Deck landing was easy with the Barracuda—with everything down, there was so much drag it had to be powered onto the carrier. When the throttle was cut, the aircraft sat down and stayed down. View was good throughout the approach, and controls were effective, especially laterally.

Performance was mediocre, with a top speed of 184 knots (210 mph) at 2,000 ft, which fell to 173 knots (200 mph) with a torpedo. Range amounted to 628 nm (724 miles) or 524.5 nm (604 miles) with a torpedo. Service ceiling was 21,600 ft, or 17,500 ft with a torpedo.

The Barracuda was armed with two 0.303-in Vickers K gas-operated machine guns on a flexible mount in the rear cockpit, plus one 18-in torpedo or 1,600 lbs of bombs carried externally.

Assessment: If the Helldiver was the cross the U.S. Navy had to bear, the Barracuda was the Royal Navy's albatross. Its performance was pathetic by contemporary standards, and its defensive armament was poor. Rudder overbalance proved to be a severe restriction on a breakaway maneuver after a torpedo attack, and it caused a number of fatal accidents in training. In the dive-bombing role the plane was much more effective, provided it could get to the target area unmolested, and it surpassed the Helldiver in dive-attack ability.

Barracuda II Versus Messerschmitt 109F, Focke-Wulf 190A-4, or Zeke 52

Against any of these contemporary fighters the Barracuda II was vulnerable, and no more so than in a torpedo attack run-in or a postattack breakaway. Its only defense was to hug the surface, keeping any attacker in the field of fire of the rear guns, but this was rather like bringing a peashooter to bear on a tank.

Verdict: The Barracuda had virtually no hope of survival against any of the German or Japanese fighters it was likely to encounter.

Corsair II Versus Messerschmitt 109G-6

The Me 109G differed from the F model in having a 1,475-hp DB605 AM engine, which gave it a top speed of 386 mph at 22,640 ft and an initial rate of climb of 3,346 ft/min. It was armed with one 30-mm engine-mounted cannon with 60 rounds and two 13-mm fuselage-mounted cannon with 300 rounds per gun.

A battle between the Corsair and Me 109G-6 would be a contest between two of the world's greatest engines, each superlative but differing from the other in ways that could determine the result of combat. The Double Wasp gave the Corsair a slight speed edge over the German fighter at medium altitudes, while the in-line engine gave the Me 109G-6 a performance advantage at low level, particularly in rate of climb and acceleration in a dive. The Double Wasp was less vulnerable to combat damage than the liquid-cooled DB605, and this was accentuated by the greater firepower of the Corsair.

The Corsair's best tactic would be to take on the Me 109G-6 in the horizontal plane. The German would favor vertical maneuvers.

Verdict: Since carrier air battles usually take place at low altitudes, the Me 109G-6 should be favored in this encounter. However, the Me 109G-6, not as good a dogfighter as its predecessor, the Me 109F, would find itself unable to afford tactical errors against the powerful American fighter.

Corsair II Versus Focke-Wulf 190A-4

This would be a contest between a heavyweight and a lightweight fighter, with virtually all the advantages on the side of the latter. Having flown both aircraft a lot, I have no doubt as to which I would rather fly. The Fw 190A-4 could not be bested by the Corsair.

Verdict: The Fw 190A-4 was arguably the best piston-engine fighter of World War II. It is a clear winner in combat with the Corsair.

F6F-3 Hellcat Versus Messerschmitt 109G-6

This would involve two fighters of almost equal performance. The Me 109G-6 would not be able to exploit its prowess in the vertical plane, and it would certainly be outmaneuvered as well as outgunned by the Hellcat, whose view would be an asset. There was really no maneuver the German fighter could use effectively to evade the Hellcat, which would, nonetheless, have to be flown to its limits to ensure a kill.

Verdict: The Hellcat had a distinct edge over the Me 109G-6 but would not be able to overcome it without a lot of pilot sweat.

F6F-3 Hellcat Versus Focke-Wulf 190A-4

This would be a showdown between two classic fighters. The German had a speed advantage of 30 mph, the American a slight advantage in climb. Both were very maneuverable and both had heavy firepower. By 1944 the Fw 190 was a little long in the tooth, while the Hellcat was a relative newcomer; still, the superb technology built into the German fighter by Kurt Tank was not outmoded. The Hellcat had broken the iron grip of the Zeke in the Far East, but the Fw 190A-4 was a far tougher opponent. Risk to the Hellcat would be high indeed.

Verdict: This was a contest so finely balanced that the skill of the pilot would probably be the deciding factor.

Operation Overlord

In the whole course of World War II there was no month more eventful than June 1944. Of this time Winston Churchill wrote, "Here then we reach what the Western Powers may justly regard as the supreme climax of the war. Africa was cleared. India had been defended from invasion. Japan, over-strained and disillusioned, was recoiling on her homeland. All danger to Australia and New Zealand had passed away. Italy was fighting on our side. The Russian armies had driven the German invaders from their country. The Hitler tyranny was doomed."*

On 5 June the mightiest operation of the war was launched with the cross-channel invasion of France, the incomparable Operation Overlord. For this immensely complicated and successful assault the RAF and the Fleet Air Arm provided aircraft that served in antishipping, minelaying, and other roles. An entire fighter wing deployed for bombardment spotting; other fighters were attached to the air defense of Great Britain.

Sixteen FAA squadrons were involved: six Avenger squadrons; three squadrons of Swordfish IIIs;† one Hellcat squadron attached to the Fighter Command; two squadrons of Seafire IIIs escorting RAF fighter-bomber sweeps over Normandy and undertaking similar missions on their own;‡ and two squadrons each of Seafire IIs and Spitfire L VBs, all flown by naval pilots specially trained in bombardment spotting and army cooperation. The spotters had flown 1,230 combat sorties by the end of the operation in mid-July, losing only fourteen aircraft, mostly to Fw 190s.

Operation Forager

The objective of this operation was to capture the Marianas, which would provide the United States with bases three thousand miles

---

*The Second World War, vol. 5, pp. 557–58.

†The Swordfish III mounted a radome containing an ASV Mk X radar scanner below the fuselage, between the landing-gear legs. It carried only two crew, a pilot and an observer.

‡The Seafire III was powered by a 1,470-hp Rolls-Royce Merlin 55 driving a four-bladed airscrew. It had manual wing folding. The main wing folded up beyond the vertical, then the tips folded outboard, parallel to the center section.

Supermarine Seafire III (Pilot Press)

farther west than Pearl Harbor. Specifically, it would allow the Army
Air Force's new long-range B-29 bombers to strike Japan.

The U.S. Task Force comprised fifteen fast carriers and eleven
escort carriers. These belonged to a fleet of more than eight hundred
surface ships supported by twenty-eight submarines. The first strike
was launched on 11 June with 208 Hellcats and 8 Avengers attacking
the airfields of Saipan and Tinian and destroying 36 Japanese aircraft.
Strikes continued for the next three days and were extended to
Guam.

On 13 June the Japanese fleet, en route to the Marianas, sortied
from Tawi Tawi, off the northeast coast of Borneo. It had a total of
seventy-three surface ships, including nine carriers, one of them the
new 29,300-ton *Taiho*. The Japanese order of battle was as follows:

	Carriers	Fighters	Dive-Bombers	Torpedo-Bombers
Carrier	*Shokaku*	71 Zeke 52	10 Zeke 32	54 Jill 12
Division 1	*Taiho*		81 Judy 33	
	Zuikaku		9 Judy 11	
Carrier	*Hiyo*	56 Zeke 52	25 Zeke 32	27 Jill 11
Division 2	*Junyo*		27 Val 22	
	Ryuho		9 Judy 33	
Carrier	*Chitose*	18 Zeke 52	45 Zeke 32	12 Kate 21
Division 3	*Chiyoda*			6 Jill 11
	Zuiho			
TOTAL:		145	206	99

Because the light carriers were too slow to operate the Judy 33 effectively, they carried Zeke 32s fitted to carry one 551-lb bomb.

The D3A2 Val 22 had the higher-powered Mitsubishi Kinsei 54 engine of 1,280 hp, giving it a top speed of 281 mph but reducing its range to 874 statute miles. It carried one 550-lb bomb under the fuselage and two 132-lb bombs, one under each wing.

The B5N2 Kate 21 was powered by a 1,115-hp Nakajima Sakae 21 engine, which gave it a top speed of 225 mph and a range of 1,220 statute miles.

The order of battle of the U.S. Navy's Task Force 58 was as follows:

	Fighters	Dive-Bombers	Torpedo-Bombers
Task Group 58.1			
Hornet	40 Hellcat	33 Helldiver	20 Avenger
Yorktown	44 Hellcat	31 Helldiver	18 Avenger
Bataan	24 Hellcat	—	9 Avenger
Belleau Wood	26 Hellcat	—	9 Avenger
Task Group 58.2			
Bunker Hill	41 Hellcat	33 Helldiver	18 Avenger
Wasp	41 Hellcat	32 Helldiver	18 Avenger
Cabot	24 Hellcat	—	9 Avenger
Monterey	21 Hellcat	—	8 Avenger
Task Group 58.3			
Enterprise	3 Corsair	23 Dauntless	15 Avenger
Lexington	42 Hellcat	34 Dauntless	20 Avenger
Princeton	25 Hellcat	—	9 Avenger
San Jacinto	24 Hellcat	—	8 Avenger
Task Group 58.4			
Essex	45 Hellcat	36 Helldiver	20 Avenger
Cowpens	26 Hellcat	—	9 Avenger
Langley	25 Hellcat	—	9 Avenger
TOTAL:	483	222	199

The Hellcats were F6F-3s, the Corsairs F4U-2s. There were also twenty-seven Hellcat night-fighters on six of the fleet carriers, in addition to three night-fighter Corsairs on the seventh. These did not take part in daylight operations.

Both quantitatively and qualitatively, the Americans were heavily favored, but the Japanese hoped to bring into play several strategic and tactical advantages: the greater search-and-attack range of their carrier aircraft; land-based aircraft in the Marianas that could support the battle; the Marianas bases, which their carrier planes could use; and the fact that their carriers would be steaming steadily toward the enemy while launching and recovering aircraft in the easterly trade-winds, while American carriers would be steaming away from the enemy during such operations.

The U.S. Task Force was aware of the Japanese fleet's advance, but search planes had not sighted Japanese ships on 18 June or on the morning of 19 June. Although expecting to be struck from the west, Task Force 58 received its first attack from an unexpected direction when two Judy bombers and six Zeke dive-bombers came in from the east. They had flown from Guam, which had been reinforced by the Japanese after the American attacks there on 12, 13, and 14 June. The raid was ineffective. One Judy was shot down by a Hellcat, one Zeke by a destroyer.

At dawn Japan's First Mobile Fleet started an intensive search for the American carriers with forty-three planes, launched in three groups at half-hour intervals. A sighting was made, and the first strike of the day was conducted by sixteen Zeke 52s, forty-five Zeke 32s, and eight Jill 11s of Carrier Division 3. This was followed by a strike force of forty-eight Zeke 52s, fifty-three Judy 33s, and twenty-nine Jill 12s of Carrier Division 1.

Just after the *Taiho* had launched her contribution to the strike, a torpedo from a U.S. submarine struck her, but she was little affected. An hour later American radar picked up Japanese raiders 150 miles away, and every available fighter took to the air in defense. Of sixty-nine Japanese attackers in the first wave, forty-two were destroyed in exchange for one Hellcat. The battleships *South Dakota* and *Indiana* were hit and slightly damaged, but no Japanese planes got through to the U.S. carriers.

The second strike of 109 Japanese planes was detected on radar 115 miles away, and again it was met by a horde of Hellcats. Six Judys got through the powerful defense to attack the *Wasp* and the *Bunker Hill*, but they inflicted minimal damage. Once again Japanese losses were huge, amounting to ninety-four aircraft.

A third strike of fifteen Zeke 52s, twenty-five Zeke 32s, and seven Jill 11s came from Carrier Division 2. There was some confusion as to the targets selected, and only about twenty raiders located the U.S. carriers. Once again radar and the Hellcats thwarted the enemy, and seven Japanese planes were shot down.

The fourth Japanese strike of the day, launched from Carrier Division 2 plus the *Zuikaku*, amounted to eighty-two planes. They failed to find the U.S. carriers and so headed for Guam, where twenty-seven Hellcats from the carriers *Cowpens*, *Essex*, and *Hornet* set about them. Altogether, seventy-three of the eighty-two Japanese planes were lost in the raid.

By three o'clock in the afternoon enemy reserves were exhausted. The Japanese had lost 253 carrier planes, Task Force 58 only

twenty-nine. The worst blow to the Japanese was being deprived of
the carriers *Shokaku* and *Taiho* and their twenty-two aircraft. The
Shokaku sank after being hit by three torpedoes from a U.S. submarine, the *Taiho* because of inept damage control after an earlier
torpedo hit.

The Japanese fleet had still not been found by Task Force 58, so
twelve U.S. carriers steamed west to find them. Task Group 58.4
remained behind to keep Guam and Rota islands under surveillance.
This it did to good effect, shooting down twenty-one enemy aircraft
and destroying another fifty-two on the ground.

In the afternoon of 20 June Japan's First Mobile Fleet was at last
sighted by an Avenger from the USS *Enterprise*. Launching a strike
would stretch the range of the American planes to their limits and
entail their recovery in darkness, but the decision was made to pro-
ceed. Eighty-five Hellcats, seventy-seven Helldivers and Dauntless,
and fifty-four Avengers took off. In fading light contact was made
with the Japanese ships. First an oiler group was struck; two oilers
sank. Carrier Division 3 was then sighted and Hellcats shot down
seven enemy planes. Only one bomb hit, on the *Chiyoda*'s flight deck.

The Americans attacked Carrier Division 2 with more success.
Avengers dropped two torpedoes, which sank the carrier *Hiyo*, while
two bomb hits on the *Junyo* together with six near misses stopped
that ship's air operations.

About fifteen miles from Carrier Division 2 was the lone *Zuikaku*
with a light screen of two cruisers and eight destroyers. She was
attacked by Avengers, which scored one direct hit and six near misses.
Altogether the dusk attack cost the Japanese sixty-five planes.

American strike planes now had the job of finding Task Force
58 in the dark and landing on their carriers at night. The task force
commander made a risky decision to light up his ships for the returning planes, but in spite of this operational losses were heavy: seventeen fighters and sixty-three bombers. With combat losses amounting
to 6 fighters and 14 dive- and torpedo-bombers, a total of 100 of the
216 strike aircraft, 46 percent, were lost. Only 12 percent of the
aircrew died.

The Battle of the Marianas was both a strategic and a tactical
victory for the U.S. Navy, although some historians now feel that a
more aggressive posture would have resulted in more decisive losses
to Japan's First Mobile Fleet. This remains questionable, in the light
of what was going on at Saipan, where seven escort carriers with their
Wildcats and Avengers had to cover the assault of the island while
the fast carriers went west. As long as the exact whereabouts of
Japanese ships were unknown, there was always the danger of Task
Force 58 being outflanked by a Japanese detachment sent to attack
amphibious shipping at Saipan.

U.S. escort carriers bore the brunt of close-air support for the Marianas assault troops, combat air patrols, and antisubmarine patrols. These duties were not without cost. On 22 June, after an airfield had been captured ashore, the escort carriers began to fly off their considerable number of army fighters.

On the evening of 17 June an attack by Japanese planes put the escort carrier *Fanshaw Bay* out of commission, flinging a bomb into her after elevator. The American combat air patrol, which had to land on board after dark, lost nineteen aircraft in the process. It had previously shot down eight Japanese planes. This stood as a stark reminder to the U.S. Navy of its unpreparedness for night carrier operations. The lesson was to be repeated the next night when, after another enemy attack that cost the Japanese five planes, thirty-one American aircraft were lost during the night recovery.

Task Force 58 proceeded toward Saipan to refuel at sea, then split up the next day, 23 June. Three of the task groups returned to Eniwetok. Task Force 58.1 headed north to hit the islands of Chichi and Iwo Jima, where Japanese aircraft en route to the Marianas were stopping. There were 122 aircraft there, whereas the first American strike consisted of 51 Hellcats, each carrying a 500-lb bomb. Sighted by a Japanese patrol plane, the U.S. planes were intercepted halfway to the target, and most of them had to jettison their bombs before plunging into combat. The encounter cost the Japanese twenty-four Zero fighters and five Judy dive-bombers, while the Americans lost six Hellcats.

Two retaliation strikes were mounted against the U.S. carriers. The first, composed of twenty torpedo planes, was wiped out by the Hellcats. The second—twenty-three fighters, nine Judy dive-bombers, and nine Jill torpedo-bombers—failed to find the carriers. Hellcats downed ten fighters and seven torpedo-bombers.

On 4 July the Japanese sent out a small strike of nine fighters and eight single-engine torpedo planes whose pilots had been briefed to use suicide tactics against U.S. carriers. Intercepted, they lost five Zekes and seven torpedo-bombers to the Hellcats.

The capture and occupation of Saipan was complete on 10 August. The same day General Tojo's government fell.

The next assault targets were Guam, scheduled for 21 July, and Tinian, for 24 July. Task Force 58 returned to pound the islands as the troops went ashore. Seven escort carriers covered Tinian, each carrying twelve to sixteen FM-2 Wildcats and nine or twelve Avengers. Five escort carriers with Wildcats, Hellcats, and Avengers supported the attack on Guam. Task Force 58 did not directly support the invasions, for there was plenty of air support available, from both carriers and land. Tinian fell on 1 August, Guam on the tenth.

The termination of the Marianas campaign marked the end of Japanese carrier warfare in World War II. Fifteen fast carriers and twelve escort carriers of the U.S. Fifth Fleet had destroyed 1,223 Japanese aircraft and sunk 110,000 tons of shipping in a two-month campaign. The Americans lost 358 aircraft, 186 to fighting (102 fighters, 52 dive-bombers, and 32 torpedo-bombers) and 172 for operational reasons.

NAKAJIMA B6N1 JILL 11

This low-wing torpedo-bomber had an oval-section, all-metal fuselage with flush-riveted, smooth-metal skin. It carried a crew of two in tandem under a continuous transparent canopy. Landing gear, including the tailwheel, was fully retractable.

The Jill 11 was powered by a fourteen-cylinder, two-row radial Nakajima Mamoru 11 of 1,850 hp. It drove a four-blade Hamilton-type airscrew. There were six fuel tanks, three on each side of the fuselage in the center section.

The airplane, easy to take off in spite of a poor view ahead, had an initial rate of climb of 2,000 ft/min. It is reported to have had good stability characteristics and rather heavy but effective controls.

Deck landing at 82.5 mph was apparently made somewhat difficult by the poor view ahead and the long nose. The lateral control was described as sloppy.

Maximum speed was 300 mph at 16,080 ft, service ceiling 26,660 ft. Range when the aircraft flew as a torpedo-bomber was 1,080 statute miles, in the reconnaissance role, 2,300 miles.

Armament consisted of three 7.7-mm machine guns, one in the port wing, firing outside the airscrew disc, one on a swing mount in the rear cockpit, and one in the floor hatch. A 1,764-lb torpedo or six 220-lb bombs on a carrier beneath the fuselage and offset to starboard were alternative weapon loads.

The Jill 12 differed from the earlier model in having the 1,825-hp Mitsubishi Kasei 25 engine, which increased top speed to 310 mph but reduced maximum range to 1,600 statute miles.

Assessment: The Jill was considerably better than its Kate predecessor in speed and range, but it was an outmoded design unlikely to have much success torpedo-bombing defended targets. Good range made it a useful reconnaissance airplane.

Jill 12 Versus F9F-6 Hellcat

The agile Hellcat could literally run rings around the Jill, whose maneuverability offered it no escape. The American fighter would

Nakajima B6N2 Jill 12 (Smithsonian Institution)

have to distinguish the Jill from the Kate, that is, remember the ventral gun carried by the Jill, otherwise it might receive an unpleasant surprise.

Verdict: There was little hope of the Jill escaping the clutches of a tenacious Hellcat whose assets were such that a swift kill was almost inevitable.

The Philippines Campaign

On 26 August Task Force 58 became Task Force 38 owing to a command structure change. The new force, which comprised sixteen fast carriers, introduced two significant changes into U.S. carrier aviation. First, the ratio of fighters to dive-bombers was increased to more than two to one, reflecting the excellence of the Hellcat as a ground-attack aircraft. Second, a dedicated night carrier brought twenty radar-equipped Hellcats and eight similarly fitted Avengers to the force.

Task Group 38.4's four carriers attacked the Bonins for three days starting on 31 August and destroyed fifty-four Japanese planes. Simultaneously the task group struck the island of Yap, 300 miles to the north. Meanwhile, on 6, 7, and 8 September, the other three carrier groups struck the Palau islands. Then Task Group 38.4 moved in to the Palaus as the other carrier groups moved west to strike Mindanao, where fifty-eight enemy planes were destroyed. The U.S. carriers met such weak opposition that they continued to the central islands, where again the opposition was minimal. Their aircraft shot down 173 Japanese aircraft, destroyed 305 on the ground, and sank 59 ships in exchange for 8 of their own planes in combat and 1 operationally. The carrier force now turned north to the island of Luzon and started a two-day attack, destroying some 300 Japanese aircraft and sinking twenty-seven ships.

The surprising weakness of Japanese garrisons in the Philippines prompted the United States to make a major change of plan. It decided to push the invasion of the Philippines ahead two months, to 20 October.

Operation Dragoon

The invasion of southern France east of Toulon on 15 August was meant to complement the massive Operation Overlord. Operation Dragoon was to be conducted by what was, essentially, a British carrier task force of seven escort carriers, augmented by two U.S. escort carriers providing air cover for the landings. Each escort carrier had twenty-four fighters aboard. A U.S. Navy detachment of seven Hellcats and five Avengers would operate from Corsica to provide night cover for the carrier force.

The carrier-borne fighters were Hellcats, Wildcat VIs, and Seafire IIIs. The Wildcat VI was the British designation for the Eastern Motors–built FM-2, a lighter version of the F4F-4, specially modified for operation from escort carriers. Its weight had been reduced by some 500 lbs, and the outboard pair of 0.5-in machine guns had been deleted so that the number of rounds could be increased from 1,440 to 1,720.

As it turned out, enemy air opposition was nonexistent, and the fighters were used mainly for ground-attack missions. During one such armed reconnaissance 110 Seafires and Hellcats encountered 5 Ju 88s, which were quickly overwhelmed. Sixteen Allied fighters were lost to enemy antiaircraft fire, and twenty-seven, mainly Seafires, in deck-landing accidents.

Wildcat VI Versus Messerschmitt 109G-6

The agile little Wildcat could outmaneuver the latest version of the Me 109, but the performance differential had widened and the German could run rings around the Wildcat. If the Me 109G-6 was tempted to mix it in a dogfight, the Wildcat had a better than even chance of success.

Verdict: The Wildcat was no real match for the Me 109G-6, but the German could not afford to take liberties with his angry little opponent.

Wildcat VI Versus Focke-Wulf 190A-4

The formidable Fw 190 held all the advantages in this contest, and there was really no way out of the dilemma for the Wildcat. Even in a turning circle it could not evade the German fighter for the first 120 degrees, and that was more than enough time for the powerful armament of the Fw 190 to take effect.

Verdict: The Wildcat had little chance of surviving single combat with the Fw 190. Its only hope lay in overwhelming the German by force of numbers.

Survival of the Redoubtable *Tirpitz*

Repeated attacks in April, May, and July by carrier aircraft had failed to annihilate the threat of the German battleship *Tirpitz*. A force of three fleet carriers and two escort carriers launched strikes on 22, 24, and 29 August, flying 242 sorties without even damaging the battleship, which used a smoke screen to protect itself. This condemned the Barracuda naval bomber for good, confirming that it was too slow to achieve surprise and incapable of carrying bombs large enough for effective attacks.

In the July strikes a new British two-seat reconnaissance fighter, the Fairey Firefly, made its operational debut. Although from the same stable as the ponderous Barracuda, the Firefly was a different aircraft altogether.

In attacks against the *Tirpitz* the Firefly's primary tasks were reconnaissance and strafing protective antiaircraft gun positions. No enemy fighters were encountered.

FAIREY FIREFLY F-1

The Firefly was a two-seat, low-wing monoplane bearing a superficial resemblance to its predecessor the Fulmar, but with more aesthetic lines. It was conceived at the outset as a multirole aircraft with hard-hitting fighter capabilities.

Although designed in 1939 it had several innovative features. The fuselage was built in halves joined along the vertical centerline. The engine was mounted as a quickly detachable "power egg." The most important feature was the flap arrangement. Youngman flaps could be extended on tracks, increasing wing area during cruising. This contributed to the aircraft's good maneuverability, and consequently, its self-defense capability.

The wings, elliptical in shape, had stressed-metal skin and could be manually folded. The elevators were metal covered, the rudder fabric covered. The tailwheel could be fully retracted. The deck arrester hook was located under the rear fuselage.

The aircraft was powered by a twelve-cylinder, V, liquid-cooled Rolls-Royce Griffon IIB of 1,735 hp. It drove a 13-ft, three-bladed, constant-speed, wooden Rotol propeller. Internal fuel capacity was 145.5 imperial gals (175 U.S.) in the main fuselage tank and 23 (27.6 U.S.) in each of two wing tanks. The Griffon IIB had a two-speed, single-stage supercharger and was started by percussion cartridge.

Fairey Firefly (Flight International)

On entering the cockpit, I was impressed by the neat and logical layout of the instruments and ancillary controls, and mildly surprised to find the view so reasonable, in spite of the long engine and pilot position a third of the way back on the wing chord.

Takeoff with a small increment of flap was short and acceleration was rapid, but a strong torque swing to starboard required a lot of counteracting rudder. After the flaps were raised, rate of climb at 135 knots (155 mph) was 2,000 ft/min. The aircraft had neutral stability that required constant retrimming with changes of power and speed.

When the Firefly was cruising at 217 knots (250 mph), stability was still neutral around all axes. In spite of moderately heavy control forces, maneuverability with the flaps set at cruise was impressive and the Firefly could outturn the agile Spitfire. In a steep turn, sudden reduction in elevator feel gave warning of an approaching stall, and if the pull force was not immediately reduced the Firefly would flick out of the turn. In diving, as speed built up, the aircraft became tail heavy and tended to yaw to port; the Firefly had to be trimmed into a dive to avoid high "g" in recovery.

The all-up stall was preceded by mild elevator buffeting some three or four knots before the nose and port wing dropped, quite sharply, at 90 knots (103.6 mph). The stall in the landing configuration gave more warning and occurred at 68 knots (78 mph) with quite a mild wing drop.

The Firefly handled well approaching the deck at 78 to 80 knots (90 to 92 mph), and the view was reasonable, but when throttle was cut the control column had to be pulled back to counteract a tendency for the heavy nose to drop. The landing gear was resilient enough to prevent bad bounce.

Armament was four 20-mm wing-mounted cannon with 160 rounds apiece, but no rear defense gun had been fitted. Eight 60-lb rockets or two 1,000-lb bombs could be carried.

The Firefly had a top speed of 277 knots (319 mph) at 17,000 ft and a service ceiling of 29,000 ft. It had a range of 672 nm (774 statute miles) on internal fuel, and a maximum range of 1,184 nm (1,364 statute miles).

Assessment: The Firefly was a useful escort fighter because of its long range, heavy armament, and good maneuverability. Lack of defensive armament counted against it, but versatility in the ground-attack mode was to prove a strong asset. As a shipborne airplane it had pleasant handling characteristics for deck landing.

Firefly 1 Versus Messerschmitt 109G

The Gustav outclassed the Firefly in performance and therefore had the initiative, but once battle was joined the Firefly could give a good account of itself.

Verdict: The Firefly would be no match for the German fighter unless the latter were lured into mixing it, when the Firefly's turning circle and powerful armament could prove a lethal combination.

Firefly 1 Versus Focke-Wulf 190A-4

The marked superiority of the Fw 190A-4 in virtually every department would give the Firefly no chance of success. The latter could exploit its turning agility to the full, but even that would only delay the inevitable.

Verdict: The Firefly would not be an easy prey for the Fw 190A-4, but neither would it be difficult—it had no sure escape route.

The Battle of Leyte Gulf

The Leyte campaign opened on 10 October when American fast carriers of Task Force 38 struck Okinawa and the smaller islands in the Ryukyu group, destroying about a hundred enemy aircraft in exchange for twenty-one carrier planes. On 11 October the task force turned west toward Formosa to further neutralize airfields between Japan and the Philippines. There were over three hundred aircraft on Formosa, a third navy fighters of the Second Air Fleet, two-thirds army planes, half of them fighters.

The Americans struck at dawn on 12 October. A huge air battle ensued in which about one hundred Japanese aircraft were destroyed for the loss of forty-eight carrier planes. Thereafter 101 sorties were flown against the U.S. carriers. Some forty Japanese raiders were shot down without any damage being inflicted on the ships.

At this stage most of the inexperienced Japanese air groups assigned to Carrier Divisions 3 and 4 were sent to Formosa as reinforcements. One hundred fifty-four aircraft were committed to combat, which was to prove a costly error.

American strikes on 13 October met little opposition, but toward evening Betty torpedo-bombers that had returned to harass the U.S. force succeeded in torpedoing the heavy cruiser *Canberra*. It was taken in tow.

On 14 October 246 carrier planes kept up the attacks on Formosa. The Japanese retaliated with 419 sorties and torpedoed the light cruiser *Houston*, which was also taken in tow. There were now two lame ducks in the force. They became a prime target for the enemy, who flew 199 sorties on 15 October without result. Two U.S. task groups set off for northern Luzon, while two remained to cover the cripples.

The Japanese continued their attacks on 16 October with sixty-two sorties. In spite of heavy losses, they managed to put a second torpedo in the *Houston*. Incredibly, the ship survived. Task Groups 38.2 and 38.3 then withdrew to the east, nursing the two damaged cruisers on the way to safety.

The carrier attack on Formosa was the most massive battle ever fought between land- and carrier-based aircraft. The results over the period from 10 to 16 October showed a staggering six hundred Japanese aircraft destroyed in the air and on the ground, compared with seventy-six American planes in combat and thirteen operationally.

Task Groups 38.1 and 38.4 attacked northern Luzon on 15 October, shooting down some twenty enemy aircraft. In the process the carrier *Franklin* received a bomb hit, but this caused only slight damage.

In the Philippines the Japanese navy's First Air Fleet had been so badly mauled by Task Force 38's strikes in September and October that its operational strength amounted to only thirty Zeke fighters and thirty Betty bombers, augmented by a few army aircraft. The situation for the Japanese was so critical that the concept of kamikaze attacks was initiated on 19 October. Kamikazes were to be employed against the fast carriers in a desperate bid to protect the Japanese battle fleet, which was on its way to counter the U.S. invasion.

On 23 October the reinforced Second Air Fleet of 450 aircraft moved from Formosa to Luzon. Next day it began bombing attacks against Task Group 38.3. One Judy dive-bomber hit the light carrier *Princeton* with two 500-lb bombs and mortally wounded her, but the attackers suffered heavy losses from American Hellcats. Commander David McCampbell shot down at least nine Japanese fighters during a single combat sortie. Eventually he would become the U.S. Navy's leading ace.

Last Phase of the Pacific War

Japan's high command, realizing that the Philippines would give the Allies a perfect base for the invasion of Japan itself, decided to play for high stakes in preventing a U.S. takeover of Leyte. The attack by the Second Air Fleet had been the first step. Now the Japanese wanted to lure the American fleet far to the north, engaging it in a secondary battle while they sent two columns of warships through the navigable straits north and south of Leyte to destroy the invasion armada of the Seventh Fleet.

The planes of three of the U.S. task groups had already sighted the Southern and Center Forces. Task Group 38.3 was engaged by the Second Air Fleet before it could strike at the Japanese warships, but 38.2 and 38.4 sent off 259 aircraft to attack the powerful Center

Force, which included the 74,000-ton *Musashi* and *Yamato*, the largest battleships ever built. The *Musashi* received nineteen torpedo hits and ten direct bomb hits before she finally sank, some four hours after the last attack. Eighteen carrier planes were lost in combat, twelve operationally, and twenty-six more when the *Princeton* sank.

The Southern Force was the next to come under attack. In the early hours of 25 October began the final battleship engagement in history. The enemy force sailed into a well-laid American trap of thirty-nine motor torpedo boats, a screen of destroyers, and a force of cruisers and battleships. In the morning surviving Japanese ships were further harassed by Avengers from the eighteen escort carriers of the invasion force.

The Northern Force, acting as a decoy in the enemy plan, included the fleet carrier *Zuikaku* and the three light carriers *Chitose*, *Chiyoda*, and *Zuiho*, but only 116 aircraft. These consisted of fifty-two Zeke fighters, twenty-eight Zeke dive-bombers, seven Judy dive-bombers, and twenty-five Jill and four Kate torpedo-bombers. On the morning of 24 October the carriers flew off an eighty-seven-plane strike against Task Group 38.3. It was thwarted by U.S. fighters and flew on to Luzon. The twenty-nine aircraft remaining on the Japanese carriers were inadequate for both defense and attack.

On the morning of 25 October Task Force 38's planes sighted the enemy carrier force and attacked with a force of sixty Hellcats, sixty-five Helldivers, and fifty-five Avengers. They achieved one direct bomb hit on the *Zuiho* and three on the *Chitose*, which had only a handful of fighters to defend them. The *Zuikaku* took one torpedo hit, and a destroyer was sunk. The *Chitose* sank two hours after she was bombed.

A second strike of thirty-six aircraft concentrated on the light carrier *Chiyoda,* causing severe damage. Then followed a huge strike of two hundred planes, which sent three torpedoes into the *Zuikaku*, causing her to capsize and sink. The *Zuiho* was again hit, and would later be finished off by the fourth strike of thirty-five aircraft. The fifth strike of ninety-six planes and the sixth of thirty-six inflicted little damage; many of the aircrew, participating in their third attack of the day, were physically and mentally exhausted. Admiral Halsey, commander of the Third Fleet, presumably came to that conclusion. He sent two heavy and two light cruisers and ten destroyers after the fleeing Japanese fleet. They sank the damaged light carrier *Chiyoda* with gunfire.

At the sacrifice of four carriers and three screening ships, the decoy Northern Force had successfully lured Task Force 38 away from Leyte Gulf and made it possible for the Center Force to turn back toward Samar, just north of the gulf. There it pounced on the unsuspecting U.S. escort carriers, sinking the *Gambier Bay* and damaging the *Kalinin Bay, Fanshaw Bay, Kitkun Bay,* and *White Plains.* Strafing Wildcats and torpedo-dropping Avengers of Carrier Divisions 25 and 26 put up a spirited defense, reinforced by Carrier Divisions 24 and 27.

The Kamikazes

Escort carriers of Carrier Divisions 22 and 28 became the first victims of Japan's new suicide tactics when kamikaze Zekes hit the *Santee* and the *Suwannee.* This attack was followed by another on Carrier Divisions 25 and 26, which sank the *St. Lo* and further damaged the *Kitkun Bay.* Then came fifteen Judy dive-bombers, which obtained further hits on the *Kitkun Bay* and *Kalinin Bay.*

On 26 October the kamikazes returned to harass Carrier Divisions 22 and 28. Carrier Wildcats shot down about a dozen Zekes and Judys but were unable to prevent a Zeke from badly damaging the *Suwannee.*

Thus ended the Battle of Leyte Gulf and the career of the Imperial Japanese Navy. A terrible new weapon had been born in the kamikaze, but it was a tool of desperation, and though it would take a heavy toll on the Allies, it was forged too late to change the outcome of the war.

The Philippines invasion still required carrier air support, because captured shore airstrips were not able to handle army aircraft. Task Force 38 returned from its encounter with the Northern Force to bolster the escort carriers, which were running short of aircraft and weapons. Now it was the fast carriers' turn to face the dreaded kamikazes. On 29 October the *Independence* was hit, and on 30 October the *Franklin* and the *Belleau Wood.*

These attacks forced the U.S. carriers to mount larger combat air patrols, thereby reducing the strength of their bomber escorts, but such was the excellence of the Hellcats that their air superiority went undisputed. In spite of the tight fighter ring around Task Force 38, a kamikaze Zeke struck the flagship *Lexington* on 6 November.

Task Force 38's aircraft continued to ravage shipping supporting beleaguered Japanese troops in the Philippines. Antiaircraft fire accounted for most of the American losses. On 25 November a large Japanese strike caught Task Force 38 with only seven carriers on station. Kamikazes hit the *Intrepid, Cabot,* and *Essex,* and lightly damaged the *Hancock.*

It is a measure of the huge effort of Task Force 38 in the Philippines campaign that in November alone its planes destroyed 875 Japanese aircraft and sank almost forty ships, thus preventing rein-

Zero Kamikaze Attack on the USS St. Lo (UPI)

forcement of the Leyte garrison. American losses, by contrast, totaled ninety-seven aircraft in combat. Five carriers had been damaged.

Japanese sources claim that in the Philippines campaign 447 aircraft left on kamikaze missions, of which 201 completed their attacks and 179 returned to base; 74 percent of the aircraft involved were Zekes, which completed 79 percent of the attacks.

New air defense tactics were devised early in December 1944 to counter the kamikaze threat, and these required a change in U.S. carrier air group composition. Fighter strength was increased to seventy-three, bomber strength reduced to fifteen dive- and fifteen torpedo-bombers. Thus in three years there had been a 400 percent increase in the carrier fighter complement.

Revised tactics called for blanket fighter cover of Japanese airfields when carriers were within range of enemy land-based aircraft. An increased combat air patrol would be kept over the carriers. These duties would be assigned to the latest Hellcat F6F-5 and -5N nightfighters, whose ground-attack capability made the reduction in bomber strength acceptable.

Task Force 38 had withdrawn to an anchorage at Ulithi atoll in the Carolines at the end of November to replenish and regroup into three task groups totalling thirteen fast carriers. These put to sea on 11 December, heading for Luzon to support General MacArthur's drive north for Manila.

The fighter sweeps over Luzon started on 14 December and continued for three days, producing a tally of 269 Japanese aircraft destroyed in exchange for 27 planes in combat and 38 operationally. The task force then pulled off 500 miles to the east to refuel and was hit by a typhoon on 18 December. This did more damage than the enemy had managed to achieve in three days of operations over Luzon. The task force lost 146 aircraft to the storm as well as two destroyers and some eight hundred men.

Task Force 38 withdrew to Ulithi to recuperate. There the carrier *Essex*, whose squadron of Helldivers was off to Guam, embarked thirty-six F4U-1D marine Corsairs, giving her a total of ninety fighters and fifteen torpedo-bombers. This first marine carrier assignment got off to a bad start. Thirteen Corsairs and seven of their pilots were lost in accidents over the course of nine days.

The powerful carrier fleet put to sea again on 30 December, heading for Formosa and the Ryukyus. It now had full control of the seas, with a force of aircraft that could take control of the skies for hundreds of miles and deliver hammer blows to ground targets within that compass. And so by the end of 1944 U.S. carrier aviation had mastered its operational role and possessed confidence that augured well for the ultimate outcome of the Pacific war.

Hellcat F6F-5

The Hellcat F6F-5 introduced aileron servo tabs, provision for two 20-mm cannon to replace two of the 0.5-in machine guns, a closerfitting engine cowling to reduce drag, an increase of 242 lbs in the weight of protection, elimination of the laminated plate-glass windscreen, incorporation of the flat, bullet-resistant panel as an integral part of the windscreen, and built-in provision for underwing bomb or rocket loads. The F6F-5 Hellcat could carry three 1,000-lb bombs and six 5-in rockets.

Maximum speed was 330 knots (380 mph) at 23,400 ft and 286.5 knots (331 mph) at sea level. Initial rate of climb was 3,410 ft/min, normal range, 903 nm (1,040 statute miles), or 1,328 nm (1,530 statute miles) when the aircraft carried a drop tank of 125 imperial gals (150 U.S.). Service ceiling was 37,300 ft.

The F6F-5N Hellcat had AN/APS.6 radar in a radome on the starboard wing, which reduced its maximum speed to 318 knots (366 mph).

Too Little Too Late

It is worthwhile to reflect on Japanese naval aircraft development at this stage of the war. Reliance on the Zeke had been virtually total for five years, but now the fighter was outclassed and incapable of further improvement in performance. Naval bombers were not faring much better, with the Jill and Judy now easy prey for potent American fighters.

Because of their early carrier successes in the Pacific the Japanese had not felt any urgency to further develop shipboard aircraft. When the tide of war started to turn they made an effort to catch up, and though this came too late, it had produced two interesting projects by 1944, the Sam fighter and the Grace bomber.

Mitsubishi A7M Sam

The Sam was to have replaced the Zeke. The design for this single-seat, low-wing shipboard fighter was begun in 1942 under the direction of Jiro Horikoshi, who had been responsible for its formidable predecessor. The first flight took place on 6 May 1944. The prototype is reported to have displayed excellent stability and control characteristics, but, with the 1,790-hp Nakajima Homare, an eighteen-cylinder radial engine, it was underpowered. The maximum speed was 343 knots (395 mph), and the maximum range with drop tanks was 1,250 nm (1,440 statute miles). Armament consisted of two 20-mm cannon and two 13-mm machine guns.

The sixth prototype received a new engine, the upgraded 2,200-hp Homare, and was redesignated the A7M2. It flew on 13 October 1944, performing significantly better than the F6F-5 Hellcat. Another six prototype A7M2s and one production model were built before the Mitsubishi factory at Nagoya was rocked by an earthquake early in December 1944. Destruction of the plant was completed in a bombing raid conducted by Superfortresses on 18 December.

Aichi B7A1 Grace 11

The B7A, the largest carrier-based aircraft produced by the Japanese, was a two-seat, low-mid-, inverted-gull-wing attack bomber of all-metal

Aichi B7A1 Grace (Pilot Press)

structure. It had flush-riveted, stressed-metal skin, and all control surfaces were fabric covered. The outer portion of the wings folded up for carrier stowage. The crew sat in tandem under a continuous, transparent canopy. Landing gear, including the tailwheel, was fully retractable.

Power was supplied by a 1,800-hp, fourteen-cylinder radial engine, a Nakajima Mamoru. It drove a four-blade, hydraulic, constant-speed, Hamilton-type airscrew. Tanks in the wings contained all the fuel.

The aircraft, first flown in May 1942, was reported to have good stability but to be heavy on the controls. It had a top speed of 304 knots (350 mph) and a range of 1,042 nm (1,200 statute miles).

Armament was two 7.7-mm machine guns in the fuselage cowling and one 7.7-mm gun operated by the rear gunner. The Grace could carry a 1,760-lb torpedo or a bomb load of equivalent weight, but the latter was limited to 1,100 lbs if the aircraft was dive-bombing.

Only 117 Grace aircraft were built before the war ended. There was no carrier to take them, for, in addition to those lost in the Marianas and Leyte Gulf battles, the giant new 68,059-ton carrier *Shinano* was sunk on 30 November, the *Junyo* was put out of action on 9 December, and the new *Unryu* sank on 19 December, all losses caused by U.S. submarines. Thus eight major Japanese carriers were lost in the second half of 1944. In the same period the Japanese lost three escort carriers to submarine attack.

Assessment: The Grace's performance would have given her a better chance of survival as a dive-bomber against the American fighters. Size would have made her particularly vulnerable in a torpedo attack. In the latter role, she was still a worthwhile advance over her predecessor, the Jill.

Royal Navy Buildup in the Far East

For part of June HMS *Illustrious* was the only fleet carrier in the Indian Ocean. On 22 June her Barracudas and Corsairs struck the Andaman islands, producing disappointing results. When she changed her complement to forty-two Corsairs and was joined by HMS *Victorious*, carrying twenty-one Barracudas and twenty-eight Corsairs, an effective strike was launched against Sabang's oil tanks.

After this sortie, the *Illustrious* left the Eastern Fleet for a refitting and was temporarily replaced by the *Indomitable*, carrying Barracudas and Hellcats. A two-carrier strike was mounted at the end of August against Sumatra, the main target being the biggest cement works in Southeast Asia, at Indaroeng. They were badly damaged. A similar effort against the Sigli rail center on Sumatra was less successful and again highlighted the shortcomings of the Barracuda.

The Eastern Fleet's next task was to carry out an operation designed to divert Japanese attention from the American invasion assault on the Philippines. From 17 to 19 October the *Victorious* attacked airfields on the Nicobar islands while the *Indomitable* went for Nancowry Harbor. Japanese army Oscars provided air defense in the Nicobars. As if realizing that these were to be their last strikes in the Far East, the Barracudas obtained excellent results, losing only one aircraft to flak. In defense of the carriers, seven Oscars were shot down at a cost of two Corsairs and a Hellcat.

Between October and December the Eastern Fleet was strengthened by the return of the *Illustrious* and the arrival of the *Indefatigable*. Its four armored-deck fleet carriers could now deploy more than two hundred aircraft: fifty-six Corsair IIs, twenty-eight Hellcat IIs, eighty-four Avengers, thirty-two Seafire IIIs, and twelve Firefly Is.

The status of the Eastern Fleet underwent a crucial change in November when it became the British Pacific Fleet. The first task for the newly constituted fleet was a series of raids on sources of enemy oil. For their supplies of aviation fuel the Japanese relied heavily on Sumatran oilfields. These had an annual production capacity of three million tons of crude oil, and nearby refineries supplied three-quarters of Japan's total requirement of aviation fuel. American attacks had depleted the number of tankers carrying oil to Japan, but the sources of production remained relatively intact.

When the British Pacific Fleet launched its first strike on 20 December against the refinery at Pangkalan Brandan, it was thwarted

Nakajima Ki 43 Oscar

by bad weather. The strike aircraft turned their attention to the alternative target, the tanker port of Belawan Deli. Though opposition proved minimal, damage was limited.

This was a disappointing start to the new fleet's operations. At least it had posted notice before the end of 1944 that it was in business.

THE NAKAJIMA KI 43-2 OSCAR 12

The Oscar, a single-seat fighter, was remarkably similar in appearance to the navy Zeke and was almost identical in performance to the Zeke 22. It was powered by a Nakajima type 2, a fourteen-cylinder radial engine of 1,150 hp, but its armament was only two 12.7-mm machine guns in the fuselage. These were synchronized to fire through the airscrew.

Carriers to Russia Again

After the escort carrier *Avenger*'s effective protection of Russian-bound convoy PQ 18 in September 1942, the Germans changed their tactics against the Russian convoys. Heavy losses caused them to reduce the weight of aircraft attack and rely more on U-boats, and so protection devolved on convoy escort vessels.

It was not until February and March 1944 that another escort carrier was again used for protection of a Russian convoy. HMS *Chaser*, with eleven Swordfish IIs and eleven Wildcat Vs, had incredible success on the return trip, sinking three U-boats and damaging two others. Then in March and April the escort carrier *Activity*, with a similar complement of aircraft, and the *Tracker*, carrying fifteen Avengers and seven Wildcat Vs, sank two U-boats and damaged three others. They also shot down six enemy shadowers of assorted types.

The next convoy was escorted by the *Activity* and the *Fencer*, the latter carrying eleven Swordfish and nine Wildcats. This team sank three U-boats on successive days.

At this point in time the most monumental land battle in history was taking place in Europe, and in the Far East some of the biggest naval battles had already been fought. The United States was heavily involved in the European theater; and Great Britain was now seeking to lend a hand in the Far East. By the end of 1944 the military might of the Allies was crushing the enemy on all fronts.

7

1945

Climax

WITH THE ADVENT OF 1945 the Allies were applying unrelenting pressure on their enemies. The emphasis of carrier operations had now moved almost completely into the Pacific. In the Atlantic, after ceaseless action against German U-boats, the Allies had gradually gained the upperhand, and by September 1944 it was considered unnecessary for escort carriers to be further employed there. Convoy protection was now assigned solely to the MACs. To protect the Russian convoys, British escort carriers were still striking at enemy shipping off the Norwegian coast and at shore targets in Norway.

Task Force 38

U.S. Task Force 38 launched its first strikes of 1945 on 3 and 4 January against Formosa, destroying an estimated 111 Japanese aircraft in exchange for twenty-two of its own, mostly operational losses.

On 5 January the carrier *Enterprise* joined the fast carriers with an air group consisting of radar-equipped aircraft for night operations—sixteen F6F-5N Hellcats, two F6F-5P Hellcats, and twenty-seven TBM-3D Avengers. She and the other night carrier *Independence* formed Task Group 38.5.

The idea of a special night carrier was first tried out when the *Independence* joined Task Force 38 in August 1944. By January 1945 her air group had twenty-seven night kills to its credit. Task Group 38.5 operated as the first independent night-carrier group, but the two carriers joined up with 38.2 in the daytime to provide added defense.

The strikes on Formosa were made in support of the Allied landings at Lingayen Gulf, to be carried out by the Seventh Fleet

172

assault force of eighteen escort carriers plus the antisubmarine escort carrier *Tulagi*. Kamikazes attacked this force on 4 January, sinking the escort carrier *Ommaney Bay*, and on 5 January, damaging the escort carrier *Manila Bay*. Further attacks on 8 January damaged the *Kadashan Bay* and the *Kitkun Bay*, despite spirited efforts on the part of the Wildcat combat air patrol, which shot down four wouldbe kamikazes. The American invasion force landed on 9 January.

Meanwhile Task Force 38 had returned to strike Luzon on 6 and 7 January. Though the attacks were hampered by bad weather, the strike force managed to destroy 111 Japanese aircraft in the air and on the ground for the loss of forty-five planes, in combat and operationally. The task force then headed back toward Formosa for another series of strikes. These proved more productive against local shipping than against enemy aircraft, which were relatively scarce.

The U.S. Third Fleet entered the South China Sea with 101 ships in the darkness of 9 January. There were thirteen fast carriers in Task Force 38 and two escort carriers protecting the replenishment group. The fleet's main objective was to destroy the Japanese battleship carriers *Hyuga* and *Ise*. These were battleships which, after two 14-in-gun turrets had been removed, were fitted with a flight deck and a hangar on the quarterdeck. Two revolving catapults were positioned forward of the flight deck. The aircraft complement was to be twenty-two Judy bombers, but these were in such short supply that the ships never embarked any planes. These hybrids were still a great menace with their eight 14-inch guns.

On a night passage through the Balintang Channel three Japanese planes were shot down by night-fighters from the *Independence*. After two more days of passage Task Force 38 launched 1,457 sorties. These failed to find the battleship carriers but succeeded in sinking forty-six enemy ships, shooting down fourteen aircraft, and destroying about a hundred more on the ground. American losses amounted to twenty-three carrier planes.

The task force turned north and hit Formosa again on 15 January, destroying thirty-four Japanese planes for twelve of their own. On 16 January the force moved along China's coast and attacked Hong Kong, where fierce antiaircraft fire cost it dear. Thirteen Japanese aircraft were destroyed, forty-nine U.S. carrier aircraft. Finally on 20 January the task force exited the South China Sea, shooting down fifteen Japanese planes on the way.

After its successful foray into the enemy's "own sea," Task Force 38 headed toward Formosa again and flew off a strike early on 21 January. Opposition in the air being minimal and sharply dealt with, the American aircraft destroyed 104 Japanese planes on the ground and sank ten ships. About midday kamikazes swept in like avenging demons on the carriers *Langley* and *Ticonderoga*, whose wooden flight decks proved vulnerable to attack. A third carrier, the *Hancock*, became victim of a 500-lb bomb released by one of its own Avengers while the plane was on the flight deck.

On the night of 22 January six Avengers struck a harbor in Formosa and achieved blind bomb hits, but three of the raiders were lost. Meanwhile, during a daytime strike launched against Okinawa to get photographs for the coming invasion, some twenty-eight Japanese planes were destroyed on the ground.

With all Japanese air power in the Philippines effectively destroyed, Task Force 38 returned to Ulithi for rest and replenishment. While there, it underwent a change of command and became Task Force 58 again.

Allied Action in the Indian Ocean

On 4 January, in another strike against the Pangkalan Brandan refinery, the British Pacific Fleet introduced a European tactic known as ramrod. This was an offensive sweep of fighters over specific ground targets, the object being to suppress flak and fighter opposition. An air coordinator supervised the operation in the air, where he remained for the duration, exercising control of the various components of the strike and taking photographs to render a more detailed damage assessment and briefing.

In this strike sixteen Hellcats and Corsairs of the fighter ramrods went after four airfields in the target area. The main strike force of thirty-two Avengers and twelve Fireflies extensively damaged the refinery. The escort, thirty-two Corsairs and Hellcats, shot down five Japanese Oscars. There were no Allied combat losses.

The main refineries on Sumatra were at Palembang, on the southern end of the island, and these were attacked on 24 January by 134 aircraft. Forty Seafires remained to protect the fleet. The attack was very successful, accounting for six Nicks, four Oscars, and a Tojo, as well as thirty-four aircraft on the ground. Allied losses totaled two Avengers, six Corsairs, and a Hellcat. The strike managed to reduce the output of the Pladjoe refinery by half.

The Palembang raid—part of Operation Meridian—had only been directed against one of the two refineries in the area, that at Pladjoe. The decision was therefore made to mount another strike against the second refinery at Soengei Gerong. This one, made on 29 January, consisted of forty-eight Avengers, fifty escort fighters, twenty ramrod Corsairs, two Fireflies for armed reconnaissance, and two PR Hellcats. Again strong Japanese fighter opposition was encountered, and seventeen Avengers, eight Corsairs, a Hellcat, and a Firefly were lost in combat or ditched because of combat damage. Another fourteen were lost in deck-landing crashes. Japanese fighter losses amounted to five Nicks, five Oscars, three Tojos, and a Zeke 32. The refinery was heavily damaged.

The two Fireflies had a remarkable combat initiation. That flown by the air coordinator shot down an Oscar and a Tojo, while the other shot down an Oscar that had already delivered a mortal blow to the Firefly.

The two Operation Meridian strikes were the largest carried out by the Fleet Air Arm during the entire war, and their losses were higher than those of U.S. Navy attacks on Japanese land targets. The explanation for this clearly lies in the low ratio of escort fighters to bombers employed by the British, whose policy it was to use bombers rather than fighter-bombers.

Shortly after the return of the second strike the fleet was attacked by seven Sally bombers acting as kamikazes. Although slower and fitted with self-sealing fuel tanks, the Mitsubishi Ki 213 Sally 3 was in effect a slightly smaller version of the navy Betty. The Seafire combat air patrol over the fleet pounced on the kamikazes, successfully disposing of all seven attackers for the loss of one Seafire, whose pilot was saved. After this eventful day, the British Pacific Fleet headed for Australia to join the Americans.

Nakajima Ki 44 Tojo 2

This army single-seat interceptor was the smallest Japanese fighter, its low-wing having a span of only 31 ft. It was an all-metal structure, and controls were fabric covered. The pilot's cockpit, set over the trailing edge of the wing, had a blister-type canopy that gave an excellent view in the air. The landing gear could be fully retracted.

The Tojo was powered by a 1,500-hp, fourteen-cylinder radial engine, a Nakajima type 2 with a two-speed supercharger. It drove a three-blade, Hamilton-type, constant-speed airscrew. Fuel was contained in the wings and fuselage.

The aircraft had a high initial rate of climb at 3,940 ft/min and was reported to be marginally stable longitudinally and laterally, and stable directionally, although it had no rudder trim tab. The aircraft had to be constantly retrimmed with changes of speed and power.

Apparently the Tojo had a higher rate of roll than the Zeke but was not quite so maneuverable—hardly a grave shortcoming, considering that the Zeke was one of the most agile monoplane fighters ever built.

Maximum speed was 383 mph at 17,000 ft. Service ceiling was 36,000 ft, range 575 miles or 775 miles with drop tanks. A total of 1,233 Tojos was built.

Armament consisted of two 7.7-mm machine guns in the fuse-

Kawasaki 45 Nick (Peter Bowers's Collection)

lage, synchronized to fire through the airscrew, and two 20-mm wing cannon. It was only lightly armored in the cockpit.

Assessment: The Tojo was a match for both the Hellcat and the Corsair except in firepower and acceleration in a dive. Its size made it a difficult target, and with the advantage of normally operating at short range in a defensive role, it was unencumbered. Still, the aircraft lacked adequate armor protection.

KAWASAKI 45 NICK 2

This design, started in 1937, was Japan's first long-range, twin-engine escort fighter, conceived in the style of the Me 110. It was a midwing monoplane with an oval-section fuselage of all-metal, semimonocoque structure. The skin covering was flush riveted and stressed. Wings were also of all-metal structure, and controls were fabric covered. The main landing gear was fully retractable, the tailwheel semiretractable. The pilot's cockpit was over the leading edge of the wings, the rear gunner over the trailing edge.

The engines were 1,050-hp, fourteen-cylinder, two-row radial Mitsubishi type 1s. They had two-speed superchargers and drove three-blade, constant-speed, Hamilton-type airscrews. Fuel tanks were in the wings.

The Nick had an initial rate of climb of 2,400 ft/min and exhibited good stability and control characteristics, although it was somewhat heavy on the ailerons.

Its top speed was 355 mph at 16,400 ft. Service ceiling was 35,000 ft. At normal range the Nick flew 640 miles, but this could be increased to 1,300 miles with drop tanks. A total of 1,700 Nick 2s were built.

Armament could be varied considerably, depending on the role of the aircraft, but the daylight fighter version normally carried two

12.7-mm machine guns and a 20-mm cannon in the nose of the fuselage, and two 7.7-mm machine guns on a flexible mounting in the rear cockpit.

Assessment: The Nick's design was a fine effort. Although the Japanese lagged behind the West in technology, they produced an aircraft that was slightly superior to the Me 110 in performance, if not in firepower or ability to absorb punishment. Inevitably, it was outdated by 1945, but it could still give a good account of itself against anything except the high-performance Allied fighters.

Hellcat II Versus Tojo 2

This would be a classic contest whose outcome was determined by pilot skill—if the Hellcat did not use the right hit-and-run tactics and became embroiled in a dogfight. The Hellcat was better able to survive hits from the enemy, who was himself ill protected.

Verdict: This was a near-even contest, but favored the Hellcat if that aircraft performed correctly.

Corsair II Versus Tojo 2

This should be similar to the Hellcat-Tojo encounter, except that the Corsair would be at more of a disadvantage mixing it with the Tojo. Again the Allied fighter was endowed with superior firepower and protection.

Verdict: Not much favored either aircraft except a choice of tactics, and that choice rested largely with the Corsair.

Firefly I Versus Tojo 2

The Firefly was outclassed in speed but by using its maneuver flaps could outturn the Tojo. It also had powerful forward armament to bring to bear. However, if the Tojo elected to maneuver in the vertical plane the Firefly was vulnerable, particularly because it lacked rear defense armament.

Verdict: The Firefly had little hope of success in such a combat. The initiative would lie with the Tojo, which was unlikely to give the Firefly a sighting chance.

TBF Avenger Versus Tojo 2

The bomber would present a large, slow target for the agile Tojo, which would have to be wary of its opponent's rear defense armament. With a considerable speed advantage the Tojo would be able to attack the forward quarter of the bomber and so minimize the chance of being hit by its turret or tunnel armament.

Hellcat II Versus Nick 2

The Hellcat did not have a large speed advantage over the twin Nick, but the margin, combined with superior climb and maneuverability, was sufficient to give it the initiative in every phase of combat. The Hellcat would have to execute its attack skillfully, keeping out of the fields of fire of the Nick's forward and rear armament. The Hellcat's optimum approach would be diving from the forward quarter to get at the unprotected fuel tanks, then breaking away under the Nick.

Verdict: The Hellcat should never really be ousted by the Nick, unless its pilot got overconfident and made a careless attack, exposing himself to the enemy's rear gunner.

Corsair II Versus Nick 2

This situation should be similar to the Hellcat-Nick encounter, but with the Corsair having a slightly better speed advantage and more of a maneuver disadvantage.

Verdict: The Corsair would have as much success as the Hellcat against the Nick, provided it used the same tactic for the attack.

Firefly I Versus Nick 2

The Firefly, outperformed by the Nick, could not hold the initiative in an attack, but once combat was engaged it could outmaneuver the Japanese fighter and bring its powerful forward armament to bear. The Nick's best chance of success against the undefended rear of the Firefly would be a hit-and-run attack.

Verdict: The Firefly would only have a chance of success if the Nick could be lured into a dogfight, and the Nick would probably not get a kill from anything but a well-judged hit-and-run attack. This combat situation was really a well-balanced stalemate.

TBF Avenger Versus Nick 2

The Avenger's best chance of survival would be to keep at low altitude, forcing the Japanese fighter to come in from above, and then to bring its turret guns to bear against the attacker. The Nick would be lethal, however, if it made a frontal attack against the bomber.

Verdict: The Avenger's prospects of survival against the Japanese twin fighter would not be high, and its chances of a kill would be low.

Seafire III Versus Sally 3

The Seafire was one of the most agile high-performance naval fighters ever built. With a speed advantage of 100 mph over the Japanese bomber, it had full initiative. Because the Sally was well armed defensively, though only with small-caliber machine guns, the Seafire would be wise to come in on the weakest defended arc, which was head-on.

Verdict: The Sally stood little chance against the spritely Seafire, which was a small, well-armed target.

Escort Carriers in the Indian Ocean

When the British Pacific Fleet was formed the remainder of the Eastern Fleet became the East Indies Fleet. It continued to operate in the Indian Ocean and Bay of Bengal from its base at Trincomalee. Its seventy ships, which included seven British escort carriers, were to give close support to the Fourteenth Army in Burma, to sever Japanese supply lines to that area and garrisons in outlying islands, and to attack shipping, harbors, and oil targets.

On 21 January the fleet began to bombard Ramree Island, off the Arakan coast of Burma, in preparation for its invasion. Hellcats from HMS *Ameer* provided cover for the landings on Ramree and adjacent Cheduba Island on 26 January.

The fleet also had the task of undertaking aerial reconnaissance before the invasion of Malaya and the reoccupation of Singapore. The main photo target was Phuket Island, which commanded the northern mouth of the Malacca Strait and was envisioned as a base for assault on Singapore.

PR Hellcats from HMS *Empress* overflew their targets above 30,000 ft from 26 to 28 February. They had fighter cover from the *Ameer*. On 29 February enemy aircraft attacked the fleet. Hellcats from the two escort carriers shot down two Oscars and a twin-engine Dinah.

Mitsubishi Ki 46 Dinah 3A

The Dinah, a low-wing, multipurpose aircraft carrying three crew members, was the Japanese army's outstanding aircraft. A total of 1,738 were built. The model 3A was powered by two 1,500-hp Mitsubishi type-2 radial engines driving three-bladed, controllable-pitch airscrews. It had a maximum speed of 395 mph at 20,000 ft, a service ceiling of 36,300 ft, and a range of 1,800 miles. Armament consisted of two 20-mm nose cannon and a 7.7-mm rear gun on a flexible mounting.

Hellcat II Versus Dinah 3A

The Dinah, a fine, high-performance aircraft with a significant speed advantage over the Hellcat, would have to be caught at a tactical disadvantage if the Allied fighter were to have a chance to close for combat. The Hellcat could not afford to attack in the forward sector—with its speed disadvantage it would have little chance of a

Japanese Ki 46 Dinah 2 Captured by U.S. Forces (National Archives)

second attack, and in any case the Dinah had useful forward arma-ment. Therefore an attack from the quarter, drawing around to the rear, was advisable, as this would give the longest firing time and only bring the Hellcat under fire from a single, defensive rear gun.

Verdict: The Hellcat would not find the Dinah an easy kill, unless it caught the Japanese aircraft unawares or had a height advantage. Once engagement occurred, the Hellcat had a high probability of success.

Attack on the Japanese Homeland

The 116 warships that made up Task Force 58 left Ulithi on 10 February to take part in Operation Detachment, the invasion of Iwo Jima, a small island about halfway between Saipan and Tokyo and thus of immense strategic importance. But Task Force 58's first goal was to attack Japan itself.

On 16 February strikes involving over a thousand aircraft were launched against industrial plants in the Tokyo area. Poor weather hampered the effort, but a full-blooded fighter battle developed over Tokyo Bay when the carrier planes encountered about a hundred enemy fighters, forty of which were shot down. The next day another strike of about six hundred carrier aircraft attacked industrial plants, but weather conditions put an end to the day's activity. Task Force 58 turned toward Iwo Jima.

Claims of aircraft destroyed appear to have been wildly exagger-ated by both sides after these raids. The carriers lost 60 aircraft in combat and 28 operationally, while the Japanese appear to have lost 77 fighters in combat and an indeterminate number on the ground (the American claim was 190 of the latter).

One thing both sides agree on was the remarkably courageous and aggressive performance of navy Flight Warrant Officer Kinsuke Muto, one of Japan's top fighter aces. Flying one of the new George 12s over Yokohama on 16 February, he got into a major skirmish with twelve Hellcats, which had been mixing it with a formation of Zekes. The Hellcats had already accounted for ten of the Japanese fighters when they turned their attention to Muto, who accepted the challenge and shot down four Hellcats before the others had to break off the combat, having expended their ammunition. This illustrates perfectly the truth that experience backed by aggressive skill can be the decisive factor between fighters almost equally matched in other respects. In fact, Muto was combat-testing the George 12 and deliberately seeking a challenge, though certainly not with odds of twelve to one. His aircraft, an improved version of the George 11, was the fighter on which the Japanese navy was pinning its hopes for a last-stand defense of the homeland. It was land based, not intended for shipboard use.

Another example of the success that comes of pilot skill occurred on 17 February when the Japanese navy's senior fighter ace, Sublieutenant Sadanori Akamatsu, shot down two pairs of Hellcats on two successive sorties in his Zeke 52.

The U.S. assault force of more than a thousand ships included twelve escort carriers. Task Force 58 would support the landings on 19 February. On 21 February the *Saratoga*, carrying a mixed day/night air group, became the target of determined kamikazes. She was badly damaged and lost forty-two aircraft as a result of the action. That evening the kamikazes unleashed their fury against the escort carrier *Bismarck Sea*, which sank, taking with her thirty-six aircraft.

The fight for the small island of Iwo Jima was one of the bloodiest battles of the war, costing the Americans 5,200 men (15,800 wounded) and the Japanese 22,322. On 6 March U.S. Army Air Force fighters flew in from Saipan. The island was declared secure on 16 March.

The 70-mile-long island of Okinawa, lying midway between Formosa and Japan, would be a strategic staging point for the eventual invasion of the enemy homeland. The assault on Okinawa required an armada of well over a thousand ships, spearheaded by Task Force 58, which had returned to Ulithi on 4 March to prepare for Operation Iceberg. A twin-engine Francis bomber made a kamikaze attack on the carrier *Randolph*, at anchor in the lagoon, and put her out of action, thus reducing the fast carriers to fifteen.

Task Force 58 departed Ulithi on 14 March to strike the Japanese home islands, its mission the suppression of kamikaze operations against the invasion force. On 18 March Kyushu was attacked with little result. The Japanese counterattack was equally ineffective: only one bomb, dropped by a Judy, hit the *Yorktown*.

Next day the task force concentrated its attacks against ships spotted the previous day. Single bomb hits were obtained on the battleship *Yamato*, the battleship carriers *Hyuga* and *Ise*, and the carriers *Amagi* and *Katsuragi*, while four hits were made on the light carrier *Ryuho*. The Japanese retaliated with a bomb hit on the carrier *Wasp* and two bomb hits on the *Franklin*, which put her out of action.

On 18 and 19 March U.S. planes attacked the naval base at Kure and ran into an unexpected fury of opposition from Japan's most powerful fighter unit, based at Matsuyama on the island of Shikoku. The 343rd Air Corps was manned by the Imperial Navy's most experienced fighter pilots and was equipped with George 12 interceptors. The corps appears to have severely mauled the marauding carrier aircraft that came within its orbit, though the overall tally again seems blurred by exaggeration. The Americans claimed to have destroyed 482 enemy aircraft in the air and on the ground, while the Japanese claimed 119 victories.

It is interesting to reflect that at the same time in Europe, the Luftwaffe formed an elite squadron of their best surviving fighter pilots. These would fly the formidable Me 262 in a last-ditch effort to save the crumbling Third Reich.

On 20 March the withdrawing Task Force 58 was again attacked, and the *Enterprise* suffered damage. Along with the previously damaged *Wasp*, and *Randolph*, she returned to Ulithi, and the thirteen remaining fast carriers were formed into three task groups. These headed for Okinawa to support the assault armada, which included eighteen escort carriers, and an additional four loaded with marine fighters to be based on Okinawa, two protecting the Fifth Fleet's logistic group, and four with replacement aircraft for Task Force 58.

The task force started launching preinvasion strikes against Okinawa on 23 March, the day the British Pacific Fleet, whose battle force was now designated Task Force 57, sailed from Ulithi to join Operation Iceberg. The British force was under the overall command of the commander in chief of the Pacific Fleet, and its four carriers had on board over two hundred aircraft—twenty-nine Hellcat IIs, seventy-three Corsair IIs, forty Seafire IIIs, nine Firefly Is, and sixty-five Avengers. The Seafires were to be used for combat air patrol only.

On 26 and 27 March Task Force 57 launched strikes against airfields on islands southwest of Okinawa to prevent the enemy from sending air reinforcements to the scene of the main assault. Three Avengers and two Corsairs were lost to flak, twelve aircraft, mostly

Sinking of the Japanese Battleship Yamato, *17 April 1945 (U.S. Navy)*

Seafires, to deck-landing accidents. This pattern was repeated on 31 March when two Avengers were lost to flak.

On 1 April the assault marines landed on Okinawa. That day Task Force 57 was subjected to a group kamikaze attack during which a Zeke exploded on the armored flight deck of the *Indefatigable*. Three Zekes and an Oscar fell to the Seafire combat air patrol. Strikes against the airfields resulted in the loss of a Corsair and another crop of Seafire deck-landing accidents. On 2 April fighter sweeps were carried out against the enemy, with considerable success.

Task Force 58 had been strengthened by the return of the carriers *Enterprise* and *Randolph* when a full onslaught hit the Okinawa area—355 suicide planes and another 341 on conventional attack missions. On 6 April the kamikazes crashed into nineteen U.S. ships, six of which sank. Combat air patrols from the fast and escort carriers took a heavy toll on the raiders, destroying about half of them.

The same day the super battleship *Yamato* set sail from Japan on a suicide mission toward Okinawa, accompanied by a light cruiser and eight destroyers. On 7 April they were attacked by two strikes launched from Task Force 58. Ten torpedoes and five direct bomb hits sent the giant warship to the bottom. The light cruiser and one destroyer were sunk outright, while three other destroyers were so badly damaged that they had to be scuttled. The four remaining destroyers suffered extensive damage. Task Force 58's losses to flak amounted to two fighters, four dive-bombers, and three torpedo

Avengers. In addition, the carrier *Hancock* was hit by a kamikaze; she departed for Ulithi on 9 April to have the damage repaired.

On 7 April the four ferry escort carriers began to fly 192 Corsairs and 30 Hellcats to Okinawa's shores. The Corsairs were the F4U-1C version, armed with four 20-mm cannon and a more powerful engine that gave them a top speed of 446 mph at 26,200 ft and 381 mph at sea level.

Task Force 57 was also busy conducting strikes on the Sakashima islands southwest of Okinawa. Three Corsairs were lost, and a Francis torpedo-bomber, two Judy dive-bombers, and some Oscars were shot down by the Seafire combat air patrol. One Judy, flown by a kamikaze, gave the *Illustrious* a glancing blow, destroying two Corsairs on the flight deck.

The kamikazes returned on 11 April. This time Task Force 58 was better prepared, having listened to a captured Japanese pilot boast about the power of the suicide squads. Nonetheless a picket destroyer was hit, and the *Enterprise* received glancing blows from two Judys. Near-misses from bombs damaged the carrier *Essex* and two destroyers.

Task Force 57, scheduled to attack the Sakashimas again on 10 and 11 April, was diverted to Formosa, where suicide raids were being mounted against the Americans. There British pilots would meet some new types of enemy aircraft. The task force struck Formosan airfields on 12 April and lost one Avenger. Two Fireflies escorting an American air-sea-rescue flying boat encountered five Sonias, shooting down four and damaging the fifth. The combat air patrol kept busy: the Seafires shot down a Zeke, a Tony, and a Dinah; the Hellcats destroyed four Oscars and a Tony; and the Corsairs splashed a Val and an Oscar. One Seafire was lost in combat, one operationally. Next day the strikes continued and Corsairs in the combat air patrol shot down two Zekes.

It was back to the Sakashimas on 16 and 17 April, HMS *Formidable* replacing the *Illustrious*. Seven escorted Avenger and Firefly strikes bombed the airfields by day; the enemy repaired them at night. An Avenger and a Corsair were lost. Two more days of strikes, 19 and 20 April, cost another Avenger. On the evening of 20 April Task Force 57 sailed for a week's replenishment at Leyte.

Task Force 58, in continued support of the Okinawa campaign, struck Okinawa and Kyushu on 15 and 16 April, claiming twenty-nine Japanese planes in combat and fifty-one on the ground. On the second day the carrier *Intrepid* became victim of a kamikaze attack and had to retire from the operational area.

Kawanishi N1K2-J George 12

This low midwing, single-seat fighter was developed from the Rex fighter seaplane and looked like the American Republic Thunderbolt. It was of all-metal structure with flush-riveted, stressed skin, and all controls were fabric covered. The cockpit was set over the trailing edge of the 39-ft, 4-in wing and was fitted with a blister-type canopy. The pilot had armor protection.

Model 12 had an uprated 2,000-hp Nakajima Homare 21, an eighteen-cylinder, two-row radial engine with a two-speed supercharger and ejector exhausts. It drove a four-blade, constant-speed airscrew. The fuel tanks in the fuselage were self-sealing.

Rate of climb was 4,000 ft/min. The aircraft is reported to have had barely positive stability around all three axes, light and effective controls, and a rate of roll somewhere between that of the Zeke and the Tojo. It does not appear to have been quite as maneuverable as the Hellcat, being more on a par with the Corsair.

The predecessor model 11, with a top speed of 315 knots (363 mph), had been much used in the defense of Formosa. Model 12 had a maximum speed of 353.5 knots (407 mph) at 19,000 ft. Range was 929 nm (1,070 statute miles).

Armament consisted of four 20-mm wing cannon and two 7.7-mm machine guns in the fuselage, synchronized to fire through the airscrew.

Assessment: The George 12 was a high-quality, high-performance fighter that appeared too late and in too few numbers to influence the course of the air war. It was well armed and protected—the Japanese having learned from their combat experience against the Americans.

Hellcat II Versus George 12

The George had a significant edge in performance that would give it the initiative in a combat situation, and it could optimize this advantage with hit-and-run tactics. A dogfight should be a fairly even affair, with pilot skill determining the outcome.

Verdict: The odds would slightly favor the George, but that aircraft would find the Hellcat to be a challenging foe.

Corsair II Versus George 12

This would bring together two aircraft very similar in performance and handling characteristics. Pilot skill would play a vital role in deciding the winner.

Verdict: A critical analysis of all the facets of performance, ma-

Kawanishi N1K2 George 11 (U.S. Naval Institute)

neuverability, firepower, and ruggedness would probably show the
Japanese plane to be at a small—a very small—advantage.

TBF Avenger Versus George 12

The Avenger would be an easy target for the fast and well-armed
George. With its speed, the Japanese plane could hammer repeatedly
at the bomber's vulnerable nose.

Verdict: The Japanese fighter could run rings around the
Avenger, which would have virtually no chance of survival.

Seafire III Versus Zeke 52

This should be another classic battle between two great aircraft. They had identical top speeds, but at low level the Seafire had the edge in both speed and rate of climb. There was not much difference in maneuverability. The Seafire had heavier firepower, better protection, and faster acceleration. The two aircraft were so well matched they would not able to play hit and run; they would inevitably get locked in a dogfight.

Verdict: The odds favored the Seafire by a small margin, but when the Zeke was used in the kamikaze role and carried bombs, it was very vulnerable to the lethal Seafire.

Seafire III Versus Oscar 12

The advantages the Seafire held over the Zeke 32 were even greater against the Oscar, but not to the extent that the pilot could relax.

Verdict: The Seafire should be able to deal effectively with the Oscar, especially when the latter was used in the suicide role.

Mitsubishi Type 99 Sonia

This was a low-wing reconnaissance light bomber similar in appearance to the German Ju 87, having fixed, spatted landing gear. It was an all-metal structure with fabric-covered control surfaces and provision for a crew of two or three in a long, enclosed cockpit.

The Sonia was powered by a 900-hp, fourteen-cylinder, two-row radial Mitsubishi Kinsei IV, which drove a three-bladed metal airscrew. Fuel capacity was 140 gallons.

It had a maximum speed of 250 mph at 11,000 ft, a service ceiling of 25,000 ft, and a range of 280 miles carrying 560 kg of bombs.

Assessment: The Sonia was an obsolescent airplane that would be lucky to survive more than a single attack by any Allied naval fighter.

Kawasaki 61 Tony 31

This low-wing, single-seat fighter, of which 2,750 were built, was the first and for a long time the only Japanese warplane to have an in-line engine. The fuselage and wings were an all-metal structure with smooth, flush-riveted, stressed skin, but all control surfaces were fabric covered. The pilot's cockpit was over the rear spar of the wing and had a sliding canopy faired into the rear fuselage, so that the backward view was poor.

The Tony was powered by a 1,000-hp, twelve-cylinder, inverted-V, liquid-cooled Kawasaki type 2. The engine, which drove a three-blade, constant-speed airscrew, was the German Daimler-Benz 601A

Kawasaki 61 Tony (Smithsonian Institution)

built under license. There was a ventral radiator beneath the pilot's cockpit and self-sealing fuel tanks in the wings.

The Tony had a rate of climb of 2,400 ft/min and apparently handled rather like the Hawker Hurricane, which it resembled in appearance. However, it performed better, with a maximum speed of 348 mph at 16,400 ft and a normal range of 1,100 miles.

Armament consisted of two 20-mm wing cannon and two 7.7-mm machine guns in the top of the engine cowling, synchronized to fire through the airscrew. Two 220-lb bombs could be carried on racks beneath the wings, outboard of the cannon.

Assessment: The Tony was the sort of fighter seen in Europe in 1939–40. Its obsolescence would put it at a significant disadvantage against Allied fighters in 1944.

Hellcat II and Corsair II Versus Tony 31

The Hellcat and Corsair were superior in every aspect of performance except dive acceleration, and the Tony could take advantage of that for nothing other than escape. The Japanese fighter had a better turning circle, so Allied fighters would seek to avoid a dogfight, opting for hit-and-run (climb) tactics.

Verdict: The Hellcat and Corsair should have little real trouble dealing effectively with the Tony, which was slightly inferior to the Zeke 52.

Seafire III Versus Tony 31

These two fighters were evenly matched in performance and maneuverability, but the Seafire had superior climb, which it could exploit in a dogfight to get on the Tony's tail or escape from it.

Verdict: The Seafire held an ace in its hand, which if correctly played should win the combat.

Firefly 1 Versus Tony 31

This should prove to be a classic struggle between two aircraft on a par in almost every respect. The Firefly was a two-seater but had heavier firepower. Once again, pilot skill should be the decisive factor.
    Verdict: This combat could go either way.

Avenger Versus Tony 31

Here the Avenger would be at a disadvantage. Still, the Tony's liquid-cooled engine was very vulnerable to bullets, so the Japanese fighter would have to be wary of the Avenger's defensive armament. This might force the Tony to make a frontal attack, and the speed difference between the two aircraft might not permit him more than one pass.
    Verdict: The odds weighed against the Avenger, but it had a slim chance of survival.

Operations Continue in the Indian Ocean

The East Indies Fleet continued its extensive photo reconnaissance, targeting locations in northern Sumatra in March and April. On 11 April the escort carriers *Empress* and *Khedive* were attacked by Japanese planes off Sabang. Hellcats shot down an Oscar and a Dinah.

In May—the month the Germans offered their unconditional surrender in Europe—four escort carriers covered the landings in Rangoon. Two others took part in an operation to prevent Japanese intervention from Singapore. The six carriers flew four hundred sorties in eight days, losing only two Hellcats. Later in the month four of the escort carriers struck enemy airfields in the Andaman and Nicobar islands.

June was an active month for the East Indies Fleet. From 18 to 20 June the final photo reconnaissance sorties were flown over the Penang area and southern Malaya. With a mass of target intelligence now available, heavy strikes were launched against shipping, communications, and airfields on Sumatra and in southern Burma. There was little fighter opposition but heavy flak. Only one Hellcat was lost.

In July British escort carriers conducted their final operations in the Indian Ocean. Fighter strikes were launched against Car Nicobar, where fierce flak downed four Hellcats. Further strikes on Sumatra cost another Hellcat, while Hellcat raids on airfields in the Kra Isthmus destroyed thirty enemy aircraft. On 26 July the fleet was attacked by kamikazes, which sank a minesweeper and damaged the carrier *Ameer*.

In six months of operations the East Indies Fleet had destroyed more than one-third of the operational Japanese aircraft in Burma, Malaya, and Sumatra, inflicted severe damage on the enemy transport system, and helped to deny enemy use of sea-lanes in the region.

Okinawa Takes Its Toll

Task Force 58 continued to support the Okinawa campaign. On 15 and 16 April there were strikes against Okinawa and Kyushu, pilots who had raided the latter claiming to have shot down twenty-nine Japanese planes and destroyed fifty-one on the ground. On the second day the *Intrepid* sustained a direct hit and a near miss by kamikazes and had to withdraw to Ulithi.

In spite of unabated suicide attacks Task Force 58 remained intact for almost a month. During that period it was strengthened by the return of the *Enterprise* and the arrival of the *Shangri-La,* bringing the fast-carrier strength to fifteen.

The eleventh of May was a fateful day for the *Bunker Hill,* which was bombed and crashed by a Zeke and received similar treatment from a Judy. These attacks put the carrier out of action for the rest of the war. On 12 and 13 May Task Force 58 struck the Japanese islands of Kyushu and Shikoku with two task groups. The *Enterprise's* air group hit Kyushu's airfields the first night and shot down twelve enemy night-fighters. On the second night *Enterprise* aircraft destroyed four enemy planes in combat and more on the ground. In between these operations there were heavy daylight raids, giving a total of seventy-two Japanese planes destroyed in combat and seventy-three on the ground—conservative estimates.

The Japanese retaliated on 14 May with a twenty-six plane suicide raid. One kamikaze got through, crashing the *Enterprise* and putting her out of action.

Task Force 57, having returned from Leyte, was in action against the Sakashimas by 4 May. It became the target of kamikazes, one of which hit the *Formidable,* destroying eleven aircraft, and another two of which caused minor damage to the *Indomitable.* The day's combat tally was eleven Japanese Zekes and Judys, and, on the Allied side, one Avenger.

Normally, when Task Force 57 was replenishing, four U.S. escort carriers stood in for the British fleet carriers. On 4 May one of these escorts, the *Sangamon,* was severely damaged by a kamikaze. She had been the first escort carrier to operate night-fighters.

On 9 May strikes on the Sakashimas continued and one Corsair was lost. The inevitable kamikaze attack materialized, during which two Zekes crashed the *Victorious* and another the *Formidable.* Four

Corsairs from the *Victorious* and eighteen Avengers and Corsairs from the *Formidable* were destroyed, but other damage, to the armored flight decks, was not severe. A total of 201 sorties was flown against the Sakashimas on 12 and 13 May, the pattern of two days of strikes followed by two days of replenishment continuing until 25 May, when the task force departed for Sydney.

The British Pacific Fleet flew 5,335 sorties in Operation Iceberg and lost 203 aircraft, only 33 in combat or to flak. As Task Force 57, it had been supported by a fleet train that included four escort carriers. Replenishment aircraft had been ferried from Australia.

A change of command on 27 May again called for the restructuring of Task Force 58. Now 38, it only had two task groups, but this did not in any way reduce its aggressiveness. Strikes made against airfields on Kyushu on 2 and 3 June met with little opposition.

Task Force 38's next battle was against nature. On 5 June a typhoon battered the carriers, resulting in sixty-nine planes lost and twenty-three severely damaged. In spite of this the task groups were able to provide air support over Okinawa on 6 June, when they were reinforced by the arrival of the *Bon Homme Richard* with a night air group.

The Kyushu airfields were hit again on 8 June, and again there was a scarcity of targets and air opposition. The June raids on Kyushu destroyed seventy-seven enemy aircraft at a cost of fourteen carrier planes, downed mainly by antiaircraft fire. The Fast Carrier Force struck for the last time in the Okinawa campaign and retired to Leyte Gulf, where it anchored on 14 June and was rejoined by three more carriers.

On 22 June Okinawa was subdued, after nearly three months of fighting in the largest and most prolonged amphibious operation of the Pacific war. Officially the campaign ended on 2 July, and it was an outstanding victory for naval aviation. The Fast Carrier Force destroyed 2,336 Japanese aircraft in exchange for 790 of their own, of which only 269 were lost in combat.

The Final Thrust

On 1 July Task Force 38, with fourteen fast carriers, sailed against Japan. Strikes against Tokyo started on 10 July, then on 14 and 15 July against northern Honshu and the island of Hokkaido. Intense flak was virtually the only opposition.

The British Pacific Fleet—Task Force 37, with four fleet carriers carrying six Hellcat IIs, seventy-three Corsair IIs, eighty-eight Seafire IIIs, twenty-four Fireflies, and sixty-two Avengers—joined Task Force 38 on 16 July. The first combined raids were made against Tokyo on

17 and 18 July. For these Task Force 37 had only three carriers available, as the *Indefatigable* had engineering problems and could not join the others until 24 July.

On 24 July Task Force 37 flew 416 sorties, and one of them located the enemy escort carrier *Kaiyo*. The first attack secured one direct hit, later attacks obtained two more and broke her back. This was the Fleet Air Arm's only attack of the war on an enemy aircraft carrier.

On 25 July bad weather curtailed operations, but the dusk patrol of Hellcats from HMS *Formidable* intercepted four Grace torpedo-bombers heading for the fleet at 20,000 ft. Three were shot down and the fourth damaged.

Meanwhile Task Force 38 attacked the ports of Kure and Kobe, sinking the battleship *Haruna* and the battleship carriers *Hyuga* and *Ise*. Hits were also secured on the carriers *Amagi* and *Katsuragi*, which were attacked again on 28 July. The former was sunk and the latter severely damaged.

Both task forces spent the twenty-eighth and thirtieth of July punishing Japanese shipping of all types, with Task Force 37 in the south of Honshu and 38 in the north. They were withdrawn before the first atomic bomb was dropped on Hiroshima on 6 August.

While Nagasaki was being devastated by the second atomic bomb on 9 August, the combined carrier fleets concentrated on northern Honshu's airfields and shipping. Task Force 37 flew 407 sorties, dropping more bombs and firing more ammunition than the Fleet Air Arm had on any other day during the war. Similar action continued on 10 August.

On 11 August Task Force 38.5 was formed with HMS *Indefatigable* and thirteen warships from Task Force 37, which now departed for Sydney. In eight days of strikes off the Japanese coast the British Pacific Fleet had flown 2,615 sorties, destroyed or damaged 341 enemy aircraft, and sunk 356,760 tons of shipping. It had lost 101 of its own aircraft, 39 in combat or from antiaircraft fire.

Task Force 38.5 hit Tokyo on 13 August, claiming 254 Japanese aircraft on the ground and 21 in the air, of which 5 were downed by *Indefatigable* Seafires on combat air patrol.

The last strike of the war was flown against Tokyo on 15 August, before the fleet received word of Japan's surrender. It was a memorable day for the *Indefatigable*'s Seafires, which shot down eight of twelve attacking Zekes. Even after the strike returned, the task force was kept on the alert, which proved a wise precaution. With the final shots of the carrier war, the combat air patrol downed eight kamikazes making a desperate last stand.

It was 2 September 1945 before the Pacific war officially ended.

Task Force 38.5 remained at sea in the period between the cease-fire and the surrender, ready for action if the peace negotiations failed.

In Retrospect

During World War II the scale of aircraft carrier operations in the Far East was gargantuan, far exceeding that in Europe. The number of Japanese aircraft destroyed amounted to 6,826. There were very high kill rates for the U.S. Navy once the Hellcat appeared on the scene to master the deadly Zeke, which up to that time had ruled the tropical skies.

The Japanese aircraft industry had rested far too long on the laurels of the Zeke's early success. In particular, the development of aircraft engines had been neglected. Moreover, when the realization came that more and better planes were needed, Japan was under severe aerial attack. The lack of a factory-dispersal plan had catastrophic results on production, a situation exacerbated by the fact that the homeland was cut off from vital resources. The Japanese had also made a gross miscalculation about the probable length of the war and, as a result, did not have a long-term pilot-training program in place. Crowning their problems was an aviation fuel shortage that severely restricted flying when the crisis came.

In comparison, German aircraft and engine technology were highly advanced, and they were never outstripped by the Allies. Their aircraft and aero-engine production was severely tested by Allied bombing, but considering the circumstances was maintained at an astonishingly high level because of preplanned factory dispersal.

In the matter of pilot training, Germany had not so much miscalculated the probable length of war as failed to account for the resilience of the relatively unprepared British nation and for the vagaries of its own dictator, who committed the fatal error of fighting on two fronts. The British fought like tigers, as did some other European nations. In addition, Britain had the fortune to be an island nation with the most powerful navy in the world and two superb fighter aircraft for aerial defense. The Russians were saved by the vastness of their land and population, and the devastating conditions of their winter.

Like Japan, Germany had blooded its pilots in combat before the main conflagration of World War II began. This experience paid handsomely in the initial stages of war, but the advantage rapidly evaporated with attrition against the determined Allies. Later, flight training was severely constrained by enemy harassment and a shortage of aviation fuel.

The training methods of the Japanese and Germans varied little from those of the Americans and British, and in spite of varying ideologies all the pilots shared one thing—determination. The Allies were much more fortunate than the enemy in having more manpower from which to select pilots and a larger number of secure areas in which to train them.

The inevitable question, bound to be argued as long as World War II is discussed, is which was the tougher theater for aerial combat, Europe or the Far East? To this there is no simple answer. In Europe the standard of Axis opposition was likely to be higher in terms of technical quality, but in the Far East there was the phenomenon of the kamikaze, which added a new dimension to aerial combat and survival.

From a naval aviator's point of view the weather in the Atlantic and its adjacent seas was more unpredictable than in the Pacific, and a downed aviator had a better chance of survival in the latter. Against this must be weighed the constant apprehension of pilots flying over Japanese-occupied territory as to what their fate would be if they were taken prisoner.

The morale of pilots is much affected by their living conditions—for example, whether they enjoy amenities such as regular mail delivery and how far they are from home. In this respect there is little doubt that those in the Far East theater were the less fortunate. Their situation was made worse in the months after VE-day; a state of euphoria settled over Europe and the United States at the very time that kamikaze attacks peaked. The Japanese were fiercest when fighting like trapped animals. During these months the British Pacific Fleet tagged itself the Forgotten Fleet.

Aside from the academic question of which theater was tougher, the naval aviators in both were a special breed who accepted the limitations of operating from a mobile base. They flew single-engine airplanes over vast tracts of hostile sea, and if they were lucky enough to survive aerial combat and the natural hazards of their operational environment, they ultimately faced the test of landing on their mobile base, the aircraft carrier. Records show that many more aircraft were lost operationally than in combat. The men that accepted these risks as a matter of routine had to be of a unique caliber.

8

Theoretical Combat

The Greatest Fighter of World War II

MANY POTENTIALLY CLASSIC combats between Allied and Axis powers did not take place because the combatants fought in different operational theaters. It is to these theoretical cases that I now turn, using my own experience test-flying the aircraft to assess how they would have fared against each other in single combat. Later in this section I will go one step further, pitting friend against friend. If we then compare these cases with actual ones, it should help us determine which was the greatest fighter of World War II.

The list of top fighters in the single-seat category are generally accepted as the following:

German	American	Japanese	British
Focke-Wulf 190D-9	Grumman F6F-5 Hellcat II	Mitsubishi A6M5 Zeke 53	Supermarine Spitfire F.XIV
Messerschmitt 262A-1a	North American P-51D Mustang IV	Kawanishi N1K2-J George 12	Hawker Tempest V

Only three of the above are naval aircraft, but that is enough to set up some interesting theoretical combats.

The essential data for assessment are as follows:

Focke-Wulf 190D-9

Aircraft	Engine	Maximum Speed (mph at ft)	Rate of Climb (ft/min)	Armament
Hellcat II	1 X 2,000-hp radial	376 at 22,800	3,650	6 X 0.5 MGs
Mustang IV	1 X 1,590-hp in-line	432 at 24,000	4,000	6 X 0.5 MGs
Spitfire XIV	1 X 2,035-hp in-line	447 at 25,600	4,580	2 X 20-mm cannon 2 X 0.5 MGs
Tempest V	1 X 2,400-hp H-type	426 at 18,500	3,750	4 X 20-mm cannon
Fw 190D-9	1 X 1,776-hp in-line	426 at 21,326	6,250	1 X 30-mm cannon
	1 X 2,240-hp in-line (with MW injection)	440 at 37,000 (with MW injection)	(with MW injection)	2 X 20-mm cannon 2 X 13-mm MGs
Me 262A-1a	2 X 1,984-lb axial jets	540 at 19,685	3,937	4 X 30-mm cannon
Zeke 53	1 X 1,120-hp radial	370 at 15,700	4,100	2 X 20-mm cannon 1 X 12.7-mm MG
George 12	1 X 2,000-hp radial	407 at 19,000	4,000	4 X 20-mm cannon

FOCKE-WULF 190D-9

The Fw 190D-9 entered service in the autumn of 1944. It was the first version of the fighter to be fitted with a liquid-cooled engine, the 1,776-hp, inverted-V Junkers Jumo 213A-1 with MW 50 power boost. This lengthened the fuselage by just over 4.5 ft but lowered the profile by 2 ft.

The Fw 190D-9 preserved all the superb handling characteristics of the earlier versions and in addition had significantly enhanced engine and firepower.

Assessment: This was, in my opinion, the finest piston-engined fighter to enter Luftwaffe service.

Messerschmitt 262A-1a (National Archives)

MESSERSCHMITT 262A-1A

The Me 262A-1a was Germany's and the world's first operational jet fighter, and as such it made for itself an immortal name in aviation history. It could also claim the innovative feature of a low wing swept back just over 18 degrees.

The aircraft's all-metal fuselage—a near triangle with the single-seat cockpit mounted midway along the chord of the wing's center section—had the sinister lines of a shark. The wings each had Frise-type ailerons in two sections, with slotted flaps inboard, and full-span automatic leading-edge slats. The tailplane was mounted halfway up the fin, and the rudder and elevators were mass balanced. The tricycle landing gear retracted hydraulically into the underside of the wings. There were hydraulic brakes on all wheels, that on the nose-wheel being operated by a hand lever.

The Me 262A-1a was powered by two Junkers Jumo 004 B-1 eight-stage, axial-flow, gas-turbine units, each of 1,984-lb static thrust in a nacelle slung under each wing. Fuel tankage was 198 imperial gals (238 U.S.); a similar quantity could be carried in the rear main. The forward auxiliary tank held 37 imperial gals (44.5 U.S.), the aft up to 132 (158.5 U.S.). The fuel was 87 octane gasoline with a 5 percent mix of lubricating oil. The Riedel two-stroke starter motor ran on the same fuel.

View from the cockpit was excellent, and the instruments were logically laid out. Starting was a complex procedure, and during taxiing the throttles had to be moved with restraint so as not to exceed the jet-pipe temperature limits.

Takeoff was made with 20 degrees of flap, and at full power fumes or smoke invariably penetrated the cockpit. The takeoff run was long, and if an engine cut before the safety speed of 180 mph was reached the result was a violent, almost certainly fatal diving turn.

The initial climbing speed was 286 mph, and once the plane reached 185 it became thoroughly exciting to fly. With a tactical Mach number of 0.82, it was in a performance league all its own. In fact, pilots could get into trouble if they allowed speed to build up beyond Mach 0.83, when the nose started to drop and they had to give a two-handed pull to effect recovery. Luftwaffe pilots were instructed not to exceed an airspeed of 600 mph below 26,000 ft.

Harmony of control was pleasant, with a stick force per "g" of 6 lbs at mid center of gravity and a rate of roll of 360 degrees in 3.8 seconds at 400 mph. The Me 262A-1a had a docile stall and was very maneuverable, leaving one with the impression of a first-class combat aircraft. Its stability promised an accurate gun platform. Maximum speed in level flight on one engine was 310 mph, requiring one-third rudder application.

Landing the Me 262A-1a was straightforward with a final approach speed of 125 mph, but the landing run was long and German brakes were notoriously prone to fading.

Range with the main tank fuel only was 298 miles at sea level, 528 at 20,000 ft, and 652 miles at 30,000. The upper pair of 30-mm cannon, in the nose, had one hundred rounds each, the lower pair eighty rounds each. Their effective range was 650 yards.

Assessment: The Me 262A-1a was the most formidable aircraft produced in World War II, its performance rendering it virtually untouchable. Though its potential was never fully realized—it was powered by unreliable engines, and later in the war the supply of experienced pilots to fly it was depleted—it had a huge impact on aviation design.

NORTH AMERICAN P-51D MUSTANG IV

The P-51 Mustang prototype was designed and built in 117 days. It was saved from mediocrity by the eventual installation of a Rolls-Royce Merlin driving a four-blade airscrew, new ailerons, and improved armament. The aircraft reached its peak in the P-51D model, equipped with a modified rear fuselage and a blister hood to improve the view.

This single-seat fighter had laminar-flow wings set low on the all-metal fuselage and metal-covered ailerons, the port aileron with a controllable trim tab. The rudder and elevators were fabric covered and had trim tabs.

The cockpit was fitted with an optically flat, five-ply, laminated-glass, bulletproof front panel and side panels of safety glass. It had a

North American P-51D Mustang IV (Naval Historical Center)

stainless-steel sheet and an armor-plated fireproof bulkhead in front of the pilot, as well as two plates of face-hardened steel armor behind his seat. The thing that struck me about the whole cockpit was how small it was by American standards—but then the Mustang was originally designed to a British specification.

The engine was a 1,590-hp Packard V-1650-7 (Rolls-Royce Merlin 69), a twelve-cylinder, V, liquid-cooled engine with a two-speed, two-stage supercharger and aftercooler, driving a four-bladed, constant-speed airscrew. Self-sealing fuel cells in the wings had a total capacity of 153 imperial gals (184 U.S.), and an auxiliary self-sealing tank in the fuselage behind the pilot held 71 imperial gals (85 U.S.).

On the ground the view ahead was poor, owing to the long nose, and the aircraft had to be swung from side to side while taxiing. This, however, was made easy by a tailwheel capable of being locked to the rudder controls and steered over a range of 6 degrees either side. This steerable position was achieved by holding the control column aft, past the neutral position, which helped to control the swing on take-off. Takeoff was commendably short.

Climb rate at 160 mph was high. The aircraft was positively stable about all three axes, except when it had fuel in the auxiliary fuselage tank, which made it longitudinally unstable. This tank normally carried fuel only on long-range escort flights.

The Mustang had a rate of roll bettered only by that of the Fw 190, and with a much gentler stall than the German fighter, it was highly maneuverable.

Landing the Mustang required concentration, for at an approach speed of 105 mph the view was bad, and high-rebound-ratio landing gear made a three-point landing tricky. This state of affairs was exac-

Supermarine Spitfire XIV (Pilot Press)

erbated by the aircraft's lack of directional stability on the landing run. The U.S. Navy abandoned the Mustang's deck-landing trials on an aircraft carrier for these reasons.

Armament was the standard American fit of six 0.5-in machine guns, three in each wing.

Assessment: The Mustang was a superb aircraft exhibiting tremendous performance and agility from sea level to 40,000 ft. It was undoubtedly the finest fighter produced by the United States in World War II.

SUPERMARINE SPITFIRE XIV

The aesthetically beautiful Spitfire was developed, in a series of models, to keep pace with improvements in engine power, refinements in aerodynamic efficiency, and increases in firepower. The Mk XIV was, to my mind, the greatest Spitfire model to see operational service in World War II.

It used the 2,000-hp, twelve-cylinder, V, liquid-cooled Rolls-Royce Griffon 65. The engine had a two-speed, two-stage supercharger driving a five-blade, constant-speed Rotol airscrew. The engine mounting, designed by Supermarine, was assembled with the engine to form a complete power plant.

The airframe incorporated a teardrop cockpit hood giving rearward vision with the top line of the fuselage lowered. Armament was one 0.5-in machine gun and one 20-mm Hispano cannon in each wing.

The performance of the Spitfire XIV was electrifying. It had lost

none of the beautiful harmony of control that made the classic Mk
IX such a pleasant aircraft to fly and to fight.

Assessment: The Spitfire XIV was the greatest British fighter of
World War II, incorporating as it did so many improvements over
earlier models without losing anything in looks or handling.

HAWKER TEMPEST V SERIES 2

The Tempest was developed from the Typhoon fighter, which had
been particularly successful in the ground-attack role. The new design
featured a thin, laminar-flow elliptical wing and a more powerful
engine. The prototype first flew on 2 September 1942 and the first-
production machine on 21 June 1943. The series-2 controls were
fitted with spring tabs.

The Tempest single-seat, low-wing fighter was a pugnacious-
looking aircraft that exuded rugged power rather than sleekness of
line. It had a 2,400-hp, twenty-four-cylinder, H-type, liquid-cooled,
sleeve-valve engine, a Napier Sabre 11B. It drove a four-bladed,
constant-speed de Havilland Hydromatic airscrew. A low-velocity duct
beneath the engine, housing coolant radiator and oil cooler, gave it a
bulldog chin. The air intake was positioned in the center of the
assembly. A main tank carried fuel in the fuselage, forward of the
pilot, and there were additional fuel tanks in the wings. All were self-
sealing.

The cockpit, located over the wings' trailing edges, had a bulletproof windscreen and armor fore and aft of the pilot. With the long
nose the view on the ground was poor, but in flight the blister hood
gave an excellent all-round view. There was a powerful swing to
starboard on takeoff, but the aircraft could be held comfortably on
rudder, provided full port trim had been applied.

The initial rate of climb at 185 mph was 3,750 ft/min, slightly
below that of contemporary fighters in early 1944. The aircraft was
stable directionally and laterally, but slightly unstable longitudinally.
The elevator control was light and effective, the ailerons reasonably
light and effective, the rudder moderately light and effective. Elevator and ailerons became sluggish at low speeds.

The stall occurred without warning, and the left wing dropped
sharply at 85 mph all-up, at 75 mph all-down. The high-speed stall
reminded one of the Fw 90: the ailerons snatched, and if the "g" was
not immediately eased the aircraft would become inverted and spin.

The Tempest could dive to a maximum indicated airspeed of
540 mph below 10,000 ft. It tended to become tail-heavy in a dive.
Above 10,000 ft it had a maximum safe Mach number of 0.80, at
which limit slight buffeting was accompanied by a marked nose-down
pitch.

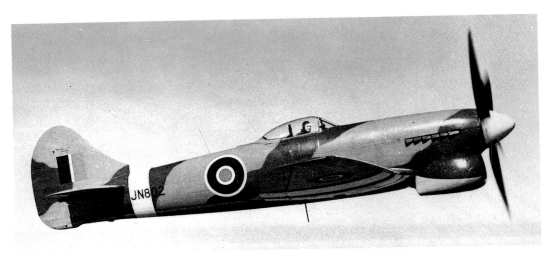

Hawker Tempest V (RAF)

With a top speed in level flight of 426 mph at 18,500 ft, the Tempest had a service ceiling of 36,500 ft. Normal range was 740 miles. Armament consisted of four 20-mm wing cannon, and there was provision for two 1,000-lb bombs under the wings or eight rocket projectiles.

Assessment: The Tempest was one of the most highly successful large, single-seat fighters of World War II. With a loaded weight of 11,400 lbs it was twice as heavy as the Zeke 52, but it was surprisingly agile and able to absorb punishment. It had a powerful punch as a fighter, and it also excelled in low-level ground attack.

Hellcat II Versus Fw 190D-9

The Fw 190D-9 held all the aces in combat, even without the addition of water-methanol injection. The aircraft's rate of roll and acceleration with water methanol would get it out of any tight situation and turn the encounter rapidly to advantage.

Verdict: This would be virtually no contest. Disparity between the two aircraft in performance, handling, and firepower gave the German fighter the upper hand.

Hellcat II Versus Messerschmitt 262A-1a

This would be a classic only in one sense: pitting the greatest jet-engine fighter of World War II against the greatest Allied naval piston-engine aircraft. But it would strictly be a battle for survival on the part of the Hellcat, completely outclassed in performance and firepower. The only superior feature the naval fighter had to offer was its turning circle, and in any case the German jet was unlikely to try and mix it; he would go for scything passes. The speed of the Me 262A-1a was such that the Hellcat pilot would have to exercise some fine judgment about when to initiate his turn. Strangely enough, the Schwalbe was not at its best, as one would expect, at high altitude; compressor stall gave the engines a tendency to flame out, so it was better suited to combat at low or medium level.

Verdict: This should be a one-sided affair, though the German jet would probably need more than one pass because its high closing speed gave it a firing time of only about two seconds.

Mustang IV Versus Zeke 53

The Zeke, if flown to its limits, was never going to be an easy enemy to take on, for its turning circle was second to none and it had a rate of climb common to fighters a whole generation later. Its weaknesses against an aircraft such as the Mustang were lack of speed and firepower. The Zeke could never afford to take on the American interceptor in the vertical plane, because of lack of acceleration in the dive, and in the first 90 degrees of a turn in the horizontal plane, the Mustang could unleash a lethal burst of fire against the fragile Zeke.

Verdict: This would be a certain if not easy victory for the Mustang, which the Zeke should find difficult to shake off.

Mustang IV Versus George 12

In this battle, a small edge in speed and maneuverability belonged to the Mustang, but it had little margin for error. Its high rate of roll, giving the advantage both in attack and defense, should be the deciding factor in this cat-and-mouse game.

Verdict: The Mustang could use its all-round advantage to good purpose, but the pilot would have to work hard for victory.

Spitfire XIV Versus Zeke 53

The Zeke would find itself facing a fighter par excellence, with no weakness to exploit and huge advantages in performance, view, and firepower. Even its legendary maneuverability would be matched for once.

Verdict: The Zeke would be overwhelmed swiftly and surely by a fighter outclassing it in virtually every department.

Spitfire XIV Versus George 12

This might be a tussle, if the Japanese fighter exploited its considerable performance to the full. Ultimately, however, it had no hope of escaping the all-round superiority of the Spitfire.

Verdict: There could only be one outcome of this combat between the excellent George and the superb Spitfire.

Tempest V Versus Zeke 53

This would be a meeting of David and Goliath, with the small, spritely Zeke against the large but surprisingly nimble British fighter. There would be no point in the Tempest engaging the Zeke in a dogfight. It would have to resort to the same tactic the Hellcat had used so successfully—using its superior speed for swift passes with short bursts of heavy armament. However, the Tempest, not as maneuverable as the Hellcat, might find combat with the Zeke rather like trying to swat a fly. Certainly the British fighter should not be lured into a tight turn or it might present itself as a helpless target to the enemy.

Verdict: Although the odds favored the Tempest V, this could end in a stalemate, with neither aircraft really able to come to grips with the other.

Tempest V Versus George 12

The performance gap between these two aircraft was not sufficient to be decisive. There would be a classic struggle, an inevitable dogfight in which the Japanese fighter's superior maneuverability would, along with pilot skill, play a vital role.

Verdict: The George should have the edge, but this combat would be finely balanced indeed.

Zeke 32 Versus Focke-Wulf 190A-4

This would have been a sizzling combat in mid-1942. Although the German fighter had a 50-mph speed advantage, it could not match the turning circle of the Zeke. The superb aileron control of the 190 would more than offset this disadvantage, allowing it to follow the Zeke around the first 120 degrees of an evasive turn, or allowing a lightning half roll and pull-through if it had the Zeke on its own tail. One burst from the Fw 190A-4's considerable armament should kill the fragile Zeke, but drawing a bead on the Japanese aircraft would not be easy.

Verdict: These were two truly great fighters, but designed to different philosophies. The more advanced technology evident in the Fw 190A-4 would give it the supremacy to win an interesting conflict.

F6F-3 Hellcat Versus Spitfire IX

The Spitfire IX was the best of the Spitfires outfitted with the Merlin engine; indeed it was regarded by most as the supreme example from the original mold. It had the Rolls-Royce Merlin 63 of 1,650 hp and was armed with two 20-mm cannon and two 0.5-in machine guns in the wings. It had a top speed of 408 mph at 25,000 ft, an initial rate of climb of 3,950 ft/min.

This combat (mid-1943) would be a battle of different shapes, the corpulent against the slim. The Spitfire was superior in every aspect except ruggedness. Differences between the two aircraft, which clearly illustrated the penalties inherent in carrier-borne airplane design, were not significant enough to make the contest one-sided, but they did heavily favor the Spitfire.

Verdict: The mighty Hellcat would find its match in the mightier Spitfire, and a lot of sweat would be expended before the inevitable dogfight reached a conclusion.

Mustang IV Versus Spitfire XIV

Here the two Allied thoroughbreds would be unleashed (mid-1944) against each other. The Spitfire possessed a slight speed advantage at high altitude and a significant advantage in rate of climb. In the matter of handling, the Mustang had the superior rate of roll and faster acceleration in the dive, but the Spitfire had the tighter turning circle. Both aircraft offered a splendid view and were equipped with powerful armament.

The exploitation of these relative assets brought offensive and defensive advantages, and I can see no sure way to victory for either combatant. I have flown both for many hours, and I would probably choose the Spitfire if given the choice in a fight to the death.

Verdict: I once flew a Spitfire IX against an Fw 190 over France, when after only ten minutes of thrust and parry in a "g"-loaded dogfight we both broke off the battle simultaneously, as if in mutual recognition of an indecisive outcome. Such would be the likely result of this contest, if both pilots were of similar skill and experience.

Having reviewed the eight short-listed, single-seat fighters, I feel the Me 262A-1 should be singled out as the most formidable fighter of World War II. However, it should not be considered for the title of greatest because it belonged to the new era of jet-engine aircraft and, in any case, it arrived too late for maximum operational impact.

In assessing the piston-engine contenders, it is necessary to consider not only their technological assets but also their impact on the course of the war. Some of these aircraft had operational lives that lasted for the duration of the war.

The following design features that together make a great fighter are listed in order of importance:

1. Speed (full combat power at high, medium, and low altitudes)
2. Rate of climb (a steep angle of climb is also advantageous)

3. Dive acceleration (including ability to bunt into a dive without engine-cutting)
4. Maneuverability (turning circle, rate of roll, and harmony of control)
5. Firepower (rate of fire, muzzle velocity, and caliber of guns/cannon)
6. Pilot visibility (all-round field of view without blank spots)
7. Range (particularly for offensive, escort, and naval fighters)
8. Ammunition load (sufficient rounds for multiple combats)
9. Protection (armor for crew, self-sealing fuel tanks, and engine coolant system)
10. Vulnerability (ability to absorb a reasonable number of hits and the type of engine layout)

Using the foregoing criteria, I would compile a merit list as follows:

1. Spitfire XIV (superb performance, splendid handling, but short range)
2. Fw 190D-9 (magnificent rate of roll, almost flawless except for the stall)
3. Mustang IV (only a whisker inferior to the Fw 190D, but superior in range)
4. George 12 (a good all-rounder in the tradition of the ubiquitous Zeke)
5. Tempest V (large, but agile for its size and particularly suitable for ground attack)
6. F6F-3 Hellcat (robust, and very good in every desirable fighter feature)
7. Zeke 53 (incredibly nimble, with impressive range, but fragile)

As one would expect, this list places the aircraft in almost reverse chronological order. For a realistic assessment of greatness, each fighter must be analyzed according to the time it made its operational debut.

• The Zeke made a tremendous impact on aerial warfare in the Far East, first in the war against China in 1939 and then against the Allies from December 1941 until the arrival of the Hellcat in the summer of 1943. In effect, this little Japanese naval fighter ruled the tropical skies for four years, and it developed an outstanding reputation, reflected in the influence it had on fighter design throughout the world.

Even after its reputation had been eclipsed by the Hellcat the Zeke continued, with only slight improvements, to be the mainstay of Japan's air defenses. Its wartime career spanned six years of aerial fighting, during which it met with huge success. A total of 10,938 Zekes were manufactured.

• The Spitfire had just entered squadron service at the outbreak of World War II, when its main adversary was the Me 109. Supermarine's elegant fighter was one of the prime reasons the Allies won the critical Battle of Britain, which halted German plans to invade England. Thereafter, except when the Fw 190 was introduced and the Me 262 made its late appearance, the many developed Spitfire models kept the Allies in lead position in the category of fighter.

The Spitfire also entered service as a naval aircraft, the Seafire. This gave the Royal Navy's Fleet Air Arm the speedy, low-level Seafire LIIC for the invasion of Italy and the Seafire III for operations in the Far East. The Seafire had excellent fighter features, but with poor deck-landing characteristics and short range, it was not a good naval aircraft. It served over three years on British aircraft carriers.

• The Fw 190, which first appeared in European skies in the fall of 1941, caused mild panic in the RAF when it demonstrated its superiority over the Spitfire V. For a year its command of the air went unchallenged, until the arrival of the Spitfire IX. Then it was matched in performance. The Fw 190 continued to pose a threat, appearing for the duration of the war in improved versions that kept it at the forefront of fighter technology.

• The Mustang started life inauspiciously as the Mk I with the Allison engine, but after receiving a new engine, the Packard-built Merlin, and new ailerons, it was a different aircraft. The Mustang III entered operational service at the beginning of 1944 and was followed by the more heavily armed Mk IV. These two versions, acting as escorts to the Flying Fortress in its daylight bombing raids over Germany, substantially reduced bomber losses and thereby increased pressure on Germany.

• The Hellcat arrived in the Far East theater in the late summer of 1943 and completely changed the operational scene. Ousting the Zeke from its position of dominance, the Hellcat remained superior until the end of World War II, undoubtedly altering its course. While the Hellcat may not rank as the greatest fighter of World War II, it was certainly the greatest naval fighter in the Pacific theater.

• The Tempest made its operational debut in offensive sweeps over France and the Netherlands in April 1944. Shortly thereafter it had to switch to a defensive role to combat Germany's V.1 assault against southern England. Tempests destroyed 638 of these 400-mph low-flying bombs, a third of the total destroyed by Allied aircraft. Soon afterward the Tempest resumed widespread ground attacks in support of the Allied invasion of Europe. Because it was primarily used as a fighter-bomber, the Tempest was not ultimately successful in the role of pure combat fighter.

• The George was the Zeke's natural successor but did not appear early enough to make anything other than a fleeting impression. What it might have done is open to conjecture, especially as the Mustang was beginning to enter the theater. Its impact can be summed up as too little, too late.

In determining which single-seat fighter of World War II was the best, we should take into account basic quality of design, development potential, combat success rate, and the aircraft's influence on the conduct and outcome of various operations. From this sort of analysis two fighters emerge as the most prominent: the Spitfire and the Fw 190.

To fly these superb aircraft in any of their multifarious guises was to experience the exhilaration of virtual perfection. To fight in them was to feel the thrill of confidence; to fight against them, to endure the fear of impending defeat. Each fought on many fronts and always with a high degree of success.

It is not easy to establish a winner between these two, and indeed I have vacillated so much on the choice that I feel compelled to give them equal rank, though that has meant swallowing my national pride. If the Spitfire had had the German fighter's rate of roll, I could have declared it a clear winner and eased my conscience.

Next one must look at the American fighters, and here it is easier to make a judgment. In the Far East the Hellcat almost single-handedly turned defeat into victory. The Mustang IV, though technically superior, never made such an impact on any war theater.

The fabulous Zeke, which ruled its own roost for longer than any other warplane, would rate higher than the Hellcat but for one factor—its fragility. Even after being usurped from its impregnable position the Zeke remained a menacing little wasp until the end, earning itself a permanent place in the history of aerial warfare.

The latter-day Tempest V and George 12 were unquestionably fine fighters, but according to the criteria we have been using they fall below the first five, possibly because they didn't have the time to make their mark before World War II ended.

Here, then, is the final list of greatest single-seat fighters of World War II:

1. Supermarine Spitfire and Fw 190
3. Grumman Hellcat
4. North American Mustang IV
5. Mitsubishi Zeke

6. Hawker Tempest V
7. Kawanishi George 12

The Greatest Naval Fighter of World War II

In the above list there are only two carrier-borne fighters, included on the merit of their versatility rather than performance features. There is no more demanding task for an aircraft designer than to combine performance with the robustness and handling necessary in a plane that is to be catapulted into the air with high acceleration loads and snatched back with equally harsh deceleration loads. Because of this naval fighters deserve to be judged in their own right, and a judgment will involve consideration of additional qualities. A naval fighter has more than just the rigors of combat to overcome; it must return to and land safely on a small, moving flight deck before it can be said to have survived. Both combat and landing require a high degree of skill, and to fail in one is in effect to fail in both.

The special design features required in any shipborne aircraft are:

1. View (especially dead ahead in the landing-approach attitude)
2. Viceless stall (torque stalls or severe wing dropping at low approach speeds can be fatal)
3. Low-speed aileron control (for line-up and wing pickup in turbulence)
4. Landing drag (required in the landing condition to give positive contact on cutting throttle)
5. Coarse throttle control (to give delicate alterations in speed and lift)
6. Low-speed elevator control (to hold a three-point attitude on cutting engine power)
7. Low rebound landing gear (to prevent bouncing over arrester wires)
8. Wing folding (power folding for quick turnaround)
9. Arrester hook (position on airframe can be critical in reducing landing accidents)
10. Catapult attachments (minimum number to reduce weight and drag)

Here are the monoplane single-seat fighters used by naval carrier forces in World War II:

American	British	Japanese
Grumman Wildcat	Hawker Sea Hurricane	Mitsubishi Zeke
Chance-Vought Corsair	Supermarine Seafire	
Grumman Hellcat		

F4F-4 Wildcat Versus Sea Hurricane IIc

Here were two fighters almost evenly matched in combat performance and firepower, with the British fighter holding the edge. The
Hurricane could exploit its superior rate of roll, the Wildcat its steeper
angle of climb. In a dogfight the Hurricane could outturn the Wildcat, and it could evade an astern attack by half rolling and using its
superior acceleration in a dive.

Verdict: This is a combat I have fought a few times in mock
trials. The Hurricane could usually get in more camera gunshots than
the Wildcat, but for neither was this an easy job. The Hurricane
would probably have been more vulnerable to gun strikes than the
Wildcat.

Zeke 22 Versus Sea Hurricane IIc

The Japanese fighter was superior in performance, particularly climbing and a turning circle, but the Hurricane, with its better rate of roll
and dive acceleration, would still be difficult to bring down. If the
British fighter drew a bead on the Zeke—a large if—that would
guarantee its powerful four-cannon armament an instant kill.

Verdict: This would be a contest of well-matched opponents, but
the Zeke's remarkable agility should ultimately prove lethal.

Corsair II Versus Seafire III

Below 10,000 ft the Seafire had a slight speed advantage, but otherwise these two fighters were on a performance par. With regard to
maneuverability, comparing the Corsair and the Seafire would be like
comparing a shire horse and a polo pony. Both carried a lot of firepower, but the Corsair was likely to be less vulnerable to combat hits.

Verdict: There was only one difference between these two splendid fighters, and that was agility. For that reason alone, the odds
would favor the Seafire.

F6F-3 Hellcat Versus Seafire III

Though it had a slight edge in performance, the Seafire would find
the Hellcat a rugged opponent. The latter would not be able to
employ the hit-and-run tactics it used so successfully against the
Zeke, so there was little to do but commit itself to a dogfight, thereby
gaining slim odds.

Verdict: In this confrontation, the Seafire would prove slicker on
the draw. If the British aircraft had had the range and deck-landing
capability of the Hellcat, it would have ruled the seven seas.

Assessing naval fighters according to design features given in
both previous lists, I would compile the following list in order of
merit:

1. Hellcat (scores high in every feature)
2. Zeke (scores high on most features, but low on vulnerability and protection)
3. Wildcat (a mini-Hellcat, though a generation behind in performance)
4. Sea Hurricane (a land fighter adapted to shipboard with limited success)
5. Corsair (powerful in the air, but a dog to deck-land)
6. Seafire (a thoroughbred in flight, but too refined for rough-and-tumble carrier operations)

Analysis of the war records of these six aircraft confirms the Hellcat and Zeke in their leading positions. The other four are now examined.

• The Wildcat was the foil for the deadly Zeke during the first two years of the war against Japan, and even after the arrival of the Hellcat it served in large numbers on escort carriers. In the early war years the Wildcat bolstered the Royal Navy's obsolescent carrier forces. During the entire conflict it served in the Fleet Air Arm with great distinction throughout the world.

• The Sea Hurricane was the main tool of victory in the Battle of Britain, and it was adapted for carrier use as a stopgap until more Wildcats could be obtained from the United States. The Hurricane made its mark primarily in the Mediterranean theater, but it also operated from carriers escorting the ferocious Russian convoys. In both these operational areas it had the performance necessary to ward off sustained German attacks.

• The Seafire, the shipboard version of the Spitfire, was extensively used in the Mediterranean and in the later stages of the war on a limited scale in the Far East, but its short range limited it to the combat air patrol role. Unfortunately, its deck-landing disadvantages probably resulted in more operational losses than combat successes.

• The Corsair began life inauspiciously, being deemed unfit for shipboard operations. Before being cleared for carrier use it demonstrated its tremendous fighter potential while operating from shore bases in the Far East. Though almost as potent as the Hellcat in combat, it was never as fit for shipboard operations.

With all the foregoing taken into account, my final list of the greatest single-seat shipborne fighters of World War II is:

1. Grumman Hellcat
2. Mitsubishi Zeke
3. Grumman Wildcat

4. Chance-Vought Corsair
5. Hawker Sea Hurricane
6. Supermarine Seafire

The Most Effective Dive-Bomber of World War II

The specialist dive-bomber was most widely used by the U.S. Navy, the Imperial Japanese Navy, and the German Luftwaffe. It was indeed the primary offensive weapon of the two opposing carrier forces in the Far East; the Royal Navy tended to rely more on multipurpose aircraft with a dive-bombing capability. The specialist dive-bombers used in World War II were:

American	British	Japanese	German
Douglas Dauntless Curtiss Helldiver	Blackburn Skua	Aichi Val Yokosuka Judy	Junkers 87

In effect, these could all be called naval dive-bombers. (The Germans had intended to use the Ju 87 on the aircraft carrier *Graf Zeppelin*.)

The features that make an effective dive-bomber are as follows:

1. Steepness of dive angle (a steeper angle gives greater accuracy and better sighting)
2. Moderate terminal velocity (to give sufficient time for aiming corrections)
3. Good aileron control (to correct line errors of sighting during dive acceleration)
4. Absence of dive buffet (buffet adversely affects aim)
5. Bomb load (heavy enough for sufficient destructive effect)
6. Protection (against fighter attack and antiaircraft fire)
7. Range (long-range strikes often carry an element of surprise)

Based purely on the above, my merit list would be in the following order:

1. Ju 87 (a true vertical diver, with an excellent auto-dive/release/recovery system, and heavily armored)
2. Val (near vertical diver with good maneuverability, long range)
3. Dauntless (with an initially poor sighting arrangement, slow-operating spoiler flaps, but good lateral control)
4. Skua (with a poor climb rate, a tendency to propeller overspeed in dive, and poor control harmony)

5. Helldiver (with a constant dive buffet and heavy controls, making aim and recovery difficult)

Before compiling a list of the greatest dive-bombers, however, we should examine their impact on the course of World War II. These five aircraft were all designed and four were flying before the outbreak of World War II. With the rapid increase in fighter performance and antiaircraft effectiveness the specialist dive-bomber soon became obsolete, being replaced by the speedier, more flexible multipurpose or fighter-bomber. Nevertheless, all except the Skua had a long and illustrious career.

• The infamous Ju 87 was the terror weapon wielded by the Germans during their blitzkrieg. Its startling success was due mainly to a high degree of accuracy, but for survival it had to be used in an environment of air superiority. There can be little doubt that the Stuka was a powerful factor in building the sort of confidence necessary to Germany's offensive policies; it may even have been the reason Hitler was arrogant enough to attack Russia. Though of obsolete design, the Stuka was used operationally throughout the war.
• The Skua was a useful dive-bomber if a poor carrier aircraft. It was the first airplane to sink a warship in World War II, but that was its only major success, and its operational life was terminated in 1941.
• The Val struck the first blow of the Pacific war with the attack on Pearl Harbor, and, under the umbrella of the then-all-powerful Zeke, ranged far and wide over the Indian Ocean, dominating that area with its offensive accuracy and maneuverability. It gave a good account of itself at Coral Sea and Midway and in the Solomons, but the advent of the Hellcat removed the effectiveness of its escorts and left it an easy prey to the American fighter.
• The Dauntless was the weapon primarily responsible for the U.S. Navy's victory in the carrier battle at Midway, which was a turning point in the war against Japan. The aircraft continued to enjoy success in the Solomons campaign and was the offensive mainstay of the Pacific Fleet until the arrival of the Helldiver in late 1943. Many naval aviators preferred the Dauntless to its replacement, but it was slow and vulnerable and depended heavily on its fighter escort of Wildcats and Hellcats. Despite these shortcomings, the Dauntless fought until the middle of 1944, compiling a splendid battle record over a period of two and a half years.
• The Helldiver, which arrived in the Far East to replace the obsolescent but effective Dauntless, proved a major disappointment. Its impact on the battle scene was minimal and its losses comparatively heavy if the powerful escort it normally required is taken into

account. U.S. carrier complements of these ineffective aircraft had to be reduced and much of their task allocated to fighter-bombers.

The Judy dive-bomber has not been considered because, apart from its rather ineffectual participation in the Marianas campaign, it was mainly used in the kamikaze role—hardly the basis on which to compare it with other dive-bombers.

Taking these histories into account, I would compile a list of the most effective dive-bombers in the following order:

1. Ju 87
2. Douglas Dauntless and Aichi Val
3. Blackburn Skua
4. Curtiss Helldiver

Normally, the American and Japanese aircraft were fortunate to find themselves powerfully escorted, a luxury seldom enjoyed by the Skua, which was supposed to do its own fighting to and from the target.

The Top Torpedo-Bomber of World War II

The most effective way of destroying a ship in war was by torpedo attack, and aerial delivery of this fearsome weapon called for a specialist aircraft, or at least an airplane modified for the task. The latter was usually ineffective against a well-defended target, so the following carrierborne torpedo-bombers were specially designed:

American	British	Japanese
Douglas Devastator	Fairey Swordfish	Nakajima Kate
Grumman Avenger	Fairey Albacore	Nakajima Jill
	Fairey Barracuda	

The features required in this role were largely dictated by the torpedo's delivery limitations. The drop envelope of the World War II torpedo was particularly restrictive, so the following design characteristics were sought:

1. Low terminal velocity (in a dive approach to sea level, after sighting the target, since excessive buildup of speed in a dive would throw the plane out of the drop envelope)
2. Positive stability (particularly longitudinally, at low altitude for the run-in to the target)
3. Good view ahead (for aiming)
4. Maneuverability (for an evasive break immediately after torpedo dropping)

5. Protection (the pilot was very vulnerable to a ship's defensive fire, and the aircraft, while running in, was vulnerable to fighters)

According to design, performance, and handling features, my merit list reads as follows:

1. Avenger (well armed defensively, very robust, very heavy controls)
2. Jill (speedy for the type, a good general improvement on its predecessor, the Kate)
3. Kate (very effective in its early life, but easy prey for the Hellcat)
4. Swordfish (antiquated but unbelievably effective)
5. Albacore (slow and unwieldy, but like the Swordfish a good nocturnal prowler)
6. Barracuda (plagued by a rudder overbalance)
7. Devastator (slow, unmaneuverable, and carried an ineffective torpedo)

Any further analysis of the impact of torpedo-bombers on the war would discount the last three because of their unimpressive combat records or short operational lives. The other four produced records that make interesting comparison.

• The Swordfish was already obsolescent in 1939 but remained operationally effective throughout the almost six-year-long war. From first to last, the Fleet Air Arm had twenty-five front-line squadrons equipped with this veteran biplane. The Swordfish was responsible for history's first successful air-torpedo attack against a capital ship, and it virtually crippled the Italian fleet at Taranto in an epic night attack in late 1940, thus altering the balance of sea power in the Mediterranean. It also hunted and destroyed the German battleship *Bismarck*. But it was as an antisubmarine hunter-killer in the crucial Battle of the Atlantic that the Swordfish excelled, operating from escort carriers and MACs day and night, in foul weather and fair, year after long year.

• The Kate appeared a year later than the Swordfish and, like it, served for the entire war. It created havoc at Pearl Harbor and throughout the Indian Ocean, acquitted itself well at Coral Sea and Midway, then began to decline when the Hellcat arrived in the Pacific. The American aircraft denuded it of vital escort fighters.

• The angular and portly Avenger became operational just before the Hellcat, both from the same Grumman stable. When the two operated together they made a formidable team in the Far East theater, which they dominated from late 1943 onwards. In the Atlantic the Avenger also acted successfully as an antisubmarine hunter-killer operating from escort carriers.

• The Jill first appeared in a major battle during the Marianas

McDonnell F-4K Phantom (U.S. Navy)

campaign, when it made little impact against stiff opposition and heavy antiaircraft fire. After that battle, the swan song of the Japanese fleet, the Jill was largely used for level bombing and kamikaze attacks.

With all these factors considered, my list for the top torpedo-bomber of World War II is the following:

1. Fairey Swordfish
2. Grumman Avenger
3. Nakajima Kate
4. Nakajima Jill

I did a lot of thinking before placing the obsolete Swordfish biplane before the more modern Avenger monoplane. Analysis of the facts shows that the Swordfish, in action well before the Avenger, obtained better torpedo results and suffered fewer losses. Perhaps my choice stresses the yawning gap in performance between carrier- and land-based aircraft in World War II. The advent of the jet engine, angled deck, steam catapult, and mirror landing sight has gone a long way toward removing that imbalance, magnificent modern carrier planes such as the McDonnell F-4 Phantom being proof.

I made my first deck landing in a Wildcat and my last in a Phantom, and consider myself privileged to have rounded off a naval flying career with such an alpha and omega. Of course, I have had my fair share of "dogs" to put aboard carriers, but then without the bad, how can one know what is good? The same is true in combat—without ever being the underdog one can never fully appreciate what it means to have the odds in one's favor.

It has been said that the glamor has gone out of aerial combat, but truth to tell, there never was any glamor in it. Fear, pain, almost unbearable physical and mental stress—these do not add up to glamor, and to pretend they do is to glorify war. In World War II, however, a certain chivalry attended the final stages of aerial combat; it was the closest one could get to a duel of honor. If a pilot shot down his opponent and the opponent escaped by parachute, there was an unwritten code saying the pilot would not try to kill him—even though he might live to fight again.

Since those days, airplane design and performance, weapons and equipment have changed drastically, but the pilot has not. Aside from the question of chivalry, and of the different skills that must be honed today, his physical and psychological makeup are the same. When he enters single combat he engages in one of the supreme tests of man against man—though he neither knows his opponent, nor feels toward him any sense of personal rivalry. The only prize is survival. To win it requires, above all, skill, and to exploit skill to the full, he must know the technological capabilities of the enemy's weapon. But it is the pilot, not the technology, that ultimately decides which aircraft will win a duel in the sky.

INDEX

Allied aircraft are listed by popular name, with the Allied code name being used for Japanese aircraft. French, German, Italian, and Russian types are listed by manufacturer's name and designation. Ranks are the highest to which reference is made in the text. Numbers in italics refer to maps and photographs.